Football Offense & Plays

American Football Coaches Association

Bill Mallory
Don Nehlen

EDITORS

HUMAN KINETICS

Library of Congress Cataloging-in-Publication Data

Football offenses & plays / American Football Coaches Association ; Bill Mallory, Don Nehlen, editors.
    p. cm.
   Includes index.
   ISBN-13: 978-0-7360-6261-9 (soft cover)
   ISBN-10: 0-7360-6261-0 (soft cover)
   1. Football--Offense. 2. Football--Coaching. 3. Football--Training. I. American Football Coaches Association.
   II. Mallory, Bill. III. Nehlen, Don. IV. Title: Football offenses and plays.
GV951.8.F657 2006
796.332'2--dc22
                                                       2006012393

ISBN-10: 0-7360-6261-0
ISBN-13: 978-0-7360-6261-9

Copyright © 2006 by Human Kinetics Publishers, Inc.

Acquisitions Editor: Jana Hunter
Developmental Editor: Cynthia McEntire
Assistant Editor: Scott Hawkins
Copyeditor: John Wentworth
Proofreader: Pam Johnson
Graphic Designer: Nancy Rasmus
Graphic Artist: Kim McFarland
Cover Designer: Keith Blomberg
Photographer (cover): From left to right, photos courtesy of the sports information departments of the University of West Virginia, Auburn University, and Mt. Union College.
Art Manager: Kareema McLendon
Course Diagrams: Argosy
Line Art: Roberto Sabas
Printer: Sheridan Books

Human Kinetics books are available at special discounts for bulk purchase. Special editions or book excerpts can also be created to specification. For details, contact the Special Sales Manager at Human Kinetics.

Printed in the United States of America   10 9 8 7 6 5 4 3 2 1

Human Kinetics
Web site: www.HumanKinetics.com

United States: Human Kinetics
P.O. Box 5076
Champaign, IL 61825-5076
800-747-4457
e-mail: humank@hkusa.com

Canada: Human Kinetics
475 Devonshire Road Unit 100
Windsor, ON N8Y 2L5
800-465-7301 (in Canada only)
e-mail: orders@hkcanada.com

Europe: Human Kinetics
107 Bradford Road
Stanningley
Leeds LS28 6AT, United Kingdom
+44 (0) 113 255 5665
e-mail: hk@hkeurope.com

Australia: Human Kinetics
57A Price Avenue
Lower Mitcham, South Australia 5062
08 8277 1555
e-mail: liaw@hkaustralia.com

New Zealand: Human Kinetics
Division of Sports Distributors NZ Ltd.
P.O. Box 300 226 Albany
North Shore City
Auckland
0064 9 448 1207
e-mail: blairc@hknewz.com

In Memory

Coach Randy Walker, a very special member of the AFCA and contributor to this book, sadly and suddenly passed away just prior to publication. Coach Walker was a credit to our sport and our profession and he made a positive impact that benefited us all. Coach Walker will be greatly missed.

CONTENTS

PHOTO CREDITS

All photos provided by contributors unless otherwise noted.

Pages 7 and 14 Courtesy of Auburn University

Pages 40 and 43 Courtesy of Northern Illinois University Media Services

Pages 49 and 56 Courtesy of University of Minnesota

Pages 69 and 71 Courtesy of Purdue University Sports Information Archives

Pages 75 and 78 Courtesy of BGSU Athletic Communications

Pages 86 and 98 Courtesy of Northwestern Media Services

Page 108 Courtesy of West Virginia University Sports Communications

Pages 121 and 126 Courtesy of the University of Delaware

Pages 128 and 133 Courtesy of Air Force Athletics

Pages 149 and 151 Courtesy of Texas A&M Department of Athletics

Page 164 Courtesy of University of Maryland

Pages 186 and 188 Courtesy of Mount Union College

Page 199 Courtesy of University of Michigan

Pages 207 and 209 Courtesy of the University of North Carolina

Page 218 Courtesy of West Virginia University

Page 226 (Bill Mallory) Courtesy of Paul B. Riley, Indiana University Athletics

Page 226 (Don Nehlen) Courtesy of West Virginia University

Page 227 (John Bond) Courtesy of Northern Illinois University Media Services

Page 227 (Al Borges) Courtesy of Auburn University

Page 227 (Greg Brandon) Courtesy of BGSU Athletic Communications

Page 228 (Mitch Browning) Courtesy of University of Minnesota

Page 228 (Jim Chaney) Courtesy of Purdue University Sports Information Archives

Page 228 (Fisher DeBerry) Courtesy of Air Force Athletics

Page 229 (Mike Dunbar) Courtesy of Northwestern Media Services

Page 229 (Dennis Franchione) Courtesy of Texas A&M Department of Athletics

Page 229 (Ralph Friedgen) Courtesy of University of Maryland

Page 230 (Larry Kehres) Courtesy of Mount Union College

Page 230 (Terry Malone) Courtesy of University of Michigan

Page 231 (Glen Mason) Courtesy of University of Minnesota

Page 231 (Joe Novak) Courtesy of Northern Illinois University Media Services

Page 231 (Chuck Peterson) Courtesy of Air Force Athletics

Page 232 (Tubby Raymond) Courtesy of University of Delaware

Page 232 (Rich Rodriguez) Courtesy of West Virginia University

Page 232 (Greg Studrawa) Courtesy of BGSU Athletic Communications

Page 233 (Joe Tiller) Courtesy of Purdue University Sports Information Archives

Page 233 (Gary Tranquill) Courtesy of University of North Carolina

Page 233 (Randy Walker) Courtesy of Northwestern Media Services

The Evolution of Offensive Football

Hayden Fry

The AFCA and Human Kinetics gave me the assignment of writing the introduction to this outstanding book, *Football Offenses & Plays*. While I am truly honored to be associated with this great book, I must admit writing the introduction is a daunting task. The evolution of offensive football is a huge topic that alone could fill several books. So, to narrow the scope a bit, I will focus on the changes made in college offenses, because that's the level of football I know best, and most of the noteworthy innovations and trends have either originated with the college game or found their way into it from the high school and pro ranks.

The top coaches who have contributed chapters to this book have done an excellent job explaining specific areas of offensive football. Here, I will attempt to provide an overview of how philosophies, athleticism, technology, coaches, players, and rule changes have influenced the big picture of college offense over the years.

Early Influences

The first college football game in the United States was played in 1869 between Rutgers and Princeton. The game was played using a combination of rugby and soccer rules and resembled the latter sport more than it resembled football as we know it today. Led by Walter Camp, the game of football became organized in 1876 with the creation of the Intercollegiate Football Association (IFA). Since that time, the rules have been refined to make football a more distinct and appealing sport for players, coaches, and fans.

Today's college football benefited a great deal from trial and error and the contributions of great, innovative coaches during its formative years. Among the early sideline innovators were legends such as Amos Alonzo Stagg, Glenn S. "Pop" Warner, Walter Camp, Bob Zuppke, John Heisman, Knute Rockne, and Fielding Yost. Coach Warner, for example, was somehow inspired to shift his backfield from the box formation to single- and double-wing alignments.

Coaches have won games using many different philosophies. The early emphasis on playing great defense and having a sound kicking game actually spurred many offensive breakthroughs. Some of these breakthroughs were the result of tremendous individual performers who managed to put points on the scoreboard despite facing extremely tough defenses that focused their efforts on containing them. Outstanding early offensive players such as Jim Thorpe at Carlisle, Pudge Heffelfinger at Yale, George Gipp at Notre Dame, and Red Grange at Illinois helped football gain widespread popularity.

High Entertainment Value

The evolution of college football offenses during the past half-century has made the game only more fascinating, exciting, and productive. Growing emphasis on garnering the entertainment dollar has certainly prompted those who fix the rules and strategies to open up the game. Television exposure, bowl games, and revenue sharing have made for big changes in the sport at the Division I level.

Rule changes have also brought about many positive changes in the game. AFCA executive directors Bill Murray, Charlie McClendon, and Grant Teaff have given great leadership, and rule committee director Dave Nelson has led the way to new guidelines that have benefited coaches, players, and fans alike. Elimination of the substitution rule permitted college coaches to have offensive and defensive teams as their personnel allowed. The specialization of offensive personnel significantly improved the execution of assignments and point production. The rule that limits the amount of time coaches can spend with their players has led to more highly organized practices and better execution.

At the University of Iowa, I developed the philosophy that our offense would do everything possible to be different in our strategies, formations, and plays, as long as we remained fundamentally sound. Our objective was to make the opposing teams change their practice routine by making adjustments on defense for the challenges we presented them. By doing so, we believe the time factor was on our side in preparing for games each week.

My teams were using a one-back formation in the early 1950s. In recent years, this formation has been dubbed the West Coast offense; perhaps we should have called it the West Texas offense. The game became fun for our side. The game became fun for our players, and the element of surprise motivated the team to execute more consistently. A reverse and throwback to the quarterback became a base play. We practiced our exotics as base plays, which meant execution was good.

Recurring Cycles

If you study the history of the game, it's amazing how offensive tactics have made a complete cycle over the years. Just as in the example of the West Coast offense, we still do the same things, but the window trimming is just a bit different. Old-time players and coaches recognize today's so-called innovative offenses and smile.

Modern offenses have become very productive using multiple formations to limit defensive stunts, coverages, and adjustments while still running plays made popular many years ago. For example, it's common to see blocking schemes used by single-wing, double-wing, and two tight-end formations. Option plays are now being run out of the spread or shotgun formations, as well as the full-house backfield or wishbone formations. Many quarterbacks today are basically running the same plays that the single-wing tailback ran years ago. The shotgun formation used in conjunction with the single-wing formation popular in the early 1900s through 1950 now uses the option, bend back, or misdirection play originated by the standard T formations.

Zone- and area-blocking schemes are run from one-back formations. Misdirection and cutback running plays that were popular with the full-house backfield are now productive with one back because of the spread formation and zone-blocking schemes. The change to zone or area blocking takes advantage of defensive pursuit and creates different defensive responsibilities.

Many original offensive plays and blocking schemes are now being executed from multiple formations. Once the offensive philosophy becomes successful, the defense makes adjustments to stop the offense. Once the defensive schemes slow down the offense, a new offensive scheme is created. Often, the resulting attack has a familiar look, something from the past that has been borrowed and adapted to fit the present.

Influential Coaches and Players

The list of coaches who made major impacts on modern college offenses could fill many pages. History highlights the names Frank Leahy, Bud Wilkinson, Bear Bryant, John McKay, Vince Dooley, LaVell Edwards, Earl Blaik, Howard Jones, Bo Schembechler, Woody Hayes, Darrell Royal, Bill Yeoman, Dave Nelson, Sid Gilman, Steve Spurrier, Don Coryell, Barry Switzer, Eddie Robinson, Frank Broyles, Bob Neyland, Bobby Dodd, Fritz Crisler, Bernie Bierman, Duffy Daugherty, Tom Osborne, Ara Parseghian, Joe Paterno, and Bobby Bowden.

I recall my first NCAA convention, when I had the good fortune to be seated between Coach Bear Bryant and Coach John McKay. I finally got up enough nerve to ask Coach Bryant how he had won so many games. He said, "Son, just remember one thing. If the other team can't score, you can't come out worse than a tie." Coach McKay was listening and he said, "That's good advice. On the offensive side of the ball, establish your running game and then put in a play-action pass with a fake of your best running play. That's it. Now, go get 'em!"

Among the great players who made a positive impact on the gridiron and caused many defensive coaches headaches were Sammy Baugh, Doak Walker, Bronco Nagurski, Johnny Lujack, Doc Blanchard, Glenn Davis, Jim Brown, Roger Staubach, Johnny Rodgers, Archie Griffin, Herschel Walker, Barry Sanders, Bo Jackson, and Michael Vick. Those kinds of athletes can help make any offense look pretty special.

Modern Tactics

College football offenses, plays, and talent—especially at the quarterback position—now present a wide array of challenges for defenses. In turn, defensive coaches have created many different schemes to counter those attacks, and offensive coaches have responded.

Coaches have done a great job improving blocking techniques, reading defensive stunts and coverages, and designing pass routes to take advantage of the defensive alignment. The outstanding offensive teams have incorporated motion, shifting, and audibles to create a defensive weakness to attack by pass or run. This philosophy is what I call "scratch where it itches!" In other words, take advantage of what the other team will give you.

To combat multiple defensive schemes and alignments, offenses have adopted sophisticated automatic systems. Automatics have become a necessity to exploit the weakest part of the defense, be it with the pass or run. Automatics also are valuable against stunts, blitzes, and specific secondary coverages. The use of live and dummy audibles has helped eliminate many bad plays and contributed to the consistency of moving the chains down the field. Many offensive game plans are designed to limit the adjustments, stunts, and coverages of the opponent's defense. The results are apparent in the multiple spread formations seen in today's game.

Spread formations using the width of the playing field have also served to limit defensive adjustments. This emphasis has significantly improved the passing game. In recent years, the offensive game plan has incorporated various option plays from spread formations.

Many teams today use as many as four wide receivers in their base formation. By spreading the defense, offensive personnel have a better opportunity to execute their assignments, and the offense can more easily isolate and exploit matchup advantages over certain defenders.

Another trend in offensive football has been the use of the no-huddle offense. This requires the defense to line up immediately and play more standardized alignments and coverages. Many college teams run their no-huddle and two-minute drills better than their base offenses. My wife once noticed that when our team had to score a touchdown or kick a field goal late in the game in order to win, we always used the no-huddle offense. Her question to me was, "If that system is the deciding factor on who wins the game, why don't you use it more often?" Good point. Many times in key games my teams were successful using the no-huddle offense in the first quarter and after receiving the second-half kickoff.

Training and Technology

Improvements in strength and speed training have given modern athletes greater opportunities to become successful in executing their assignments.

Players dedicating themselves year-round to conditioning and skill development are reporting to the first practice each season bigger, faster, stronger, and more talented than did the squad preceding them.

The accessibility and convenient technology of modern game tapes and discs allow coaches to capture and review every aspect of the opponent's defense and kicking game, giving coaching staffs the information they need to complete their game plans. Many years ago, the coaching staff scouted the opposing team and made notes from the stands or press box. Later, film exchanges were permitted between the two teams the week of the game. Today, most college football staffs have athletic department video personnel who provide every segment of the game on individual tapes or discs for the players and coaches to review. Many coaches record televised professional games in hopes of finding something new and useful to add to their offensive playbooks.

Advanced digital and computer technology saves hours of time, simplifies scouting, and significantly elevates the teaching and coaching process. I still recall punching holes in my down–and-distance play cards and putting all of the cards on different ice picks. Splicing the old Kodak analyst film into individual reels for coach and player review took hours. Now the individual player can study an opponent's defensive alignments and schemes on a laptop computer. "Hard drive" has indeed taken on a whole new meaning in football preparation.

Pass Happy

The passing game has made great progress since the first forward pass was recorded in 1876. Yale and Princeton were playing; as Walter Camp was being tackled, he threw the ball forward to a teammate, who ran for a touchdown. Princeton protested and claimed a foul. The official decided the only way to settle the dispute was to toss a coin. After reading the coin, he ruled the touchdown would stand.

The passing game became so popular that the size and width of the ball changed to accommodate the grip of the passer. Many teams today have made the passing game a priority, and they run only when necessary. It comes as no surprise that most major college passing records (attempts, completion rate, and yards) have been set since 2001.

Pass protection has become an art for successful passing attacks. A ball-control passing attack has become very popular on the college and professional levels. Teams that establish the running game are enjoying deep-pass success after faking their favorite running plays. Quarterback skills combined with talented receivers have truly opened up the game, and the players and fans love it.

Pass receivers today have the flexibility to adjust their pass patterns as they read the movement of the defender. In reality, they're running the equivalent of the option game with their pass pattern adjustment after the snap of the football. This type of pass-route adjustment has become very popular and productive.

The greatest pass route I ever called was "Levi get open." That told three receivers to run pass routes that would occupy the defenders in their area and permit the remaining wide receiver, Jerry LeVias, to use his speed and agility to get open. He had the option to get open. Against the 1968 national champion Ohio State team, he caught 16 passes. Years after the game, one of the assistant coaches told me that Coach Woody Hayes was so upset that he locked up his coaching staff at the stadium until the film was reviewed and critiqued. All of the coaches' families

sat in the stands waiting for their husbands. It was after midnight when Coach Hayes said good night to his staff.

Joe Montana, Dan Marino, Steve Young, and many other quarterbacks became famous using this system coupled with the hot read for blitzes. Moving the pass pocket also brought about fewer quarterback sacks. Throwing the ball to all eligible receivers has become very valuable. The teams that have incorporated screen plays and dumping the ball to backs out of the backfield, especially after a play-action fake, are enjoying great success in moving the chains.

The running game has not disappeared from college football but has been simplified through the years. Great defensive pursuit has brought about zone- or area-blocking schemes that permit the ball carrier to run to daylight. The opportunity to run to any daylight created across the offensive front has given the great backs more freedom. The bend-back play and sprint draw help keep the defense at home. In the old days, the offense ran more double-team blocking schemes and trap plays. These schemes are still popular in certain conferences.

In the forthcoming pages, you'll find many exciting tactical options available in today's game. Each chapter is written by a successful coach and contains a wealth of Xs and Os to add to your team's offensive package. Perhaps even more valuable are the coaches' insights into how to implement and teach their systems, and then how to refine, modify, and execute them.

Whatever you might draw from this fine book, learn it well. And then, before attempting to implement it, make sure your athletes can grasp your instructions and convert them into action on the football field. That is the basis of any successful offense. Enjoy!

KEY TO DIAGRAMS

$\oplus$ Center

$\bigcirc$ Offensive player

v   Defensive player

⬤   Ball carrier

▢   Zone coverage

△   Blitzing defensive player

◖   Blocking direction

⊤   Blocking route

↑   Running route

↑ / ⊤   Optional route

⟶⫽   Handoff

┄┄►   Pass/toss

∿∿∿   Presnap motion

POSITION ABBREVIATIONS

Defensive

N	Nose tackle
FS	Free safety
SS	Strong safety
WS	Weakside safety
W	Weakside linebacker
S	Strongside linebacker
M	Middle linebacker
ILB	Inside linebacker
LB	Linebacker
E	Defensive end
SE	Split end
T	Defensive tackle
R	Rover
BSG	Backside guard
C	Corner

Offensive

C	Center
TE	Tight end
FB	Fullback
WR	Wide receiver
RB	Running back
Q	Quarterback
H	Halfback
F	Fullback
T	Tailback

PART I

Two-Back Sets

I Formation

Al Borges
Auburn University

The offensive configuration in which a fullback and tailback align straight behind the quarterback has withstood the test of time. The I formation first gained popularity in college football but has long since become a very common look among professional teams. This basic set, along with the various offset looks involving the positioning of the fullback, has been a successful platform from which offenses can attack the defense at all levels of competition.

I'll discuss some of the most often used plays from I sets. Many of these plays have been run for a long time. Others have been altered to accommodate the changes in today's defensive techniques and schematics. Though little is novel about this formation, the I does provide an offense an excellent opportunity to maintain a balanced run and play-action game as well as the means to consistently get the ball to the best running back.

Over the years, coaches have implemented a number of offensive tactics from the I formation. Whether it was the University of Southern California running the student body sweep or the Nebraska Cornhuskers attacking the defense with any number of option concepts, the diverse schemes that can be run from the I make it a very appealing and versatile alignment for coaches.

Basic Alignment

In the basic alignment for the I (figure 1.1*a*), the tailback aligns 7 yards deep in a balanced two-point stance. The fullback aligns in a three-point stance with his heels at 4-1/2 yards deep. On occasion, we'll offset the fullback to either strong (figure 1.1*b*) or weak side (figure 1.1*c*). In this case, the fullback will align splitting the leg of the offensive tackle at the same depth. Although offensive line splits can vary, the base spacing we prefer is 2 feet. The tight end splits 3 feet.

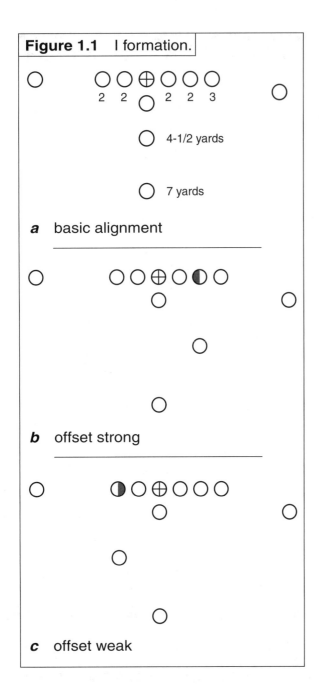

Figure 1.1   I formation.

2 2   2 2 3

4-1/2 yards

7 yards

a   basic alignment

b   offset strong

c   offset weak

Power Play

We begin with what might be considered the oldest play in contemporary football—the power play (figure 1.2). There are several advantages to carrying this play on your running game menu:

- It allows the offensive line to come off hard and aggressive in an attempt to establish the line of scrimmage.

- It can be used in many situations, such as short-yardage, goal-line, or four-minute offense.

- The nature of gap blocking allows the offensive line to handle any variety of slants, stunts, and blitzes.

- We seldom, if ever, audible this play, which allows us to use any snap count (first sound, on one, hard count).

- We can use any number of groups or formations based on how we choose to attack the defense.

- By nature, gap blocking is very simple and results in few assignment errors.

- This play can be run either toward the tight end or toward the open side.

- The downhill nature of this play reduces the possibility of tackles for loss.

The tailback aligns with his toes at 7 yards deep. He takes a short lateral step to the call side and comes hard downhill, attacking the B gap. He should always be aware of where the double team is coming from. The power play is not a cutback type play, so the tailback should be aware of staying outside the double team. He must be patient, knowing the hole could open late.

The fullback attacks the tight end's inside hip and stays on a course that allows him to kick out the first defender to show outside the tight end's block. The first defender could be the outside linebacker, defensive end, strong safety, or another defender. It's important for the fullback to maintain a tight course and not lock in to any particular defender, knowing that things might change on the snap of the ball.

The quarterback open-turns at 6 o'clock and takes the ball back to the tailback, making the exchange as deep as possible. He should carry out a bootleg fake in an effort to hold the backside contain defender.

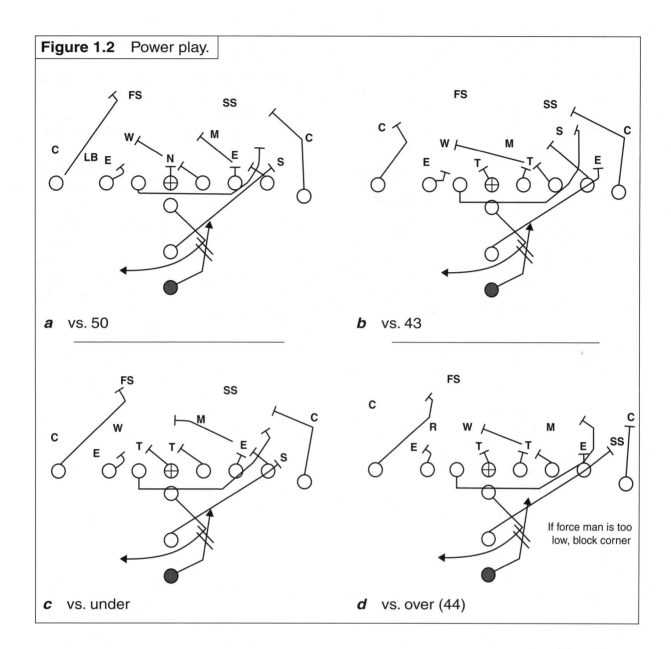

Figure 1.2   Power play.

a   vs. 50

b   vs. 43

c   vs. under

d   vs. over (44)

If force man is too low, block corner

The flanker force-blocks. The split end convoys through the free safety.

Figure 1.2 shows some blocking patterns versus four basic fronts.

Coaching Points

- The backside tackle must protect the backside B gap.

- The pulling guard must come tight off the double team in an attempt to trap the first linebacker inside. He must be aware that the tight end might engage the defensive end and must adjust accordingly.

- The playside blockers must be aggressive, particularly when double-teaming.

- Moving the line of scrimmage is critical.

- When the tackle is uncovered, the tight end must always think about blocking to the inside or cramming to the backside linebacker.

Slice Play

The slow isolation, or slice, play (figure 1.3) is one of the most popular plays in football today. This play gives the tailback an opportunity to use his vision without being rushed to do so. The slow developing nature of the slice play helps the tailback pick his hole after the defense declares its gap control. Here are the other advantages of running this play:

- The initial pass look serves to get the pass rushers upfield and to soften the linebackers, which helps the fullback execute his block.

- This is great action to use for play-action passing.

- The offensive line is not asked to blow the defense off the ball. They simply must prevent penetration to give the tailback the opportunity to exercise all his options.

- This play can be run from any two-back formation as well as from various groups, such as two backs, one tight end; two backs, three wide receivers; or two backs, two tight ends.

- The slice play is excellent to use with a hard count, which forces the defense to declare their looks.

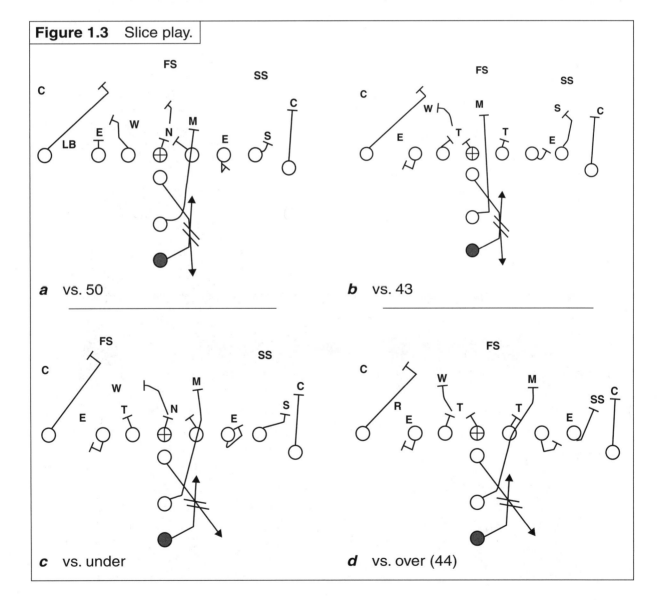

Figure 1.3   Slice play.

a   vs. 50

b   vs. 43

c   vs. under

d   vs. over (44)

The tailback aligns 7 yards deep. On the snap of the ball, he shuffles slightly to the playside, but no wider than the A gap. He starts downhill, following the fullback's block.

From his alignment, the fullback shuffles slightly to the playside, looking to block the first linebacker inside-out. The fullback must be aware of any line movement so he can adjust his track, if necessary.

The quarterback opens to his arm-side at 6 o'clock (right for a right-hander, left for a lefty). He shows pass on his first couple of steps. It's important that the ball is exchanged as deep as possible so the tailback can get a quick read of the defense's intentions. The quarterback must understand that this play should not be run against every defense and must be prepared to audible as necessary.

The flanker blocks the corner. The split end convoys through the free safety.

Figure 1.3 shows the blocking patterns for this play.

Coaching Points

- If the tight end is covered by an outside linebacker, he should use a stretch-and-turn technique to widen the C gap. He should be aware of a slant or stunt by the outside linebacker.

- The playside tackle steps slightly with his outside foot and allows the defender to declare his rush lane. He must keep his rear end out of the hole.

- The playside guard and center must be aggressive with their techniques to prevent penetration.

- The backside guard must not allow the 3 technique to slant and penetrate, which is a common way to defend this play.

- The backside tackle should get the defensive end as wide and as deep as he can by using a pass-protection technique followed by a shot-put type maneuver with his inside hand.

Wide Zone

The wide zone (figure 1.4) is one of the favorite plays in football today. This play can be run in several ways. Some teams choose to run it very wide (2 yards outside the tight end) in an attempt to stretch the defense as quickly as possible. We have taken a different approach, tightening the path taken by the tailback, off the rear end of the tight end, in an attempt to make our offensive line techniques more aggressive. Here's the upside:

- Because of the nature of contemporary defenses, our attacking mindset allows us to match the aggressiveness of the opposition's upfield charge.

- Because we're still using zone-type steps, we can handle any line movements.

- From the center to backside tackle, we use cut techniques to get defenders down on the ground.

- The offensive linemen are permitted to come off hard, knowing that

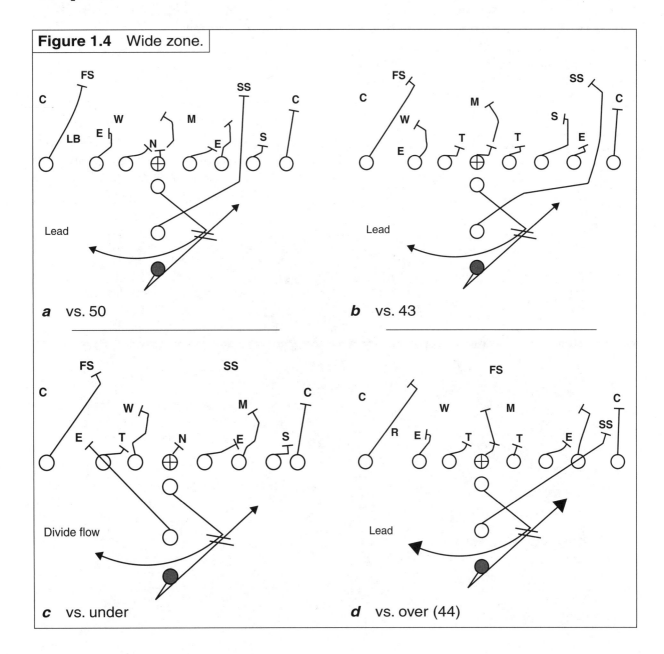

Figure 1.4   Wide zone.

a   vs. 50

b   vs. 43

c   vs. under

d   vs. over (44)

they're supported to the inside by an adjacent lineman.

- This action serves as an excellent look for a variety of play-action passes.
- The tailback can come downhill instantly, reducing the possibility of a tackle for a loss.

At 7 yards deep, the tailback drop-steps and aims at the tight end's butt. He keys the block on the first down lineman outside-in. He attacks the line of scrimmage until he's cut off by a defender.

For lead, the fullback executes much like the tailback—he attacks the tight end's butt. He finds an entry point into the line of scrimmage. He's responsible for the force man but should be aware of any second-level defender who might have gone unblocked.

For divide flow, from the called formation the fullback attacks the backside contain player. His track should be through the backside tackle's outside leg.

Driving off the backside foot, the quarterback sets his angle at 45 degrees and connects with the tailback between his second and third step. Once the exchange is made, the quarterback executes the boot fake to hold the backside contain player.

On lead, the flanker blocks the corner. On divide flow, the flanker force blocks. The split end convoys to the free safety.

Figure 1.4 shows the blocking patterns for the wide zone.

Coaching Points

- The covered playside blocker must come off hard through the outside armpit of the down linemen.
- The uncovered playside blocker should come off blocking through the midline off the defender over his adja-

cent lineman. If any opponent shows, he should knock that defender outside using the knockout technique.

- The center must neutralize the nose guard by attempting to get his head across. When blocking the second level (linebackers and safety), the center should use a cut technique, as should the backside guard and tackle.

Naked Bootleg

The first play-action that we present is the naked bootleg off the wide zone (figure 1.5), which can be very effective in slowing the pursuit of the defense. Here are other advantages to the naked bootleg:

- It gives the quarterback the opportunity to get outside, which shortens the distance of the pass.
- It equips the offense with a deceiving misdirection package.
- It complements the wide zone and in turn helps offensive linemen block the run effectively.
- It can be run from a variety of formations and groups using any number of receivers.
- It gives an athletic quarterback a run–pass option by putting stress on the contain man.
- The blocking scheme is easy to execute.
- The inside receivers (tight end and running back) can work under and behind second-level defenders.

Using the same track as the wide zone, the quarterback will reach and extend the ball in front of the tailback in an attempt to jerk the defense. Once the disconnection is made, the quarterback snaps his head around and starts his arc around the opposite end, getting no deeper than 9 yards. He attacks the corner, forcing the contain man to squeeze.

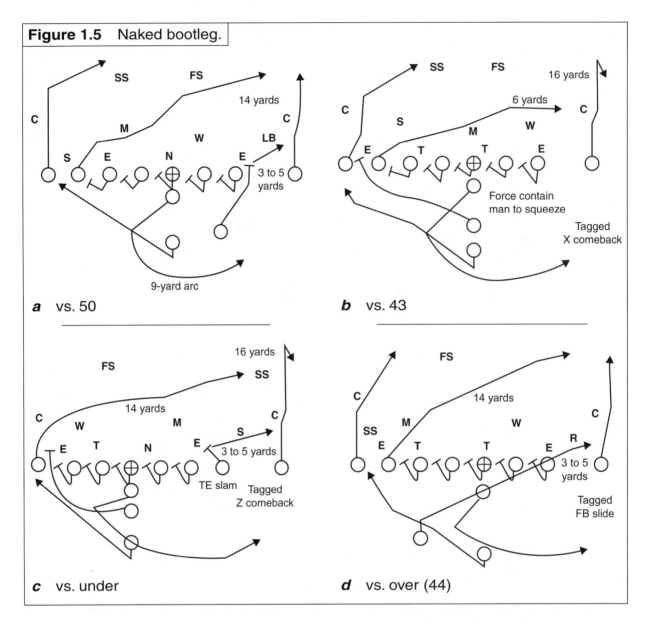

Figure 1.5   Naked bootleg.

a   vs. 50

b   vs. 43

c   vs. under

d   vs. over (44)

Using the same track as in the wide zone, the tailback takes the fake while keying any pressure blitzing outside the tight end. The tailback accelerates off the fake so that the defense continues to react to his movement into the line.

On lead, the fullback sells the wide zone by simulating that look exactly. On divide flow, the fullback slams the contain man for two seconds and releases into the flat 3 to 5 yards deep. He needs to stay aware of the rolled-up corner. The fullback will usually be offset on divide-flow naked bootlegs.

The backside wide receiver runs a post route. The playside wide receiver should clear unless designated to run a comeback route.

When playside, the tight end slams the down lineman for two seconds and then releases 3 to 5 yards into the flat. When backside, the tight end runs a 14-yard over route. He needs to read the coverage and sort his way through the second level of the defense without getting tied up. He should attempt to get under the first linebacker and behind the backside linebacker, gaining depth thereafter.

Coaching Points

- The offensive line blocks two gaps toward the fake side. Once a defender is engaged, he should be blocked toward the sideline.

- The playside wide receiver clears the corner wide and deep to protect the flat receiver.

- The tailback must explode off the fake in an effort to jerk the defense away from the naked bootleg.

- The quarterback can look upfield if he breaks contain quickly. If he sees that the defense is blatantly outflanked, he must get the ball to the flat receiver quickly.

- The backside crossing receiver has the option to throttle down if he stays in good relationship to the quarterback's movement.

Slice Pass

The slice (slow isolation) pass (figure 1.6) is one of the most potent play-action passes at all levels of football. It serves to complement the run and gives the quarterback a chance to throw the ball down the field. Here are other advantages:

- It has a great protection that sells the run play as well as protects the quarterback's backside with his best pass blockers.

- It can be used with timing routes to throw the ball quickly.

- It tends to freeze the core of the defense, allowing the quarterback to throw behind the second and sometimes third level of the defense.

- The protection can block four rushers strong and three rushers weak, which handles a large part of most blitz packages.

- It allows backs to serve as check-down receivers in the event upfield throws are taken away.

- It can be run from various two-back formations and groups.

For the quarterback, the same 6 o'clock track is used to sell the slice play. Footwork (three-, five-, or seven-

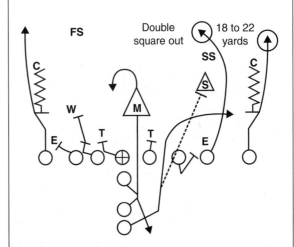

Figure 1.6 Slice pass.

a vs. 50; QB throws square-out vs. retreat coverage (cover 3 or man free), takes five quick steps, plants, and throws

b vs. 43; QB thinks TE or flanker vs. two deep, based on width of SS; WRs convert their routes to fades

(continued)

Figure 1.6   *(continued)*

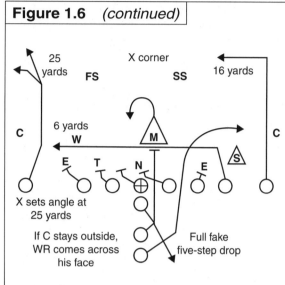

c vs. under; QB throws corner route or shallow cross based on flat coverage

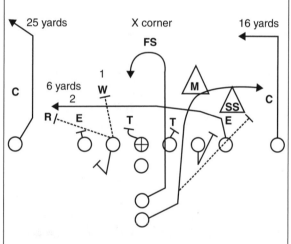

d QB sight-adjusts vs. four weak blitzes; BSG or C may double-read

step drop) is dictated by the length of the route. Token fakes are used on timing routes. More animated fakes are used with upfield throws. The quarterback must understand that this protection cannot handle four rushers weak, so a sight adjustment, generally involving the X receiver, is necessary.

The tailback is responsible for the first linebacker outside-in. Unless that defender blitzes, the tailback fakes

through the line of scrimmage, using the same technique as in the slice play. The tailback is allowed to abort his fake to pick up any blitzer.

The fullback is responsible for the first linebacker inside-out. He uses the same track as he does on the slice play. If no blitz shows, the fullback releases on the route.

The flanker, tight end, and split end run various pass routes.

Figure 1.6 shows some slice passes and protections.

Coaching Points

- Quarterback and running backs must understand the nature of the play and fake accordingly.
- Generally, the backside guard or center will double-read to any fourth blitzer on the weak side.
- Running back's routes can change based on the play called.
- X receiver and quarterback must be aware of sight adjustment scenarios.
- With no blitz coming, the play should look as much like the run as possible.

Iso Pass

On the iso pass (figure 1.7), we fake to the weak side while involving the tight end in pass protection on the strong side. We slide our line in the same manner as we did for the slice pass. At times, we use a slot formation to add one more receiver to the equation. Here are the primary reasons we like this action:

- It's a very sound play-action play in that you can pick up four defenders weak as well as strong.
- The isolation fake is convincing to the weak inside linebacker and free safety.

- The running backs can serve as checkdown receivers if no blitz shows.
- It allows the quarterback to throw the ball down the field or underneath the defense.
- Very few scenarios should require an audible.
- There's no need for any hot or sight adjustments versus blitzes.

Much like the slice pass, the faking done by the quarterback is dictated by the nature of the route. The quarterback sets up behind center, so it's important that he maintain the 6 o'clock track.

The tailback's assignment is to block the first linebacker, safety, or corner outside-in. The tailback comes downhill immediately. He may abort his fake versus any blitz.

The fullback's blocking assignment is the first linebacker inside-out, just like the slice play. His track is much more immediately downhill. He does not shuffle-step as he does on the slice. He wants to sell fast isolation right now.

Figure 1.7 Iso pass.

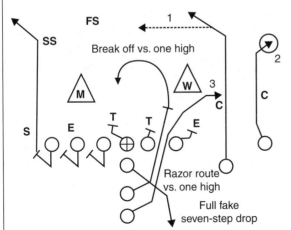

a vs. 50; QB throws square-out to X vs. one-high retreat coverage

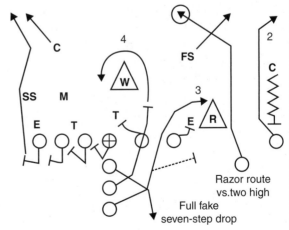

b vs. 43; QB throws off the movement of the SS vs. two deep, thinking either TE or flanker

c vs. under; QB looks flanker to SE to check down

d vs. over (44); QB looks flanker on post to SE to check down vs. two high

The tight end checks any D-gap blitzer. If no blitz shows, he'll release into a route. The flanker and split end run various pass routes.

Figure 1.7 shows examples of iso passes.

Coaching Points

- The running back may abort the fake to pick up blitzers.
- The quarterback must understand the nature of the play. This will dictate how animated the faking will be.
- The wide receivers have no concern for sight adjustments because the protection can handle four rushers weak and strong.
- The offensive line must come off with low hats to sell the run.

Quality Backs

The I is a much more effective formation when the two players lined up behind the quarterback are able to execute their respective roles fully and proficiently. The fullback must be a hard-nosed player willing to sacrifice his rushing statistics, his individual glory, and his body to play the position in this set. The fullback must be willing to block as much as 90 percent of the time and will be asked to block a number of defensive players, be it a defensive end on a power play, a safety on a wide zone, or an inside linebacker on an isolation play. The fullback must make it his mission to execute his responsibility each and every play. He also must be able to execute perfect technique to ensure effective blocks.

The I formation tailback must also be tough, knowing that he might be asked to carry the ball 25 times or more per game. He should possess great peripheral vision and efficient lateral quickness. Speed is important, as Tony Dorsett and Bo Jackson demonstrated during their careers. But good running instincts, coupled with the ability to run through tacklers, can compensate for a lack of great speed.

CHAPTER 2

Split Backs

Bill Yeoman

In my playing days and early coaching career, I benefited from a great group of teachers. Among the names you would recognize were Earl "Red" Blaik, Sid Gillman, Vince Lombardi, and Duffy Daugherty, but many more mentors helped shape my understanding of the game. As I look back, it was an unbelievable group to learn from. I didn't realize it at the time, but when Vince Lombardi diagramed and explained the Green Bay sweep and accompanying plays to me, it was my first exposure to an *offense*.

I must not have paid very good attention, because in 1962 when I went to coach at the University of Houston, I started out by running plays, not an offense. It wasn't until practice in the fall of 1964, when we tried to run a tight-slot power sweep against a split-6 defense, and the defensive tackle attacked the slot man and messed up the whole play, that I began to see the light.

You see, our two backs were aligned foot to foot behind the guards, 4-1/2 yards deep. Why? I don't know. Anyway, I told the tight end and slot man to fake the double team and go downfield. I also told the tackle to seal the 3 technique and come off on the linebacker, the guard to force his head outside the 3 technique, and the fullback to run what we called a 3 dive. On the snap of the ball, the defensive tackle took off up the

field to defeat the double team, and our slot and end let him go, as instructed. Our tackle and guard sealed off the 3 technique and linebacker. The result was a hole about 5 yards wide for our fullback. After that, the defensive tackle settled down, and we went back to running our power sweep.

It wasn't until we looked at the film that we realized this was more than just a dive play. That week we were playing Penn State. We ran the short trap and triple option, compiling nearly 400 yards of offense and scoring a touchdown on 13 veer from 20 yards out. That was the beginning of the offense that we ran for 23 years.

During spring practices in 1965, we installed the inside and outside veer, counter and counter option, and trap and trap option. We averaged 8-1/2 yards a snap in all scrimmages, which you think would have been enough to make the offense our bread and butter, but it wasn't.

During the summer, some of the coaches talked me out of running the offense to start the season. We ended up running a lot of garbage that produced a 1-5 record and put us on the brink of getting fired. I called the team together and apologized. I told them that for the rest of the season, we were going to reinstall the offense we had run so successfully during the spring and see if it worked. We had Middle Tennessee that first week we ran it, and we came out on top. Ole Miss was up next, and we beat them for the first time in the school's history, 17-3. We then knocked off a Kentucky club ranked number 7 in the nation. And we finished the season with a tie against Florida State. From that point forward, the triple option was the base of our offense. For the next five years, we led the nation in offensive stats (points, yards per game, yards per play, and so on).

After the 1965 season, I was able to define where we were going offensively. I realized that it's imperative that a coach gets *oriented* before he gets organized. By that, I mean he must recognize in his own mind how he feels the football can best be moved consistently. Until this occurs, he's wasting his time at the blackboard.

Some coaches believe in the run, and some coaches believe in the pass. When you have decided which you are, you can begin to formalize your offense. I use the word *offense;* an offense is different from merely running plays when you get the ball. Any offense must have a beginning—that is, a focal point or basic play. Once this has been established, then a logical, easily understood progression of play can be developed based on how the defense adjusts to the basic play.

At the University of Houston, we were run oriented, using the Houston option (more widely known now as the triple option) as our basic play. I hasten to add that we would throw 20 to 25 passes a game. Any more than that, and we were having a bad time; any less, and we weren't scoring enough. Several of our tight ends averaged more than 16 yards per catch, and we had one wide receiver who had four NCAA receiving records at one time. Finally, we had three 99-yard touchdown passes. Evidently, what we did when we passed the ball was effective.

In short, we used this offensive attack for four reasons:

1. It places enough of a demand on the defense that teams are forced to limit the number of alignments and stunts they use.

2. It provides the offense with a great deal of flexibility at the snap of the ball. While threatening three running lanes, it also attacks two passing areas.

3. It exploits the mental part of the game, possibly the most important facet in football.

4. Though the play is varied in its threat, the teaching and understanding on the part of the coaches and players of the offensive unit is not difficult. The ease of understanding and the ability to accomplish multiple repetitions permits more effective execution, and that's what it's all about.

By running an option offense, you decrease the advantage of having a better athlete on defense than is across the line on offense. The defensive tackle either tackles the dive man, or you hand off. The defensive end either tackles the quarterback or takes the pitch, which means basically we don't have to have an offensive lineman capable of blocking the usually outstanding athletes playing defensive tackle and defensive end.

We believe strongly that you can't stop our basic play with a balanced defense, so the opponent must adjust on defense. The defense has three groups that they can adjust: the linemen, linebackers, or secondary. It usually took no more than one series to find out what their basic alignment was and how they had been coached. This brings to the front the mental part of the game. What we had to do was take what the players had been taught and use that against them. If what we did was effective, the confidence opposing players had in their coaching was seriously diminished—which puts a defense in shambles. If you can see the coaches and players arguing on the other sideline, your chances of winning have significantly improved.

It has been noted on occasion that in football we play defense for the coaches and offense for the fans. To give the fans what they want, we must be able to hit any hole with great speed and deception. To keep the fans enthused about the game, we must have the big play. On offense, this means a long run or a long pass completion. Although we're aware of the need to control the ball, we're equally aware of the necessity to deliver the knockout punch. We feel our offense has both ball-control and knockout capabilities.

Our offense has six basic plays: the inside (13) and outside (12) veer (triple option; this is a fast-flow action); the counter and counter option (a little more deliberate action); and the trap and trap option (a slower tempo). Each backfield action has accompanying passing plays.

When we started running the triple option, or veer, nobody knew what it was. For a couple of years, we were able to stay plain vanilla and get the job done. As is always the case, defenses eventually began adjusting. This made it necessary for us to adjust—not change, but adjust. We'll get to the adjustment after we go over the basics.

In our basic set (figure 2.1), linemen line up on the ball in a three-point stance with a split of three feet, three feet, and three feet (normal splits). Sometimes the split needs to be adjusted because of the defense, but the line splits must never be less than two feet.

Backs take a normal three-point stance, aligned 4-1/2 yards from the football, directly behind the offensive guards. Depending on the quickness of the quarterback and the running back,

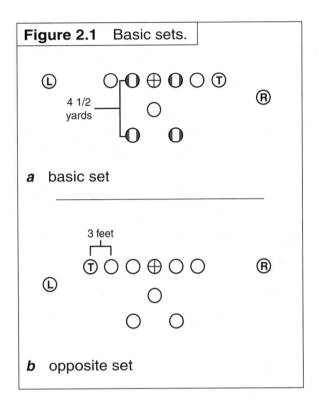

Figure 2.1   Basic sets.

a   basic set

b   opposite set

the running back can go toward or away from the line of scrimmage as long as he remains in the same vertical plane. Getting the mesh worked out is the overriding consideration.

Inside Veer (13 Veer)

The inside veer (figure 2.2) is the basis of our offense. One thing that sets it apart from all other plays is the flexibility afforded the quarterback after the snap of the ball. He has available to him the quick thrust of the dive-back, his own threat off tackle, the pitch wide, plus the threat of throwing to the tight end or R receiver or, if they are covered, coming down with the ball and running the option. Although it appears to be complicated, statistics show it's still the easiest way to get wide. The inside veer also delays commitment of the offense to run or pass, which tends to handicap the defense.

The tight end blocks the secondary man who's responsible for the force.

Splitting R so that he can't be covered by a safety from the inside means the tight end will block the strong safety. The tight end's technique is to release across the face of the defensive end, get an outside position on the safety before starting upfield, and then hang the safety on his inside shoulder as he goes upfield.

The right tackle ensures the line of scrimmage from head-on to the guard's outside shoulder. Depending on who our fullback was and who the opponent's linebacker was, if there was a 3 technique with the linebacker inside, we often would double the 3 technique and turn the linebacker loose inside. Let the fullback have it out with the linebackers. Fullbacks often respond to that kind of challenge.

The right guard blocks any down lineman from head on the center to the tackle's near shoulder. The center blocks the man on or through the playside gap. The left guard blocks base. The left tackle releases inside the 2 man and blocks the middle third. L releases to the outside of the corner and takes him deep. R makes sure the inside safety can't cover him and takes the corner deep.

The fullback is foot to foot with the right guard at 4-1/2 yards. On the snap, he accelerates at the gap between the guard and tackle. As he feels the ball on his belly, he forms a pocket and puts a soft squeeze on the ball. He must be

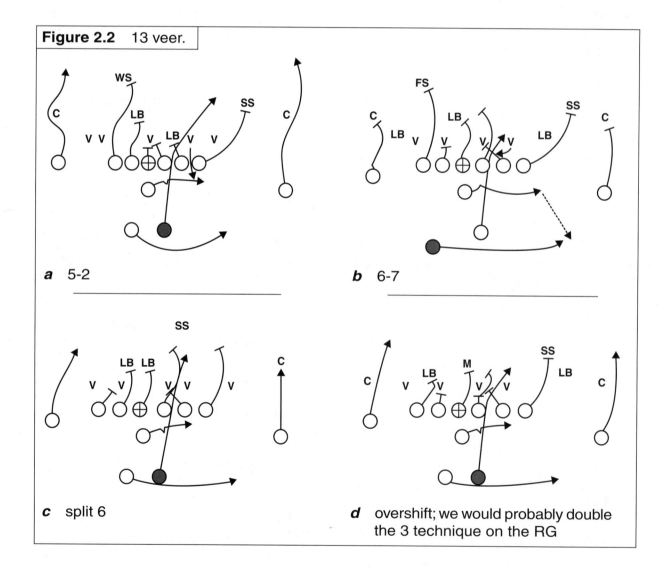

Figure 2.2   13 veer.

a   5-2

b   6-7

c   split 6

d   overshift; we would probably double the 3 technique on the RG

ready to hit the soft spot if given the ball. The decision on whether the fullback gets the ball rests entirely with the quarterback. On the snap of the ball, the halfback pushes off his left foot and establishes and maintains a pitch position. A pitch position is where the man forcing the quarterback to pitch the ball cannot pursue and make the tackle on the backs.

The quarterback takes the snap, seats the ball, pushes or drives off his left foot, and keys (or reads) the 5 technique. He meshes and settles with the fullback. If the defensive 5 technique remains stationary or comes upfield, the quarterback gives the ball to the fullback. If the defensive 5 technique closes down, the quarterback removes the ball from the fullback's pocket (or mesh) and runs a normal option on the defensive end 9 technique. The quarterback then establishes the inside running lane by getting under control and putting upfield pressure on the inside shoulder of the defensive end. He must now read the reaction of the defensive player assigned to him.

During drills, when the backs are running the plays, a coach would be the defensive end. He would jump the quarterback in a hurry; he would slow-play the quarterback; he would try to show the quarterback all the types of plays a defensive end might try. At first, the coach should make his moves quick and obvious so the quarterback can make the right decision and gain confidence. Over time, the coach should be more subtle in his moves.

Outside Veer (12 Veer)

The second play in our offense, the outside (or 12) veer (figure 2.3), is similar to the 13 veer. The 12 veer exhibits all the same pressures as the 13 veer—fast flow, and so on—but is one hole wider.

The tight end blocks the second man on the line of scrimmage. It's easy to see when it's a seven-man front. If we get an overshift or an eight-man front with the strong side end backed off the line of scrimmage, the tight end will block the 7 technique. He's still the second man. This shouldn't be confusing, but needs to be addressed.

The right tackle blocks base on seven-man fronts and combo on eight-man fronts, same as he does on the 13 veer. The right guard blocks base. The center blocks base and through the playside gap. The left tackle releases inside the two man and blocks the middle third. L and R block the same as in 13 veer.

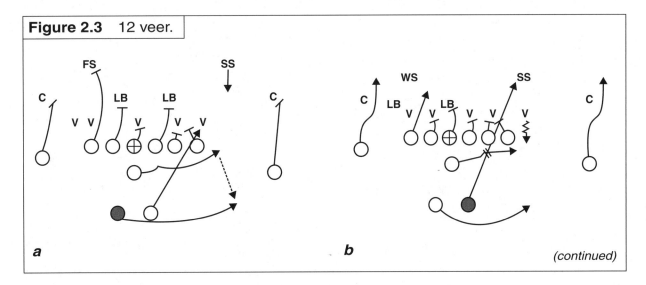

Figure 2.3 12 veer.

a   *b*   *(continued)*

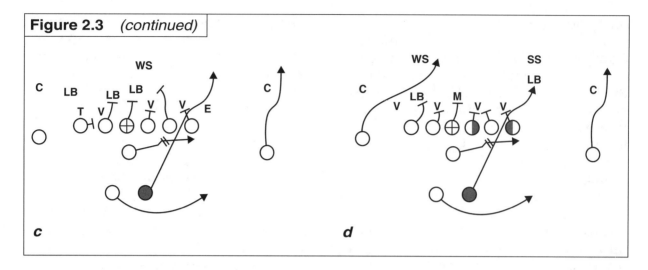

Figure 2.3 *(continued)*

c

d

The fullback slashes at the butt of the right tackle. The quarterback decides whether the fullback will get the ball. The running back is the same as in the 13 veer. The quarterback is the same as in the 13 veer but a hole wider. We don't talk about number of steps to the quarterback because some quarterbacks are 5-foot-9 and some are 6-foot-5. Talk about what you want to accomplish—the ball is in the belly of the fullback past his belly button.

13 Goal Line

Once opponents began to understand our basic attack, we had to make some adjustments. The first adjustment is a blocking that we call goal line (figure 2.4). This scheme of blocking is used as described on goal-line or short-yardage situations.

The main difference in the goal line is that there's no read by the quarterback. He rides the dive back into the line and either follows him or continues on to the end to effect an option. The blocking is the same as in the 13 veer except the dive back takes the outside leg out from under the linebacker, and the tackle turns out on the 5 technique. The blocking comes as a little bit of a surprise to the linebacker and slows his enthusiasm for the 13 veer. There was no apparent advantage to trying to run a 12 goal line, so we didn't bother with it.

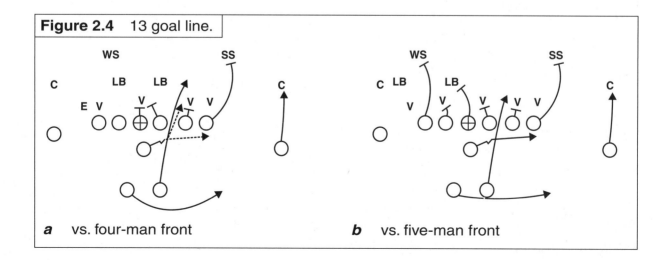

Figure 2.4   13 goal line.

a   vs. four-man front

b   vs. five-man front

13 Load and 12 Load

Another blocking that helped a great deal was the 13 load (figure 2.5) and 12 load (figure 2.6). The 13 load was okay, but the 12 load was a legitimate problem for the defense. On these plays, there is again no read by the quarterback. He gets to the dive man, places the ball in his belly, hesitates, then either follows the dive man or continues on the option. The dive man knocks the outside leg out from under the down lineman both on 13 load and 12 load. All of the blocking for 13 load is the same as for the 13 veer and 12 veer except the fullback blocks the man the quarterback usually keyed.

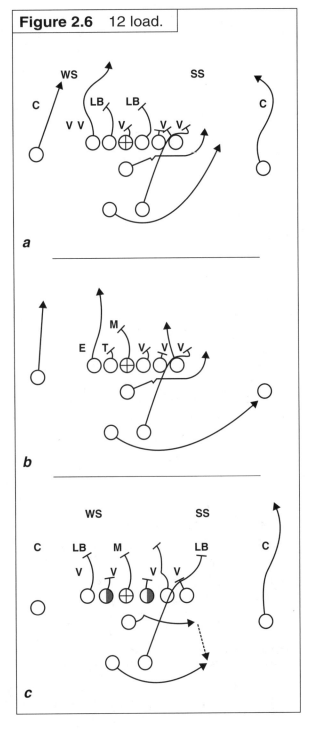

Figure 2.6   12 load.

a

b

c

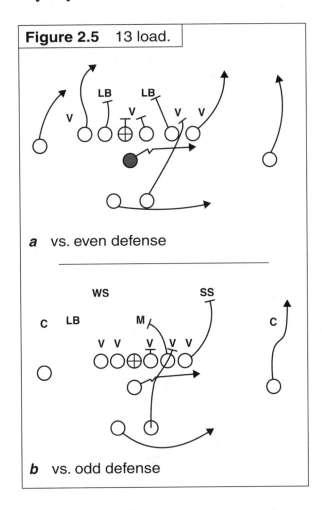

Figure 2.5   13 load.

a   vs. even defense

b   vs. odd defense

The last adjustment we made to our fast-flow offense was the 13-zone option (figure 2.7). We put in this play

our first year in the Southwest Conference, and it proved very effective. The tight end still releases and blocks the strong safety. The right tackle takes a short slide step with his right foot and puts his nose on the outside number of the defensive lineman or linebacker. He tries to hook him, but maintaining

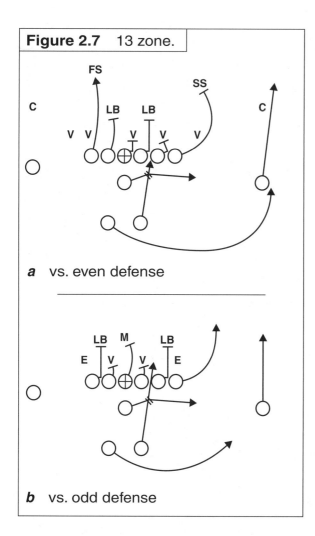

Figure 2.7 13 zone.

a vs. even defense

b vs. odd defense

contact is most important. The right guard does the same, be it against lineman or linebacker. The center and left guard also do the same. The left tackle releases inside the man over him and blocks the middle third. L runs a streak to the outside of the corner.

The big change here is the quarterback key. If the quarterback feels he can pull the ball and get to the end man on the line of scrimmage to effect an option, he pulls it. If he doesn't think he can get to the end, he leaves the ball in the fullback's belly. The worst thing you could have was a dive play. We told the quarterback to go ahead and hand off a couple of times to see how the corner of the defense reacted. H would then have a better understanding of what he could accomplish when he pulled the ball and took it wide.

Counter Plays

We have gone through our fast-flow offense. Just as the defense has available to it a change of pace with stunts and blitzes, so must the offense. One change of pace from the fast-flow triple option is the counter and counter option, which force the linebackers to be a little more disciplined in their movement. The counter also gives our backs a better chance of working the line of scrimmage.

14 Counter

The counter (figure 2.8) has been an extremely successful play for us. In fact, in one conference game we ran the counter more than 30 times. The team we were playing didn't realize we were satisfied with 4 or 5 yards at a clip. What was interesting was that after we had run about 25 counters, we ran a 13 veer, and the fullback cleared the two safeties before they got their hands off their hips.

The tight end releases outside the defensive end and blocks the strong safety. The right tackle and right guard block base. The center ensures the line of scrimmage. The left guard blocks base or comes around with the center. The left tackle releases inside and blocks the middle third. Against a defensive overshift, the counter is okay.

If you use a come-around with the center and left guard, the fullback would like to have the outside break. The first couple of times that you run the 14 counter, have the fullback hammer it straight up into the line of scrimmage. Usually, the back will cut away from the linebacker's fill. Then, if possible, start looking for the outside break. The yardage gets pretty serious.

11 Option

The counter option has been a great play for us for a long time. The time taken by

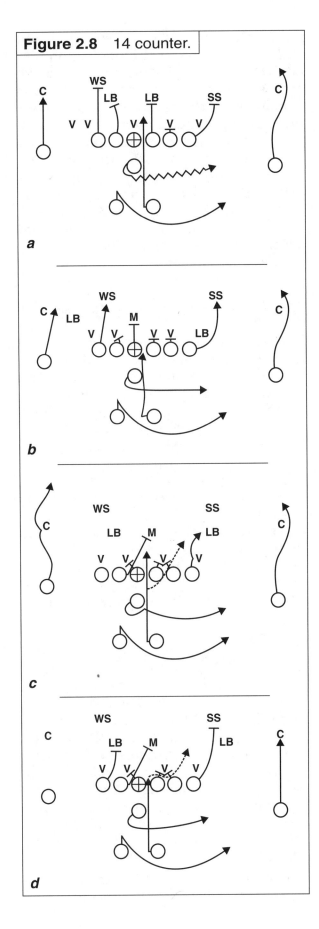

Figure 2.8   14 counter.

a

b

c

d

the fake of the quarterback and fullback allows the tight end and R receiver to force the strong safety and corner up the field a pretty good piece. Figure 2.9 shows the 11 option.

The tight end releases outside the defensive end and blocks the strong safety. R runs a streak to the outside of the corner. The right tackle can block either the second man in or the man on

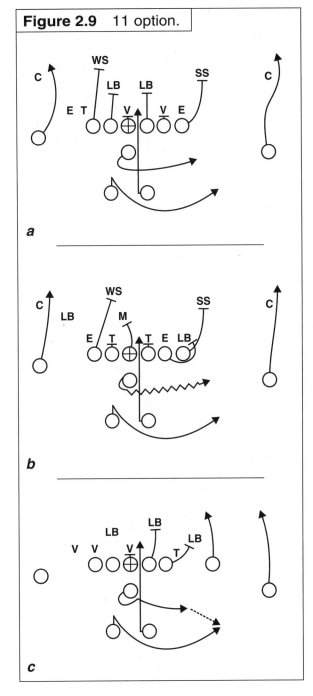

Figure 2.9   11 option.

a

b

c

the end of the line. We tell him to block whichever one he can, and we option the other one. The right guard blocks man on him and tries to log him inside. The center blocks base. The left tackle releases inside and blocks through the middle third. L streaks to the outside. The passing out of this action (figure 2.10) has been extremely effective, even when people knew what was coming.

The quarterback is the same as in the 14 counter, but we do not hand off the ball. Instead, the quarterback takes a good ride with the fullback, then continues down the line of scrimmage and options the first uncovered man past the guard. The fullback pushes off the right foot with a short jab step with his left foot, keeping shoulders parallel to the line of scrimmage. He accelerates at the

gap between the right guard and center, makes a good pocket and fake, and hits the gap between the center and guard, stopping any penetration. The running back steps with the left foot and pushes off to the right, maintaining a pitch position on the quarterback.

For the 411 play, if the tight end and R receiver are covered, the quarterback brings the ball down and options the end. On the 311 play, L always runs a post or a streak on the backside and we call the routes of T and R. (T out, R streak; T streak, R quick stop; etc.)

Trap and Trap Option

The trap and trap option represent the final two basic plays in the offense.

The trap has been good since the beginning of time. In an attempt to make the fast-flow read for the quarterback on the 13 veer more difficult, the defensive line sometimes becomes over aggressive, which helps the trap.

The trap option is harder on the secondary than any play we have. The free safety is pretty well frozen where he is until he clears the trap and then reacts to the option. This time lapse allows the tight end to threaten the strong safety to the depth of 14 to 15 yards, which makes recovery for the run very difficult.

24 Trap

On the 24 trap (figure 2.11), the tight end blocks the strong safety. The right tackle blocks the first linebacker inside. The right guard blocks the man on the center. If there's no man on the center, the right guard influences and blocks the first man outside the tackle. The center blocks head-on or back. The left guard pulls and traps the first man past the center. The left tackle counter cuts off the first man outside the left guard. R runs a streak outside the corner.

The quarterback takes the snap and seals the ball. He takes an open step

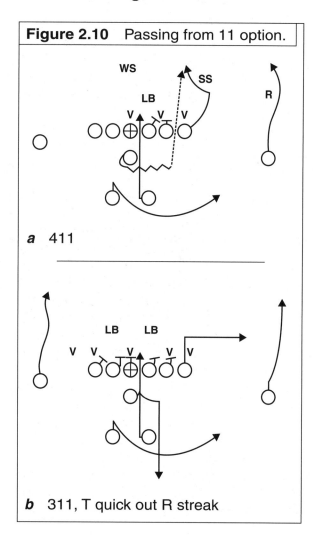

Figure 2.10 Passing from 11 option.

a 411

b 311, T quick out R streak

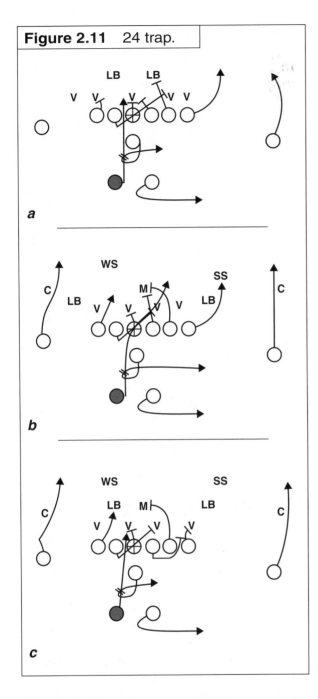

Figure 2.11   24 trap.

a

b

c

The halfback takes a slide step with the right foot. He needs to keep his pads parallel to the line of scrimmage and go at the center's near foot. The halfback meshes with the quarterback and stays as close to the center's blocks as he can.

The fullback takes a jab step with the left foot and brings the right foot up. He pushes off the right foot and makes a 180-degree turn. He picks up the quarterback and maintains the pitch position.

On an overshift, we prefer the right guard to influence the 3 technique. Run the trap option a couple of times, and you'll notice the middle linebacker just doesn't fill as fast.

21 Trap Option

The trap option (figure 2.12) has a great pull to it if you can make the trap a threat. The play requires a little more time to develop, so it's imperative that the defense is concerned with the trap.

L and R try to clear out the two corners. The tight end releases across the face of the defensive end and blocks the force. The right tackle blocks the linebacker inside. The right guard blocks any lineman from the center to the right guard's inside shoulder. When there is a man on him, he influences and logs the first man outside the tackle. The center blocks man-on or back. The left guard pulls and logs the man whom he traps on the 24 trap. If there's a backside problem, bring L in tight and have him release inside the first man outside the tackle.

If the guard on an even defense is aggressive, have the right guard block the man on him, and the pulling guard can log in the next man outside on or off the line of scrimmage.

The running back takes a short slide to the right with the right foot and then accelerates to the center's near foot. He

with the right foot at a 45-degree angle and closes with the left foot. He pushes off the left foot and pivots 180 degrees to the right to mesh with the running back. The quarterback should try to gain some depth as he comes around 180 degrees. Then he pushes off the left foot to pick up his key, the defensive end. Once he does, he moves down the line of scrimmage, trying to put pressure on the tackle being trapped.

Figure 2.12 21 trap option.

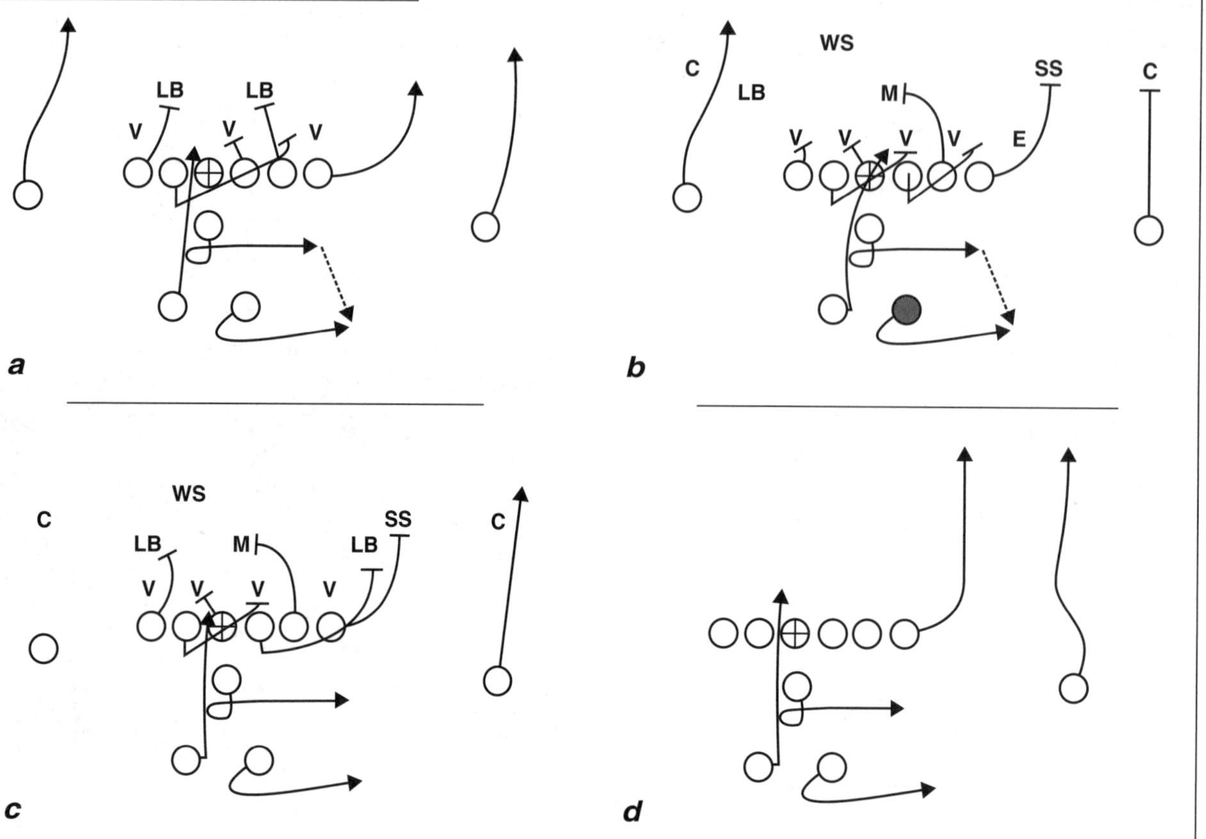

needs to make a good pocket and a great fake upfield and pick up anything that shows to his left. He goes through the playside gap.

The fullback takes short slide steps to the inside with the left foot and brings the right foot up so that he's perpendicular to the line of scrimmage. He pushes off his right foot, pivots 180 degrees, and gets a pitch position on the quarterback.

The right guard can either log the 7 technique in or go past him for the linebacker. Although we will option whomever the guard doesn't block, going after the linebacker is the better choice.

If the backside 5 technique creates problems, bring L in tight. If he's still a problem, block the left tackle on the 5 technique and tell the left halfback faking through the line to look for the backside linebacker.

Passing Game

Like our running game, our passing game is very simple. When we started the offense in 1965, we had a drop-back pass. After three or four years, we didn't see a need for it, so instead we chose to make all our passes off the running game.

If we want to throw but still keep the option alive, we put a 4 in front of the play (411, 413, 421, and so on). We throw it mostly to the tight-end side as a control, or as a short-yardage pass, usually to the tight end. On the play, the wide receiver runs a streak, and the tight end runs what we call a seam cut. The tight end releases from the line as if to get into position to block the strong safety. When the quarterback's ready to throw the ball, the tight end moves inside the safety for the pass.

To be sure the tight end knows when to make his move, we have him count to himself how long it takes for the quarterback to get ready to throw. On the fast-flow 413, the tight end is usually 5 to 7 yards deep when he makes his move. On the counter action 411 and 419, the tight end is 8 to 10 yards deep. On the trap option action 421 and 429, the tight end is 12 to 14 yards deep. Having a tight end who can get this deep on the counter and trap option creates a problem for the safety and corner. For example, in a critical conference game we were on the 8-yard line and ran a 411. The tight end and R receiver took the safety and corner all the way to the back of the end zone. Because the tight end and R receiver were covered by the safety and corner, the quarterback came down with the ball and flipped it out to the trailing halfback, who walked into the end zone for the winning score.

This brought about a little change in how defenses played against us. The teams with great athletes in the secondary started playing quarter zones on the tight-end side and trying to get the free safety across the field to help on the pitch. A strong corner and strong safety made it difficult for the receiver to get off the line. This type of play gave us a chance to use a 300 pass (figure 2.13), which was pass all the way.

From an offensive point of view, the pass gained more critical yardage than any other play we had. We faked the outside veer and ran the L receiver on a post, the tight end on a 12-yard drag, and the R receiver on a 12- to 15-yard in route. If no one blitzed from the outside, the left halfback would slide out in the flat. The quarterback went down the list of receivers and threw to the first open receiver he found.

This play is an example of how easily and quickly the offense can adjust to a change in defensive play. The pressure of the 400 series passes on the secondary helps the 300 series become more effective. The 300 series out of the counter action has been by far the most consistent part of our passing game. In the 300 series, you call the routes of the receiver you're trying to throw to. The backside receiver or receivers run a drag route at 12 to 14 yards.

If we faked the counter option and threw back to a backside receiver, usually it was after the receivers told me

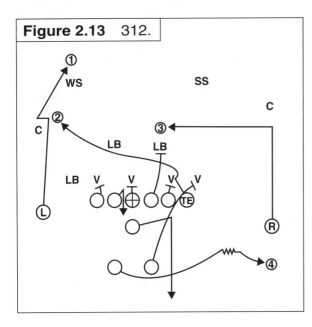

Figure 2.13   312.

someone was dreaming off. For example, if the defensive left corner was dreaming off on plays away from him, we would call 319 R streak. Interestingly, even against good teams this often worked.

We had a great time running the offense. The triple option allows you to do more with less better than any other offense I have seen. To a degree, it's a finesse offense. Our kids would attack with everything they had, but they also would enjoy taking a defensive player out of position with a fake. They enjoyed the mental part of the game. For instance, we would run 12-veer T release on the goal line because the defensive ends were told to take the quarterback if the tight end released. On the goal line or in short-yardage situations, we could hook the second man with the tackle. Because the tight end released, the defensive end took the quarterback, but the fullback had the ball in the end zone. This kind of maneuver unnerves the defensive end and destroys his confidence in what his coach has told him to do. Break down the defense mentally.

We had our share of junk plays, but the players could see why we called them. We weren't trying to fool anyone. Don't try to fool people—outexecute them. If everyone understands the basics, putting frills in is easy.

It's possible to resurrect a play. During a Cotton Bowl game, we were behind with about a minute left. I decided to run a wing right 12G (figure 2.14), a play we hadn't worked on for two or three years. Everything was the same as the 12 veer except the onside guard pulled around the defensive end. R brush-blocked the defensive end on the outside shoulder and then went down to block the safety. The tight end and right tackle blocked 12 veer, and the right guard pulled around the end and went upfield.

The defensive end leaned to the outside when the wing brushed him. The end took a couple of steps to the out-

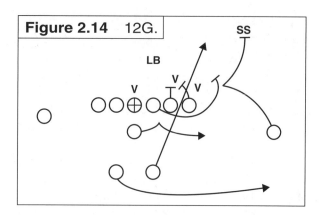

Figure 2.14 12G.

side when the guard pulled around him. The fullback went to the 4-yard line. We scored a couple of plays later.

The offense to the split-end side is the same as the offense to the tight-end side. If you don't want to go opposite or bring L in tight, you can't run 18 veer. The other plays available are 17 veer, 17 goal line, 17 load, 16 counter, 19 option, 26 trap, and 29 option.

We used the split-end side a lot for passing, but out of the 300 series, not the 400. In other words, when we went to the left or split-end side, it was pass all the way, whether we were throwing to the split end or backside to the tight end or R receiver. When we ran to the split-end side with the fast-flow offense, we did very little reading and used 17 goal line, 17 load, or 17 zone option. The counter and counter option were also effective. The trap option (29 play) was not quite as effective unless we brought L in tight and slowed down the rush of the defensive end.

When we went into the Southwest Conference, we lined up with the tight end to the right side at least 97 percent of the time. We knew exactly what we were going to run. All we had to decide was the blocking (veer, goal line, load, or zone). The counter series plays and the trap and trap option plays stayed constant as far as blocking was concerned.

One more time–don't try to fool teams–execute your offense better than your opponent executes his defense.

PART II

One-Back Sets

CHAPTER 3

H Back, Two Tight Ends

Joe Novak
Northern Illinois University

John Bond
Northern Illinois University

Our offense at Northern Illinois has evolved to using a second tight end as a fullback. Although we consider ourselves a one-back football team, and half of the time we're in traditional one-back sets, the rest of the time we're in non-traditional two-back sets. We constantly keep the second tight end on the move to make 2-×-2, 3-×-1, and unbalanced formations.

After playing against a 4-3 defense every day in spring and fall camps, we realized that using a second tight end and keeping him on the move would cause defensive coaches to burn chalk while diagramming all the different possibilities. We create many problems for the defense by using tight-end motion. Against teams that base out of a seven-man front, we create extra gaps for them to defend. Against teams that base out of an eight-man front, we can get into a 3-×-1 formation, causing alignment problems for linebackers and safeties.

We also cause defensive coordinators multiple problems in pass coverage. Motioning the tight end, or H, creates confusion for the defenders—who do they drop off of in their zone drops?

Against teams that want to play man coverage, we create confusion over who covers whom and create natural picks or rubs with pass routes.

Another reason we strongly support our system is that it allows us to gain numbers or angles at the point of attack. What more basic fundamental of offensive football is there? If you can gain a hat or gain an angle at the point of attack, you have a great chance to be successful.

The one-back with tight-end motion attack also limits the amount of blitzes defenses normally run against a two-back offense. Because of the location of the second tight end, or H, and his ability to immediately release downfield in any direction, teams treat us like a two tight-end alignment rather than a traditional two-back offense. We still have the advantage of the H being able to block the same linebackers a fullback would.

Our players believe we're using a tough, get-after-you type of attack when we have two tight ends in the game and use H with multiple motions and movements. We can be extremely physical in that style of play and run the ball against eight or even nine men in the box and still be successful. When you move H, you can iso, you can seal, and you can kick out, depending on what you want to get done on a particular drive. Our players believe that when this personnel grouping comes in the game, we're preparing to physically punish our opponents. When players are confident that they can out-physical their opponent, they have moved a long way toward defeating them from an emotional standpoint.

This style of offense also improves our ability to throw the play-action pass. Safeties who normally play 10 to 12 yards deep will play us at 8 and even 6 yards deep to stop our running attack. Linebackers also have a tendency to really bite hard on the play fake, opening lanes for the play-action pass. Besides affecting the secondary and linebackers, the running game causes defensive ends to pursue the ball rather than contain the quarterback on naked and bootleg passes. Also when defenses perceive a power running type of attack, we can drop back, get five receivers out, and benefit significantly from the defense hunkering down to stop the run.

The advantages of using two tight ends extend beyond Xs and Os. When recruiting, we have more opportunities to recruit a 6-foot-4 athletic kid who might weigh 210 pounds, red-shirt him, get him into the weight room, and end up with a kid who is 6-foot-4 and 250 pounds. If he doesn't develop into a tight end, this type of player might end up being a defensive end, an outside linebacker, or an offensive tackle. Usually, athletes with this body type play on special teams as well. This body type is more versatile than the 6-foot-1, 220-pound fullback who's really used only as a battering ram in the running game. We can find many more student athletes like this than the traditional fullback body type.

So far, we've talked about all of the advantages we gain by using two tight ends with multiple motions and movements—we create extra gaps against a seven-man front; create problems in a 3-×-1 formation versus an eight-man front; create multiple problems and confusion in pass coverage; gain angles and numbers on a defense at the point of attack; force defenses to limit the number of blitzes they would normally call against a two-back offense; develop player confidence in running the ball with this physical style of play; and aid in recruiting because the body types of tight ends are more prevalent and more versatile. To be fair, we should also mention the disadvantages of using this type of offense. A rash of injuries at the tight-end position would limit the team's ability to run this style of attack. In addition, this style of attack could cause problems for young offensive linemen. Motioning the tight end often causes linebacker movement, thus changing the blocking assignments of the offensive linemen. Finally, as opposed to a spread offense, this attack brings more defenders in the box for which you have to account.

Motion on the Field

Our initial reason for the two tight-end offense was to create an extra gap against seven-man front defenses (figure 3.1). The two tight-end set causes the seven-man front defense to be short one gap on the backside of the formation. This is an advantage for the offense because either the safety has to come out of his normal alignment to be responsible for the gap, or he has to fill the gap from his 10-yard depth. We can attack the defense with the run against a safety who plays deep or pass the ball against a safety who plays at linebacker depth.

By moving the backside tight end into a wing alignment (figure 3.2), we move

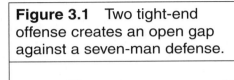

Figure 3.1 Two tight-end offense creates an open gap against a seven-man defense.

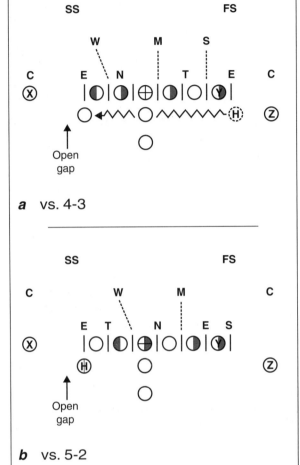

a vs. 4-3

b vs. 5-2

the extra gap from the backside of the formation to the front side. This new alignment creates different run responsibilities for the defense and causes similar problems for the frontside safety. From a wing alignment, H can be used in several blocking schemes and also release vertically and put immediate pressure on the secondary.

The same formation against an eight-man front (figure 3.3) forces the defense to decide how they're going to adjust their linebackers and secondary. If they don't shift the linebackers to the strength of the formation, the offense has a definite advantage in angles and blockers.

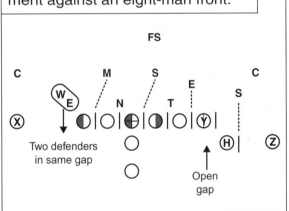

Figure 3.3 Tight end in wing alignment against an eight-man front.

Figure 3.2 Tight end in wing alignment, moving open gap to the front side.

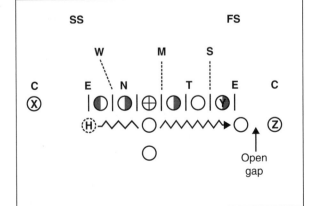

When H goes in motion across the formation (figure 3.4), it causes problems with zone coverage and creates confusion as to who to zone drop off of. The Mike linebacker in a 4-3 defense is responsible for number three, who initially is the back. When the tight end, or H back, moves, number three changes to number four, and with that change you make the defense think. Any defensive uncertainty or hesitation can lead to a defender turning a receiver loose in coverage or being unsure of what gap is his responsibility. This simple movement causes a potential change

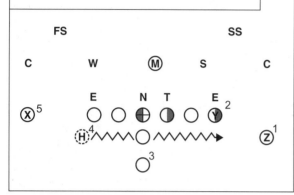

Figure 3.4 H in motion across the formation. The Mike LB has to adjust because the number three receiver becomes number four.

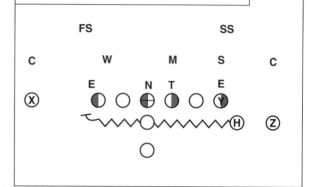

Figure 3.6 Moving the tight end creates a numbers advantage for the offense. Note the overshifted linebacker.

in coverage because of a change in formation strength, adding to defensive confusion.

Using the same motion versus man coverage, it's easy to see, with a vertical release by Y, how one can get a natural rub or pick on the strong safety who's covering H (figure 3.5).

A great benefit to moving the tight end is gaining numbers by adding movement to the scheme (figure 3.6). The Mike linebacker is shifted to the strength of the formation prior to the motion. If the Mike linebacker fails to get back in alignment over the center when the

movement occurs, it gives the offense superior numbers, helping the offense run to the weak side of the defense. We can exploit an overshifted defender by running a counter or misdirection run toward that defender and cutting the play back to the weakness of the defense (figure 3.7).

Another crucial element of motioning the tight end comes with gaining angles at the point of attack. Whether using a fold block to gain an angle in the running game or breaking contain with the motioning tight end on a sprint-out pass, the ability to gain angles signifi-

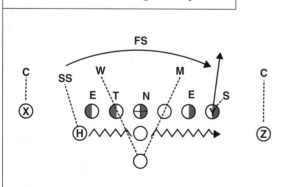

Figure 3.5 Tight-end motion vs. man coverage. Y releases vertically, creating a natural rub or pick on the strong safety.

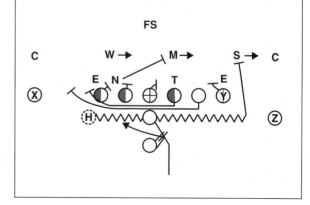

Figure 3.7 Exploiting the overshifted linebackers. The overshifted linebacker is cheating to the playside.

cantly improves your chances at successfully making plays.

A great example of outflanking a defense is to trade the tight end to try to gain an advantage and flank the defense. Because the tight end was on the other side of the formation, the defense will have a tighter technique to the weak side. By trading, or dancing, the tight end, you create the opportunity to get a better angle to get the ball outside of the defender to get a clean edge to throw a sprint-out pass (figure 3.8).

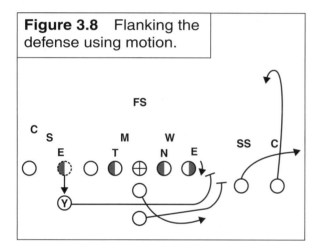

Figure 3.8 Flanking the defense using motion.

Power Play

One of Northern Illinois' most productive plays over the past few years—and a signature run in our offense—is the power play. We like to use it when we're coming off our own goal line and when we have reached the red zone. We'll even use it when we're going in to score. It's a tough, hard-nosed play that mirrors our program. Our players believe in it and want to run it, so we have confidence in it.

Because the power play has been so good to us, we have had to use eye wash with motions and movements to keep the play alive. We like the play because it gives us a double team at the point of attack. We also like the fact that it's a downhill run for the back.

One of the key coaching points is to vertical-lift the double team so we can handle linebackers running under and push to linebackers running over the top of the double team. Another key point is the backside guard square-pulling for the frontside linebacker or the Mike linebacker. We like the square pull because the guard is in the hole and running downhill on his third step; he never needs to take his eyes off his linebacker. The square-pull allows the guard to have an inside-out angle on the linebacker and keeps him from getting involved in the center's back block. The running back's key is to start on track to the A gap and stay on that track until someone makes him deviate from the hole. Because of our philosophy with the vertical push on the double-team block, the play usually hits in the frontside A gap all the way to the backside B gap.

One way we like to format the power play is to show a 3-×-1 set. We show three receivers to a side to get the linebackers and coverage bumped and then move back to a 2-×-2 look (figure 3.9). If we suspect we'll get this much overload, we motion the H back across the ball to make his block on the corner and run the power play.

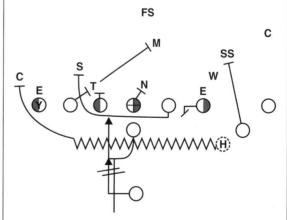

Figure 3.9 Overplayed linebackers and secondary enable offense to motion over to run the power play.

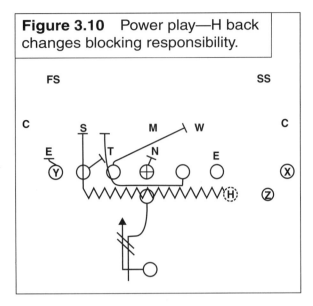

Figure 3.10   Power play—H back changes blocking responsibility.

The same formation against a different front changes the H back's blocking responsibility (figure 3.10).

The H back must attack his responsibility and protect his inside, aim for the defender's inside number, and make contact on the defense's side of the line of scrimmage. The defender is going to give a shoulder, so the H back must go blow that shoulder up. If the defender wants to spill, the H back must keep his head in front so that the defender can't penetrate. The H back needs to keep the defender covered up.

Inside Zone

A play that has become universal, and one we happen to run pretty well, is the inside zone. This is another good play coming out from our own goal line or going in to score, and it's deadly in the red zone. Using movement with the tight end creates a split-flow effect that makes the run better, seals the backside better, and sets up a great play-action pass.

The first key point to the success of the inside zone is the ability to create as many double teams as possible. We like to throw as much firepower into the point of attack as we can, and the best way to do that is to double-team. This

is another play our players have confidence in and enjoy running because it's such a physical play. We get double teams not only to the front side of the play but to the back side of the play as well, which creates seams for a good running back. We don't have to be better physically than our opponent to successfully run this play because of the double teams we create.

Another key element to the inside zone is for the quarterback to get the ball back to the running back as deep as possible at an angle that won't cut off the running back's vision of the possible cutback lane. Like most other coaches, we teach a 5 o'clock or 7 o'clock first step for the quarterback, but if we're going to err, we would rather step at 6 o'clock than 4 o'clock so the running back can see his possible cutback. Most important, the running back must start at his landmark, which for us is the guard's outside leg, and not come off that track until someone makes him deviate from it. The running back will be slow to the guard's outside leg, read the first man on or outside the guard, and then cut upfield to daylight.

Motion affects the inside linebackers (figure 3.11). With motion, you create the possibility of a zone lead. When

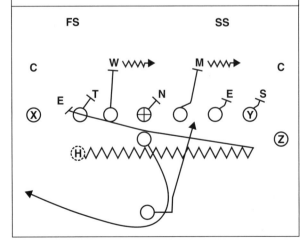

Figure 3.11   Inside linebackers respond to motion by overrunning the play.

you start the ball that way, it can contribute even more to linebackers' overrunning, increasing the possibility of a cutback.

Using a different formation and a bounce motion, we can achieve the same results (figure 3.12). The split-flow look for linebackers can possibly lead to a slight hesitation, which could be all the back needs to create a big play.

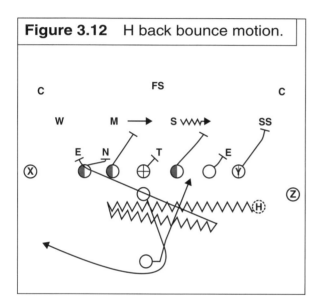

Figure 3.12   H back bounce motion.

When running the inside zone, the H back must block the first defender to show off the backside tackle. He needs to work back into the line of scrimmage. His aiming point is 1 yard on the defense's side of the line of scrimmage. The defender will give a shoulder, so the H back blows that shoulder up and keeps the defender covered up. The running back will be able to go either inside or outside of the H back's block if the H back has done his job.

Inside Zone—BOB

Another run that complements the inside zone very well is something we call BOB (figure 3.13), which is an acronym for back on backer (linebacker). The only difference between the zone

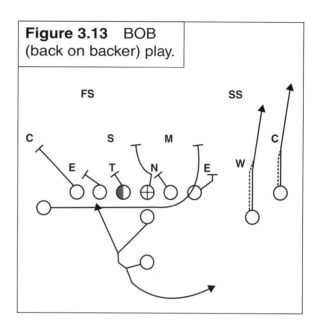

Figure 3.13   BOB (back on backer) play.

and BOB is the backside tackle and the H back, or movement guy. The same principles that apply to the inside zone also apply to this play. We base block the backside tackle on the defensive end and isolate the backside linebacker with the H back. The benefits of the play are that we give the defensive end two separate reads, and the play should hit one gap tighter. With this, we increase the stress on the safeties because the play hits more quickly and could split a two-safety shell. By creating a split-flow effect on the linebackers, we create overrun possibilities and cause hesitation.

Motioning out a fullback in the backfield who then comes back to block the weakside linebacker gives another look to the BOB concept (figure 3.14). This is nothing different for the offense but gives the defense a totally different look. If the 5 technique end stretches and the linebacker runs at all, you create a huge seam in the backside B gap.

To show the flexibility of our offensive philosophy, we can be in 11 personnel, back the tight end off the ball, and run the BOB concept (figure 3.15). If the slot receiver can dig out the linebacker, the opportunity is there for a big play.

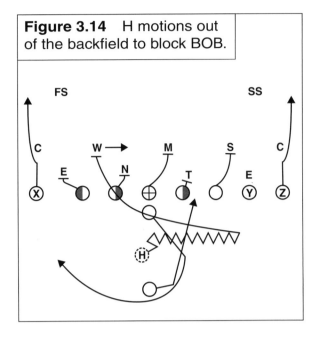

Figure 3.14   H motions out of the backfield to block BOB.

Naked Pass

A natural pass off the inside zone is the play-action naked play. By running the ball efficiently, we set up this play because we have put the backside end, backside linebacker, and flat defender in a bind. If the end doesn't squeeze the play and doesn't spill the run, it's practically impossible to stop the run. If he does a good job of spilling the run, he has a hard time stopping the pass.

With our inside zone run in 12 personnel, we use the second tight end to block back and kick out the defensive end. It's a natural complement to have him pass the defensive end on the naked play and release into the flat immediately. This route is easy to complete and even acts as a hot route if the defensive end gets pressure on the quarterback or if we see edge pressure from a blitz. Because we make the play look exactly like the run up front, we sell the play more than the fake in the back end. We make a conscious effort to have the same pad level up front and block the naked pass exactly as we would the run.

The naked pass (figure 3.16) causes definite problems for the defense. The

On the BOB play, the H back must close to his responsibility as fast as he can. He works back into the line of scrimmage. He comes tight off the center or backside guard and makes contact on the defense's side of the line of scrimmage. The defender gives a shoulder, so the H back blows it up. The H back must keep the defender covered up so the running back can get through the hole.

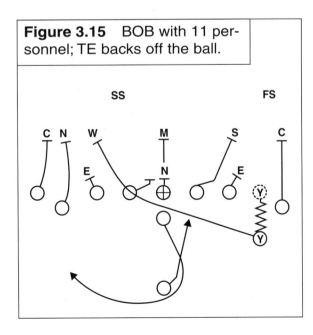

Figure 3.15   BOB with 11 personnel; TE backs off the ball.

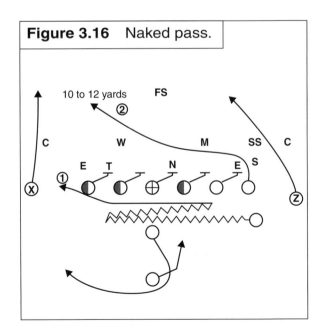

Figure 3.16   Naked pass.

aiming point for the drag route is 10 to 12 yards as the receiver crosses the opposite hash. The goal of the H back is to run a tight course and elude the defensive end at all costs. As soon as the H back clears the defensive end, he snaps his head around to look for the ball. The quarterback's progression is short route in the flat to the drag route.

A different formation and different route combination change the look of the play (figure 3.17), but the nuts and bolts remain the same. The quarterback's progression changes when he has more than two receivers to look at. He'll still look to hit H in the flat right, now as his number 1 receiver. His second progression will put the quarterback on the deep out route before the quarterback looks to the drag route as his third look. This is also a great route if you're seeing man coverage.

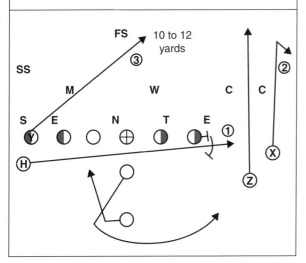

Figure 3.17 Quarterback progression changes. X becomes number 2 receiver; Y becomes number 3 receiver.

We can also create a rub on the defender responsible to cover the H back by using a different route scheme and formation (figure 3.18). The X receiver inside releases his corner and runs a shallow crossing route against man coverage. H's movement helps to show

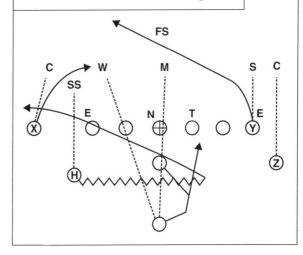

Figure 3.18 Different route scheme and formation creates a rub on defender covering H.

whether man or zone coverage is being used. If X doesn't see the defender running with the H back, he simply clears out his zone.

We do a good job putting our quarterbacks in difficult situations in practice and forcing them to make tough throws. We physically practice making them throw over defenders and around defenders. We also practice pump-faking a defensive end to get around him and get the throw off. This is an added reason why this play has been as successful for us as it has been.

Play-Action Pass

We have talked about motions and movements affecting the front seven but have yet to talk about the secondary and what movement by the H back can do. Having a solid running game will help the play-action passing game, obviously. If the running game is really going, defensive coaches have to involve their safeties. When those safeties commit to stopping the run, it creates one-on-one coverage on the outside. When you get one-on-one coverage on the outside, the opportunities for big plays are there and need to be taken advantage of.

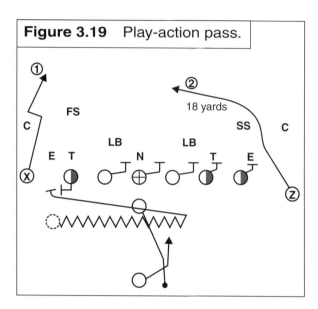

Figure 3.19   Play-action pass.

Different coaches have different philosophies of play-action protection—you have to do what best fits your people. Make the play action look like the run to the best of your ability, or slide your protection, if you want to be safe. However you decide to do it, the one constant is the deception you can add to the play with motion or movement by the H back.

If you ran the ball on first down for 7 yards, bringing up second and 3, show the same action in the backfield, add a little movement to entice the defense to bite, and then hit them over the top for a big one. Because we've been able to run the ball over the years, we've had great success hitting big throws down the field. Play-action streaks, posts, post corners, and corner posts have all been very good for us as well as H's movement to sell the run and then the corresponding routes on the outside (figure 3.19).

With single coverage on the outside and safeties down low to stop the run,

the post corner is the quarterback's first look followed by the deep over cross (DOC) route (figure 3.20). Obviously, any type of two-receiver route will work, depending on what defender you want to work against or what type of throw is most comfortable for the quarterback.

Figure 3.20   Against single coverage, the QB looks first to the post corner and then to the deep over cross route.

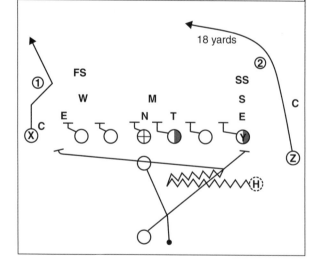

One of our favorite, and most simple, route concepts is the streak (figure 3.21). This route is good if we have a favorite matchup that particular week

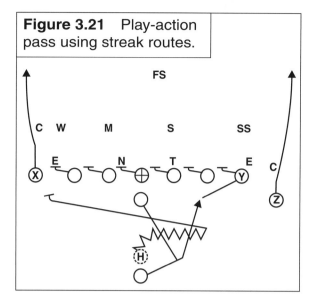

Figure 3.21 Play-action pass using streak routes.

Drop-Back Pass

One of our favorite drop-back passes comes off a two tight-end look with movement by one of them. This concept can be run out of a 3-×-1 or a 2-×-2 look. It has a shallow cross concept and a dig behind it. You can see our drive concept out of a balanced formation (figure 3.23).

We like the drive concept because we can use the shallow cross as a hot route, if needed. We also like the play on neutral downs, and it's a high-percentage throw on third down and medium. In addition, we like this route because if linebackers jump the shallow cross it creates natural windows to throw the dig behind.

If we get the back involved in the route, the triangle created stretches the defense both horizontally and vertically. If the back gets the ball, he usually has an opportunity to get upfield and make significant yardage.

The quarterback's progression is the tight end to the H back to the running back. Another thing about this play that we really like is if we know we're going to get the back out, the quarterback can reverse his progression, going to the running back first, giving the back an

or simply want to take a shot down the field. A different thought process could be to go to a two-by-two look formationally, with both receivers on the same side (figure 3.22). This creates combination routes rather than just single-receiver routes.

It's important for the H back to block his run responsibility and sell the run. He needs to come hard across the line of scrimmage. If the H back's run responsibility doesn't blitz, he looks to help one of his offensive linemen.

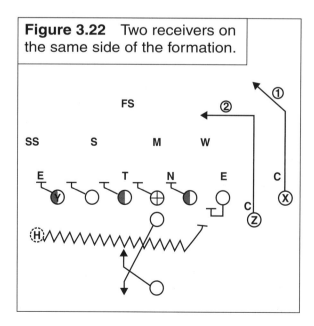

Figure 3.22 Two receivers on the same side of the formation.

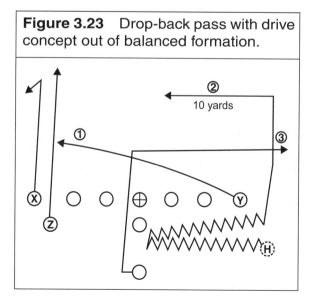

Figure 3.23 Drop-back pass with drive concept out of balanced formation.

opportunity to make yardage and possibly making the window for the tight end more pronounced.

You can also exchange the H back and tight end to create a possible rub versus man coverage (figure 3.24). In a 3-×-1 look, we show a similar scheme with the H back and tight end swapping responsibilities (figure 3.25). The quarterback's progression is the same, but it's a totally different look to the defense. We add a different movement, change the strength of the formation, and give the defense a different look, but really the play is no different for the quarterback and his progression.

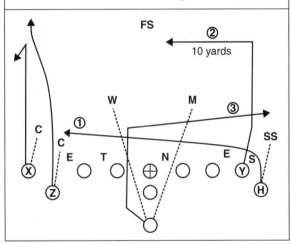

Figure 3.24   Possible rub on S and SS and W and M on crossing routes.

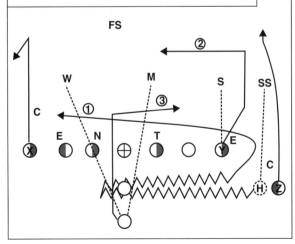

Figure 3.25   3-×-1 look; H back and TE swap responsibilities.

Gadget

A gadget play that's a natural off the plays we've already discussed is a reverse to the flanker off the inside zone (figure 3.26). We run the inside zone look in the backfield and have the H back continue around the defensive end, who's trying to spill the play. Once the H back is around the defensive end, he blocks the first defender he sees in the flat. This creates a reverse with a lead blocker.

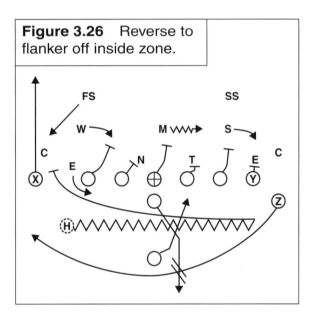

Figure 3.26   Reverse to flanker off inside zone.

For the same reasons that the naked is a good play, the reverse is a good play. If the backside end is trying hard to wrong-arm the H's block on the inside zone, he's susceptible to being run past by the H back. If the secondary player is looking into the backfield to stop the run or is conscious of covering a pass play in the flat, he's not prepared to take on the H back's block. This play marries well with the inside zone. It's a gadget play that stops defensive pursuit with little risk.

We used this play one night in a nationally televised game. We had set it up to perfection. Our opponent's defensive ends and linebackers were jumping all over our inside zone and BOB plays.

When we called this play, the end spilled the run and our H back, who had been in motion, ran past him and blocked the run-support safety. The safety had his eyes on the backfield and never saw the H back coming, which gave the flanker an opportunity for a successful play.

You can use any movement you want with the H back, or you can leave him stationary and move the Z back to get the desired mesh point (figure 3.27). This is another easy way to run the play with little risk.

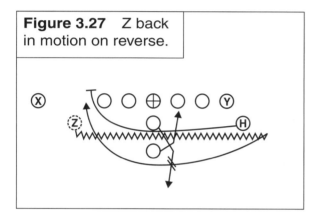

Figure 3.27   Z back in motion on reverse.

Coaches are always looking for a winning edge when it comes to finding new ways to run plays we already have or finding new schemes to help expand our packages. Tight-end motions have allowed us to have a two-back offense while retaining the framework of a one-back philosophy. Maybe the biggest thing that has come out of this particular style of attack is the psychological advantage we gain. Our players believe in the toughness and aggressiveness that it takes to run this system. They believe we're going to be able to find double teams at the point of attack. They also know that if we're having success running the ball, we can manipulate the defense by using motion to really make the defense bite hard on the run. When that happens, we're going to be able to gain big chunks of yardage on naked, play-action, and drop-back passes.

As you step out of our huddle, we hope that you have picked up one or two ideas to employ in your offensive system. We wish you the best of luck in your quest to be a champion.

CHAPTER 4

Two Receivers, Two Tight Ends

Glen Mason
University of Minnesota

Mitch Browning
University of Minnesota

When we first arrived at the University of Minnesota from Kansas in December 1996, we inherited a team that had been consistently at the bottom of the Big Ten in rushing. The year prior to our arrival, the team ranked 94th nationally and averaged only 104.1 yards rushing per game. As a staff, we were determined to establish an offense based on an effective running game.

Although our work is never finished, we have achieved marked improvement in that department. Our running game has improved to the point where we are now consistently ranked near the top of the Big Ten and have recently been ranked nationally in the top five. Many factors have contributed to this improvement, but we feel a large part of it has been our use of the two-receiver, two tight-end set, or 12 personnel, as we call it. With the right mix of athletes, you can have success using this system at any level of competition.

Several coaches have left their mark on our system as we currently operate it. We began using the 12 personnel set at Kansas during the 1994 season. Offensive line coach Pat Ruel was a big contributor to running the system at the time. When we began using this play at the University of Minnesota, line coach Steve Loney also contributed significantly to our use of and success with this system.

Anyone using 12 personnel is going to discover its many advantages. The first benefit we recognized is that the offense puts the defense on its heels. In the 2004 season we were in 12 personnel for 361 plays, more than 42 percent of our total offensive plays. Out of this personnel group, we ran nine different formations, some of which we'll cover later in the chapter. Our ability to send 12 personnel out onto the field and line up in multiple formations gives us a decided advantage over the defense. We keep them guessing.

Also, having both tight ends on the field allows us to break the huddle and approach the line in either balanced or unbalanced looks. The extra tight end gives us both a consistent blocker and a pass catcher in the huddle at all times. An extra receiver would lack run-blocking skills, and an extra running back would not be as strong in pass-catching ability.

The advantage of running this personnel group is that it gives us an opportunity to put our best players on the field at the same time. For most of our time at the University of Minnesota, our second tight end has been a better player than our third wide receiver. Part of this is by design; when recruiting, we make it a point to go after big-frame kids who can move well. We've had a lot of success in this area of the country in finding kids who fit this mold. Most of these kids are undersized when we get them out of high school, but we have had success in putting weight on them. Sometimes we're a little too successful in adding weight, but generally our overweight tight ends have thrived at offensive tackle.

An additional advantage to the system is that it's very simple to teach. We can run our entire offense from it, including our entire run package, dropback, three-step, sprint-out, and play action.

There are a few drawbacks to running the system. Obviously, if you lack the proper personnel, you can put yourself at a disadvantage. It's important to use the right kind of tight ends. If you recruit tight ends exclusively because of their pass-catching numbers, you might find you have a hard time getting them to block properly, which negates that advantage of this system. Any tight end in our system knows that run-blocking is one of his main responsibilities. We have taken it to the point that tight ends meet with and go through individual drills with offensive tackles. Any player who's afraid to stick his nose in to block someone will soon become a liability if you're running this system. Other than that, we have not found many weaknesses.

Formations

In this chapter, we'll discuss four formations that are effective against most defensive fronts you'll see. Specifically, we'll be looking at all plays against the 50 or Okie defense, the 4-3, over, and under. You will see the simplicity of many of our blocking methods out of two tight ends and, most important, you'll see how it negates many defensive schemes. The four formations we ran the most out of 12 personnel last season were ace, deuce, triple, and husker.

The ace formation (figure 4.1) was our most used formation in 2004. We were in it 45 percent of the time out of 12 personnel. This is the most basic formation out of 12 personnel. It is a totally balanced formation with one tight end and one wide receiver to each side. Each tight end is instructed to take a three-foot split from the tackle with his helmet aligned to the tackle's shoulder blades. The Y tight end is number 1, so we call the strength to that side (figure 4.1 shows ace RT). Although we label the first tight end going to the strength in every formation, we actually use them interchangeably.

On some plays, we want Y in a specific spot. For those plays, we tag the formation in a specific way. Generally, however, Y and the second tight end (labeled J) switch back and forth between front side and back side. This comes in handy during both running and passing plays; the defense can't set up based on Y.

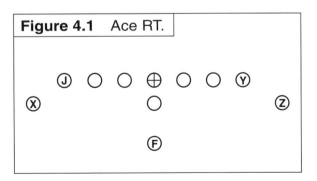

Figure 4.1   Ace RT.

In all our formations, running backs align with their heels at 7 yards, which allows them enough depth to be able to perform all their running and blocking responsibilities without having to adjust for the specific play. In ace formation, Z and X take a split halfway between the sideline and the tight end. From the middle of the field, this usually ends up being at the top of the numbers. (These alignments are based on the college field; exact placement varies for each level.)

We don't use any other formation as much as we use ace, but there are a few we like to use to give the defense a different look. One is the deuce formation (figure 4.2). In the deuce, we still line up with one tight end to each side, again changing which tight end performs the duties of Y and J. The change in this formation is that both wide receivers are off the ball to the strength side.

Generally we use this formation when on a hash, sending the two receivers to the wide side of the field. The alignment for the far receiver, Z, is the top of the numbers. X splits the difference, which ends up being about 1 yard outside of the hash.

The other two formations featured in this chapter require the movement of the tight end. This gives us the advantage of creating matchups we don't usually see and can exploit. The biggest matchup difference is when we can get the tight end lined up outside and covered by either a cornerback or safety. With our

tight ends being generally in the 6-foot-5 to 6-foot-7 range, most defensive backs don't have the size to defend a pass without pass interference.

One formation that gives us this matchup is the triple formation (figure 4.3), in which Y lines up to the side called, and J aligns to the side of the two wide receivers in a slot position. With the ball in the middle of the field, X aligns at the bottom of the numbers on the ball. The second receiver, Z, should go about halfway between the hash and the numbers. The tight end splits the difference off the line. J needs to be off the line of scrimmage, but we don't want him too deep—about the depth of the quarterback under center.

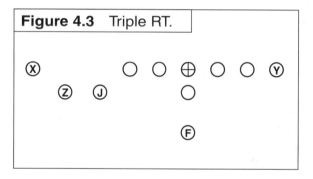

Figure 4.3 Triple RT.

It's important to work both the run and the pass out of this formation in practice and in games. This formation puts the tight end in a position he's not used to playing, so he needs to practice getting off the ball from a two-point stance. This formation can help you be successful running both ways because it forces the defense to adjust to the side with what appear to be three wide receivers. If the defense doesn't adjust, there should be a mismatch to the three-receiver side that you can run into.

The second unbalanced formation we use is called husker (figure 4.4), which sends both tight ends to the same side of the formation. The position of Y and J can be changed at any time, even

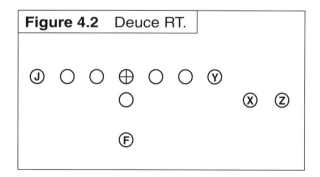

Figure 4.2 Deuce RT.

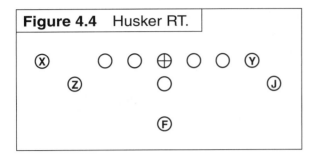

Figure 4.4   Husker RT.

going up to the line. J is placed at a two-foot split outside of Y. J should be in a three-point stance with his hand at Y's heel depth. The two wide receivers go opposite the call. X needs to be on the line of scrimmage at the top of the numbers. Z should split the difference between the end of the line and the X receiver. Typically, we run this formation from the hash with the two-receiver side going to the field.

Plays

All of these formations give us good opportunities to run or pass to either side, but with the extra blocker on the field we have a decided advantage in running the ball. Our main mode of running the ball is to use zone-blocking schemes and give the backs a chance to find a hole and get the ball downfield.

Inside Zone

Our most consistent play over the past eight years has been the inside zone running play (figure 4.5). We refer to this as our bread-and-butter play and call it many times a game. It works especially well with two tight ends because one's a good blocker on the front side who can take care of any edge players, and the

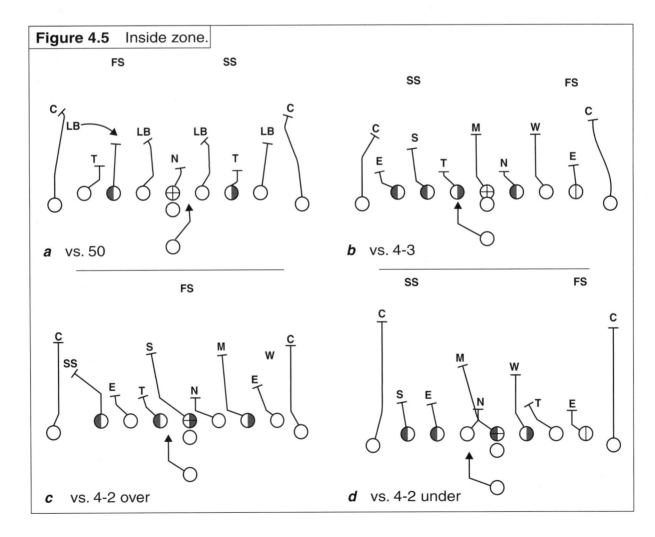

Figure 4.5   Inside zone.

a vs. 50

b vs. 4-3

c vs. 4-2 over

d vs. 4-2 under

backside tight end blocks the backside 5 or 7 technique. The problem with leaving the backside edge player unblocked is that, because the play is run between the tackles and nobody is in front of the backside 5 or 7 technique, that player has the opportunity to come off the edge unblocked and make the tackle in the backfield. With a frontside and backside tight end, we can account for him.

This is where the simplicity of the system comes in—no matter what defense is thrown at the formation, it is blocked the same way. All players have to do is block the playside gap. Figure 4.5c shows an inside zone run to the left against over defense. All of the linemen block whoever is in their playside gap. For the frontside tight end and tackle, this means making a red call and working the 7 technique out to the edge player, in this case the strong safety. Any time the tight end is covered, as shown in figure 4.5b and figure 4.5d, the tight end tries to base the man over him, and the tackle blocks whoever shows up in his playside gap. The rules are the same for the frontside guard, the center, and all backside linemen. They work the down lineman to their playside gap up to the next level. With this scheme, it doesn't matter who shows up into their gap—they are going to block him. This helps curb a lot of defensive stunting. Even if the entire line shifts or stunts to the strong side, the rules remain the same—if you have a down lineman in your playside gap, you block him. If not, work up to the next level and block the linebacker.

For the inside zone, the running back aligns his heels 7 yards from the ball and uses the footwork of open, crossover, and plant before squaring the shoulders to the line of scrimmage. The running back's aiming point is 1 yard behind the tight end's original alignment. His primary key is to run off the block of the first down defender. (In figures 4.5b and 4.5c, this defender would

be the 3 technique; in figure 4.5d, it would be the 1 technique on the center.) The running back can help the linemen tremendously by staying disciplined and pressing his hole, the B gap. This moves the linebackers and creates cutback lanes. Although this play permits for cutbacks, the running back should be looking to keep the ball front side when he has the opportunity.

During the 2004 season, the inside zone play averaged 5.7 yards per carry and was one of our more consistent running plays. In many situations, this is our go-to play, but it's not unstoppable. We consistently see eight- and nine-man defensive fronts that, on occasion, will stop the inside zone. This is why it's important to have a similar running play—you need to stop the defense from stacking up against the inside zone exclusively. In our offense, we also use an outside zone play to give us a two-headed rushing attack.

Outside Zone

Our outside zone (figure 4.6) has been a dependable complementary run to our inside zone for the past several years.

It's a different play but is blocked in about the same way. The difference is that we pull our linemen to get them out in front of the play and cutting. In general, whenever one of our linemen is uncovered on the front side of the play, we want him to pull around the end of the line of scrimmage and get his shoulders squared downfield.

The exception is when the linemen can get straight up to the linebacker level, as shown in figure 4.6b. Against the 50 defense (figure 4.6a), the frontside tight end is uncovered, but because there's nowhere to pull, he attacks the first man in his playside gap, in this case the outside backer. The frontside tackle is covered, so he reach-blocks the 5 technique. The frontside guard is

uncovered, so he pulls front side. His man is the linebacker covering him, but we want him to pull around to give himself a better blocking angle. The center is also covered, so he's going to scramble-block the nose front side. The center is the only frontside lineman we want scrambling; otherwise, we want the defender blocked up top.

On the back side, all linemen get the same instruction—cut the defender in your playside gap. It doesn't matter if it's a defensive lineman, a linebacker, or a safety. You work the levels of the playside gap—first line, then up to backer, then to secondary. Despite how fast backs are in this day and age, a backside defensive lineman or linebacker is fast enough to, on occasion, chase down the

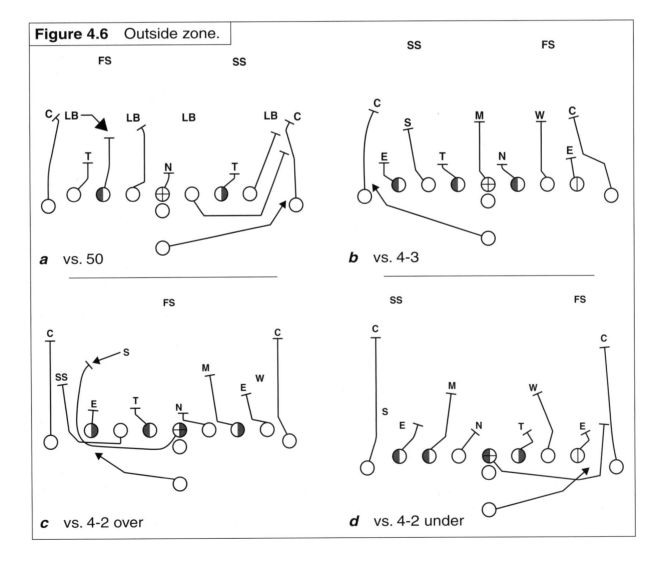

Figure 4.6   Outside zone.

a   vs. 50

b   vs. 4-3

c   vs. 4-2 over

d   vs. 4-2 under

running back. To eliminate all chance of that, we tell linemen to cut on the back side.

Other defenses dictate that other linemen pull, but to keep things simple the rules remain the same. Against 4-3, over, and under defenses, backside linemen are told to cut in all cases (see figures 4.6b, 4.6c, and 4.6d). Those on the front side and uncovered are going to pull.

Against over defense (figure 4.6c), we're going to have the most pulling. Both the frontside tackle and center are uncovered to the front side, so they're going to pull. The frontside tight end is covered, so he's going to block man-on. The tackle pulls around to block the first opposite-colored jersey he comes across. On occasion, the defender is across the line of scrimmage before the tackle can get his shoulders squared. When this happens, the tackle turns the block into a kickout and drives the defender to the sideline. The center pulls around for clean-up—any opposite-colored jersey he sees he will block. If he gets downfield, he cuts either a linebacker or a defensive back. It's unrealistic to ask a lineman to block a defensive back in the open field, so cutting is the best option. The frontside guard is covered, so he's going to reach-block. All of these rules remain the same regardless of where on the line the player is. This makes offensive linemen interchangeable, allowing us to get our five best linemen on the field at once no matter which position they play.

Figure 4.6b shows outside zone to the left against the 4-3 defense. We include this play to show that we'll run it to both sides, but ideally we like to run to the right against this defense. However, it's important that you can run to the right and left out of all formations. In this particular example, there would be nobody pulling. This is not ideal, but we'll do it from time to time.

What makes this play such a good complement to the inside zone play is that for the first two steps the quarterback and running back use the same action as in the inside zone. As in the inside zone, the running back's footwork is open and crossover, but instead of planting on the third step he works toward the mesh point with the quarterback. The quarterback uses the same footwork for the first two steps as well, which involves opening up to 5 or 7 o'clock, depending on whether the play is going to the left or right, and then working to the mesh point. For the outside zone, the quarterback opens up and works out behind the guard to get the running back the ball. Every day at practice the running backs and quarterbacks spend a minimum of five minutes working on backfield action so that it looks the same every time. Outside zone is strictly a frontside play; unlike the inside zone, the outside zone should never cut back. If there's any point at which the running back stops his feet, he's usually in trouble, so he just needs to hit the hole hard.

Speed Option

The other running play we use in our two tight-end set is the one-back speed option (figure 4.7). This play has been a good alternative for us for the past few years, and it's especially useful in the red zone. In 2003, we scored 10 touchdowns and ran 300 yards using the speed option.

The linemen rules for this play are similar to what they do in any of our zone blocking. All linemen block the playside gap, and the backside linemen and tight end cut. The main difference is that the frontside tight end leaves the end man on the line of scrimmage unblocked for the quarterback to pitch off of. It's easy when a linebacker or safety is outside and can be used as the pitch man. In these cases (figures 4.7a and 4.7c), the frontside tight end simply needs to work up to the linebacker level.

Figure 4.7   One-back speed option.

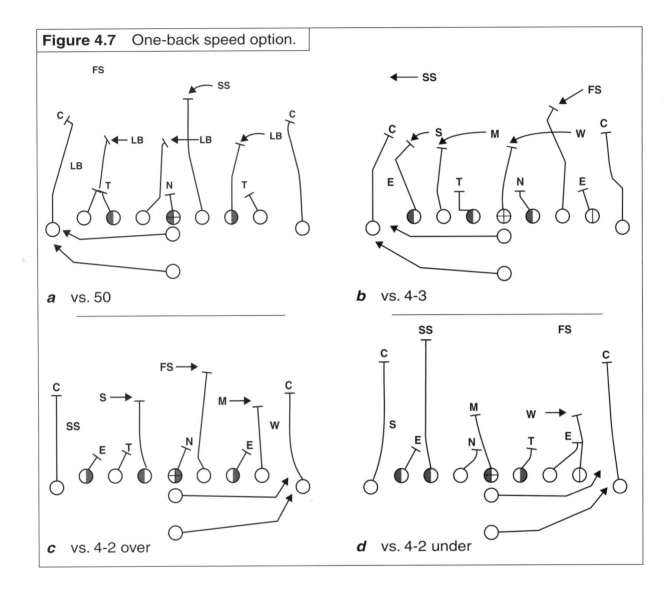

a   vs. 50

b   vs. 4-3

c   vs. 4-2 over

d   vs. 4-2 under

It's more difficult when there's a tight 9 technique on the tight end (figure 4.7b) or the tight end has a head-up 6 technique (figure 4.7d). In this situation, the tight end needs to make a judgment call. If he feels he can get up to the next level and block the linebacker without chipping the end man on the line of scrimmage, we want him to do that. In some cases, that's impossible; see figure 4.7d against under defense, for example. With a head-up 6 technique, the tight end is unable to get up to the linebacker level without hitting the end man. When this happens, we tell the tight end to turn it into a reach block. The instructions to the quarterback are that any time he sees the end man blocked he should tuck the ball and turn the play into a quarterback sweep. In every other case, we want the ball pitched to the running back because we don't want to make a living on the quarterback sweep.

Naked

With the amount that we run the ball, we need to have a play that compliments our run game and gives us a shot downfield but is not straight drop-back. The three-step passing game is a large part of our offense, but it rarely gives us an opportunity to take a shot downfield.

Five-step passing gives us a shot downfield but doesn't look like the other things we do. We find it's best to have a good play action and naked pass protection. When we run naked (figure 4.8), we're able to get both wide receivers and tight ends out on pass routes. We run this play when the defense starts to overplay the run. This changes from game to game; sometimes they overplay the run from the beginning, and then we run naked early and often.

The protection in naked is very simple—every lineman is responsible for his playside gap. As long as he pulls flat and denies penetration, you build a nice wall at the line of scrimmage. With all of the linemen going the same way and good backfield action, you can gen-

erally get the linebackers
line out of the play. One
routes is shown in figure
side wide receiver runs
frontside wide receiver
takeoff or comeback. Th.
going to be part of the protection for the
first three steps. From there, the frontside tight end runs an over route at 10 yards, and the backside tight end plants and reverses out of the block to run an under route. It's key that the backside tight end gets into the block before he plants and reverses out. If he doesn't, the defensive end will be upfield and into the quarterback's face. The under route is the quarterback's first option. If no one is covering the under, it's a safe short pass that nets good yardage.

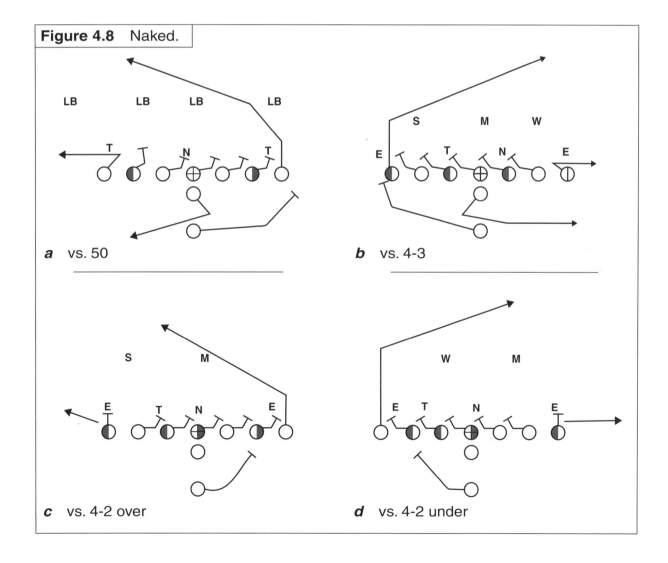

Figure 4.8 Naked.

a vs. 50

b vs. 4-3

c vs. 4-2 over

d vs. 4-2 under

Figure 4.9 Naked passing routes—backside WR runs post; frontside WR runs take-off or comeback; backside TE runs over route; frontside TE runs under route.

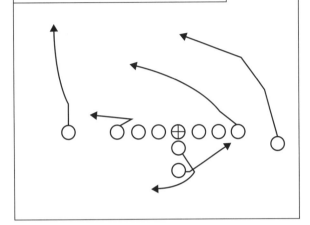

This play is often run by other schools out of a one tight-end or no tight-end set. We find that we get a better run fake look and have safer pass options if we run it out of the two tight-end set. Generally, you want to run naked out of ace formation, but it can also be run from deuce or triple if you're not in the middle of the field.

The Inside Zone Play-Action Pass

Off the inside zone play, we have consistently run a successful two-route play-action pass (figure 4.10). You have several options as far as the route is concerned; figure 4.11 displays four route options we use. If you keep using the same route combinations, the defense catches on, so last season we used 30 different route combinations.

All that remains the same here is the protection and backfield action. Call the routes any way you want to in the huddle; we tend to switch ours on a weekly basis to keep the defense guessing about what routes they'll see.

Figure 4.10 Two-route play-action pass.

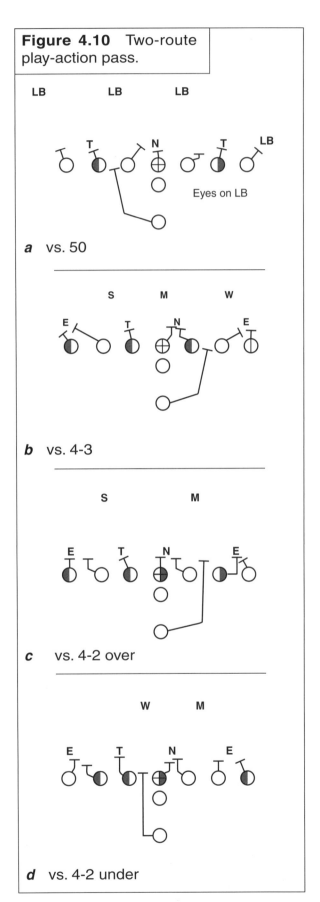

a vs. 50

b vs. 4-3

c vs. 4-2 over

d vs. 4-2 under

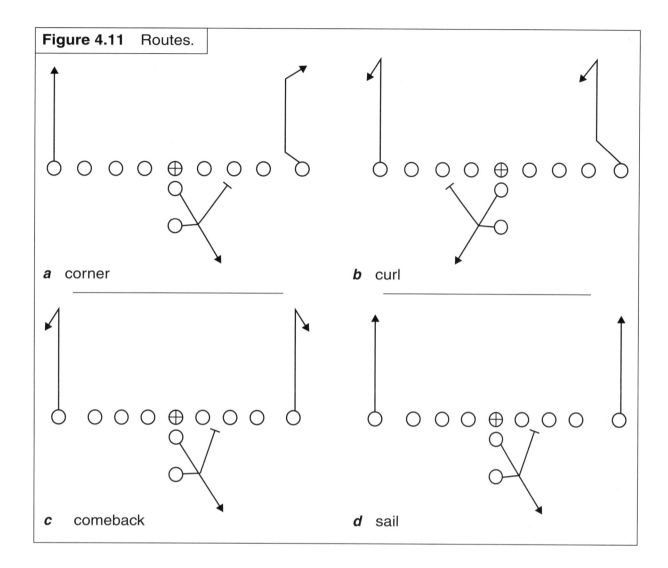

Figure 4.11 Routes.

a corner

b curl

c comeback

d sail

The protection has fairly simple rules, so the line can account for everyone, no matter what look or stunt the defense brings. Because it's a two wide-receiver route only, it's important for us to max protect. We use all five linemen as well as both tight ends and the running back. This eight-man protection gives us time to develop our routes, and the play action sucks the linebackers up into the line of scrimmage.

The frontside and backside tight end and tackle double-team any player in their shared gaps. If the tackle is covered, the tight end steps down to double-team the defensive end. He's also responsible for any linebacker who runs through his gap. If the tight end is covered, the tackle comes off the ball like a runner and covers the gap inside the tight end. Again, we want the tight end and tackle to cover any run-through from a linebacker. We coach the tight end and tackle to use four hands on the down lineman and four eyes on the linebacker. Because the blocking is the same for the front side and back side, players can easily remember their tasks.

Similar to the tackle and tight end, the guards and center work together to block both the down linemen and the linebacker. If the frontside guard is covered with a 3 technique (figure 4.10d), he blocks man-on. This is the only man block in the whole protection.

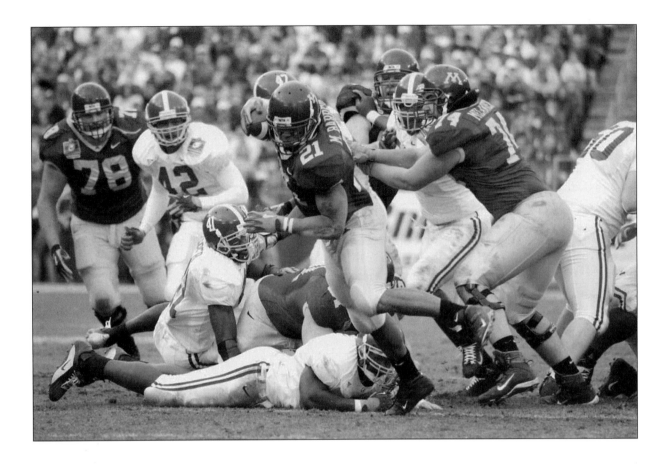

It's difficult to hold these blocks for long, so we try to minimize the number of solo blocks we ask of our line. If the frontside guard is uncovered or covered with an inside technique (figures 4.10a, 4.10b, and 4.10c), he works a double team with the center. Again, we want to have four hands on the down lineman and four eyes on the linebacker in case of any run-through. The backside guard works the same rules as the frontside guard. If he's covered with a 3 technique (figure 4.10d), he blocks man-on. If he's uncovered or covered with an inside technique, (figure 4.10a, 4.10b, and 4.10c), he double-teams with the center with eyes on the linebacker.

The running back is the eighth man in the protection. He blocks the open hole on the front side. If the guard has a 3 technique and is blocking the B gap, the running back hits the A gap and blocks any run-through (figure 4.10d). In all other instances, the running back is in the frontside B gap, waiting for a block. The running back's and quarterback's first responsibility is to carry out a good fake because without that you'll get no movement out of the defensive backs or linebackers, and it will be hard to get a receiver open.

Halfback Pass

Last season, during a Big Ten Congerence game, we found it difficult to run any sort of outside zone play. They were bringing their free safety down into the box on the outside any time they saw our wide receivers coming in to crack block. This left us in a tight spot, especially when we tried to run in the red zone. They were able to bring the free safety in to support so quickly that our tackles couldn't get a good kickout, and the play was getting stuffed. At halftime, someone suggested the halfback pass (figure 4.12). We felt that because of the way their safeties were supported we could run a crack-and-go with the wide receiver and get behind them.

In the fourth quarter we saw a perfect opportunity to use it. We called the play on a fourth and 8 from the 22-yard line. As all coaches know, plays called don't usually work the way they're drawn up. This case was no exception. Their defense was aligned similar to figure 4.12a. On the snap, instead of flowing to the line of scrimmage as he had done all game, the safety stayed deep. Luckily, the backfield action was just enough to freeze him for half a second, and our receiver was able to get behind the free safety. By the time the free safety recovered, the running back had

already thrown the ball; the pass was completed for a touchdown to put the game out of reach.

It would be difficult to pull this kind of play out more than once or twice a year and complete it against any good defense. The routes need to be changed to increase the chance of completing the pass. Figure 4.12d shows an example of one such change-up. If the free safety is playing down hard, run a tight-end delay. In this example, the tight end blocks just long enough so that the free safety plays down. From there, he can run a delay route and slip out for a pass. This play is not for all situations but is a good gimmick to use every once in a while.

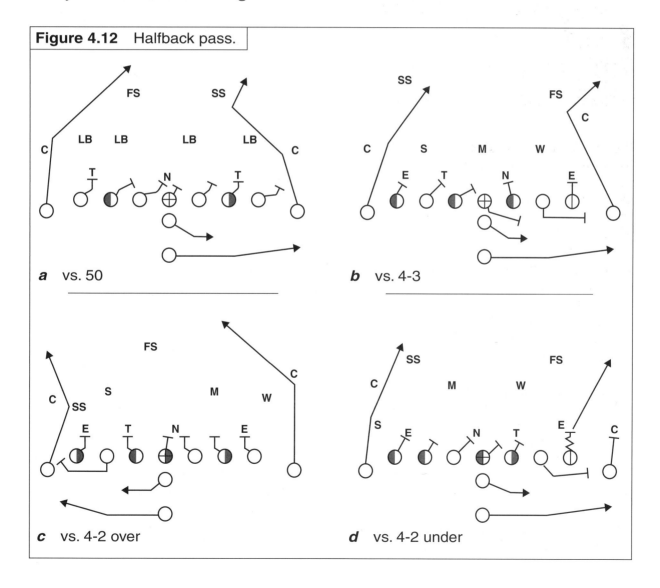

Figure 4.12 Halfback pass.

a vs. 50

b vs. 4-3

c vs. 4-2 over

d vs. 4-2 under

The way we run the plays presented in this chapter is a result of many years of tweaks and adjustments. The two wide-receiver, two tight-end set has worked best for us in our time here at Minnesota. Still, we've modified virtually everything about the system through the years as we've learned more effective ways to get the job done.

When implementing this system, select the parts you can accomplish effectively instead of trying to install it all. You can be successful with this system as long as you have the tight ends for it and you want to run the ball. After that, the system just takes hard work and lots of practice. The beauty of the system is that once players learn what to do (assignments) and how to do it (techniques), it is simple to execute and very productive. As someone once said, "the good news is, to succeed is simple; the bad news is, it isn't easy."

CHAPTER 5

Three Receivers, One Tight End

Joe Tiller
Purdue University

Jim Chaney
St. Louis Rams

Implementing offensive strategy can be a difficult task. Many questions are asked. What style? Do we throw or run? Do we want balance? At Purdue, all offensive questions are personnel driven. Who are our best 11 players? We identify who is on the field by using groupings (table 5.1).

We use four to six personnel groupings in every game. Our base grouping is what we identify as Normal. In the remainder of this chapter, we'll analyze the pros and cons of the Normal grouping, the different formations we use with it, and our base offensive plays.

Table 5.1   Purdue Personnel Groupings

Group name	Wide receivers (A, F, X, Y, Z)	Tight ends (Y, X/H)	Running backs (T, F)
Pro	2 (X, Z)	1 (Y)	2 (T, F)
Normal	3 (A, X, Z)	1 (Y)	1 (F)
Heavy	2 (X, Z)	2 (Y, A)	1 (F)
Lite	4 (A, X, Y, Z)	N/A	1 (F)
Tough	1 (Z)	2 (X, Y)	2 (T, F)
Goal line	N/A	3 (X, Y, Z)	2 (T, F)
Speed	5 (A, F, X, Y, Z)	N/A	N/A
Fleet	4 (A, F, X, Z)	1 (Y)	N/A
Jumbo	1 (X)	3 (W, Y, U)	1 (F)
Eagle	3 (X, Y, Z)	N/A	2 (T, F)

Table 5.2   Advantages and Disadvantages of Normal Grouping in the Spread

Advantages	Disadvantages
■ Forces the defense's hand—do they play base or nickel?	■ Team loses some vertical speed at the tight-end position.
■ Creates mismatches between the inside wide receivers and tight ends on the linebackers versus base defense.	■ Must move tight end for a lead back driven play.
■ Against nickel defenses, makes perimeter blocking favorable for inside wide receivers.	■ Must be creative within G-man protections to block the zone pressures.
■ Can maximize protections versus all-out blitz.	■ Defenses will force uncovered throws; team must have an answer.
■ Allows team to run strong and not worry about overhangs to the open side.	■ Weakside running game can be taken away by a defensive alignment (overhang).
■ Multiple formations can be aligned easily.	

Normal grouping became our base at the University of Wyoming years ago. We couldn't recruit a quality fullback, but we could find undersized tight ends who were good players and an abundance of wide receivers who liked our style. We needed an equalizer to compete with teams that had more talent. The spread offense fit our needs perfectly. Coach Dennis Erickson had used the spread effectively at many stops. By spreading the field we were able to match our guys on their guys in ways that favored us. For example, we would match up our tight end on their slowest linebacker. Today, we find Normal grouping within the spread the most important thing we do. Sixty to 70 percent of our snaps are committed to this grouping. Table 5.2 lists some of the advantages and disadvantages of using Normal groupings within the spread.

As you contemplate the use of three wide-receiver and one tight-end (Normal) offenses, consider your tight-end position first. Simply put, this position must be able to hold his own on a defensive end in the run game and defeat linebackers one on one in the passing game. If he can't do either, try a different grouping.

The need for a tight end on the field is fundamental. Having two open sides (no tight ends) makes it difficult to develop a running game. You can expect good defensive coordinators to overhang you and force you to throw the ball. Having a tight end on the field makes this more difficult to achieve.

There are two contrasting philosophies regarding spread offense. Some spread to throw all the time, and others spread to run the ball. Normal grouping allows us to fall somewhere in between, philosophically. We'll always use the pass at Purdue. Our belief that teams can scheme the running game and sometimes be better up front will keep us throwing. But if the running game is available to us, we'll take it all day.

Before we move into discussing specific plays, let us outline our system of calling plays. Our three-step passing game is our 90 series. Within this series, as well as our drop-back series, our routes or patterns are mirrored. Our graph for our 90 series is very simple (table 5.3).

Our systems can be learned quickly and efficiently, which allows wide receivers and tight ends to play quickly. Playing quickly is very important in college

Table 5.3   90s Route Structure

	Outside-most receiver	Inside-most receiver	Middle receiver
90	Hitch (7 yards)	Hitch	Hitch
99	Fade	Decision	LM seam

football. Our drop-back series is our 70 series. The routes and patterns are mirrored in this series as well. Frequently, we use tags or concepts to break the wide receivers' rules. Our running game is called by whole numbers: 0, 2, 4, 6, 8 to the right, and 1, 3, 5, 7, 9 to the left. If the running back is the ball carrier, a 3 is the first digit. If the quarterback is the ball carrier, a 1 is the first digit. We call grouping first, formation second, protection third, and route or pattern fourth. For example, doubles RT Ralph 73 or doubles LT 34 for a run play.

Formations

The alignment of personnel in formations is essential for success. Using our Normal grouping, we can line up in many different formations. We'll be addressing a 2-\x\-2 formation we refer to as doubles and an empty formation we call fox. In all of our formations we have the following positions to align: A, Z, X, F, and Y. Using Normal grouping, A, X, Z are receivers, Y is the tight end, and F is the running back.

In doubles formations, X (split end) and A (inside receiver) are aligned on the weak side of the formation, away from Y (figure 5.1).

All of our formation strengths are to the Y position. X is on the line of scrimmage, aligned on the numbers. Depending on where the football is and what the play is, X will move to either the top or bottom of the numbers. A receiver will always split the difference between the offensive tackle and X positions. A will always align in the

backfield, which allows him to legally be in motion. The tight end (Y) is located to the call side of the formation next to the offensive tackle. If we're aligned in shotgun, the tight end uses a two-point stance. If the play is called under center, the tight end uses a three-point stance. A 2- to 3-foot split from the offensive tackle is consistent. The Y is on the line of scrimmage. The Z receiver (flanker) is on the strong side of the formation toward Y, off the line of scrimmage, and on the numbers. Similar to the X position, Z can go from the bottom of the numbers to the top of the numbers based on the play called. The F (running back) is located in the backfield, 6-1/2 yards behind the football.

Our fox formation is an empty formation, with no backs in the backfield (figure 5.2). F (running back) and X (wide receiver) align on the weak side of the formation. Y (tight end), A (inside wide receiver), and Z (wide receiver) align on the strong side. F aligns on the numbers off the line of scrimmage. X aligns between F and the offensive tackle on the line of scrimmage. On the strong side, Z aligns on the numbers and will

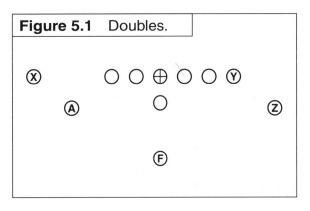

Figure 5.1   Doubles.

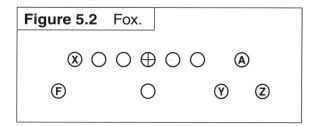

Figure 5.2   Fox.

be the widest wide receiver. Y aligns off the line of scrimmage 4 to 5 yards from the offensive tackle. A aligns between Y and Z and the line of scrimmage. All alignments vary based on the play called. In fox formation, Y is always in a two-point stance. In all empty formations, the inside receiver to the field aligns off the line of scrimmage. This allows us the bubble screen as an uncovered answer.

Many formations can be used. Doubles and fox are simple. They provide nice answers against man coverage and spread the field to attack zone coverage. Flexibility is important and vital to proper use of Normal grouping.

Inside Zone

Running the football from a one-back offense with Normal personnel has been extremely good to us. You're forced to use zone blocking schemes at some point. We'll touch on some man blocking plays later.

Our base running play is our inside zone play (figure 5.3). By definition, this is a zone-blocked run designed to find vertical seams in the defensive

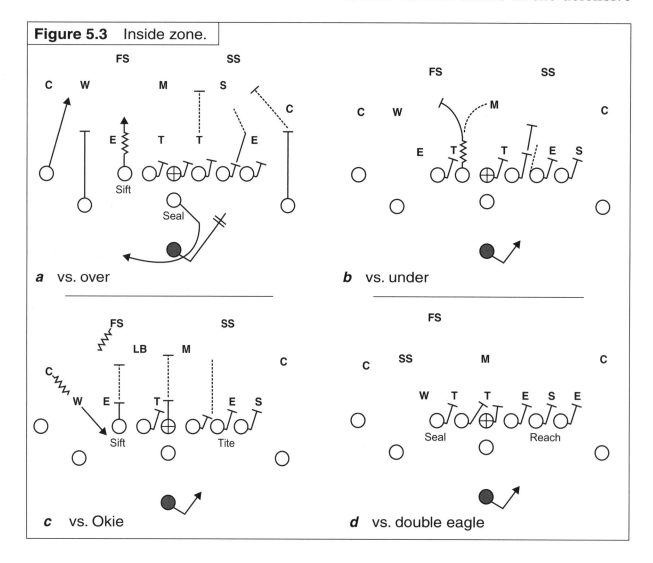

Figure 5.3   Inside zone.

a vs. over

b vs. under

c vs. Okie

d vs. double eagle

front created by an unsound defensive scheme or by creating a block well enough to force a breakdown in a gap-control defense. This is our bread-and-butter play. Our players understand that for us to be successful we must execute the inside zone play. This is a drive-block play. There's no room for finesse in this scheme.

The tight end through backside lineman are all ruled to the playside gap. Their techniques are determined by covered and uncovered rules. If covered, their targets are

1. triangle fits down the sternum; and,
2. second-step power step on top of the defensive lineman's inside foot.

If the defensive lineman is playing inside shade, we execute a hard-shoulder technique. If uncovered, the player's angle of departure is predicated on the location of the linebacker and the tightness of the defensive lineman. Covered linemen alert uncovered linemen of a possible line slant by saying "tight." If defensive linemen are in an uncovered man gap, either through postsnap movement or the defensive alignment, we execute a wedge block with the covered lineman to push the defensive lineman back to the linebacker. The offensive linemen and tight end know this as an over-and-up play. If everything goes wrong, they just go over and up.

The widest lineman playside is responsible for any overhang pressure. The tight end frequently has to make a reach call against the overhang. We will not check out of the play. We must make it work against all fronts and blitzes. We use a hard count or snap the ball on first sound with this play. Zone blocked plays are much more forgiving for the offensive line when trying to trick the defensive line.

The running back's steps mirror that of the offensive line. He slide-steps and then heads downhill at the playside offensive tackle's inside leg. His read is the first defensive lineman to the playside of the center. A common mistake by the running back is not to press the line of scrimmage enough. Without the press to the line of scrimmage, it's very difficult for the offensive lineman to successfully block his linebacker.

Our preference for years has been to run the play at the smallest shade or away from the 3 technique. This gives us two double teams at the point of attack on the G and 3 technique defensive tackles. Out of Normal grouping, we like the tight end to be on the backside of the play, cutting off the defensive end. If we can't move him there, we must have an answer for the defensive end—read his penetration (must be done from shotgun) and bootleg toward him in hopes of holding him from closing.

Draw

The next running play is essential to putting together the entire offense. It's the glue that makes the offense stick. Our common draw play (figure 5.4) has been extremely effective. As much as we throw the ball, it goes without saying that we must make the draw work. This play is similar to a slow dive play. The rules are simple and the techniques sound.

Our base offensive line rules are those of our five-man protection. For a little more than one count, the defense must see pass. The only way to judge if the play is too fast is by asking a simple question—did the inside receivers have a chance to make a block? Did we stall their underneath coverage enough with our action so that our people could be successful? The tight end is always ruled on the stud linebacker. By free-releasing him to a second-level player, it helps the sell.

Offensive tackles have the easiest job. Set firm and quick on the line of

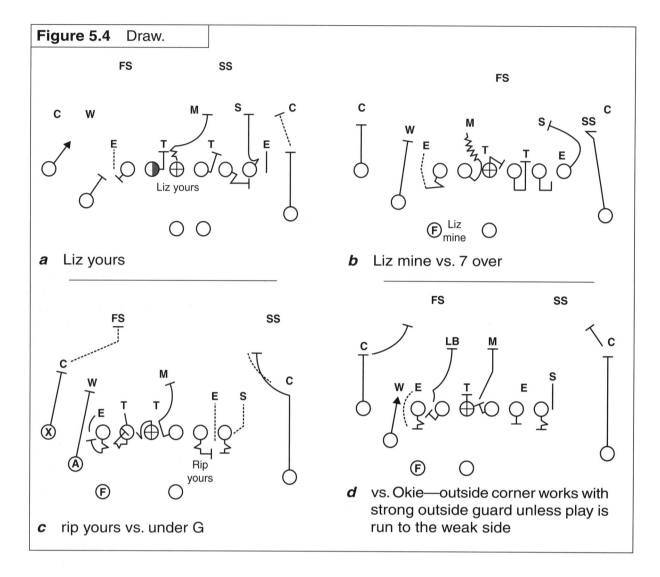

Figure 5.4   Draw.

a   Liz yours

b   Liz mine vs. 7 over

c   rip yours vs. under G

d   vs. Okie—outside corner works with strong outside guard unless play is run to the weak side

scrimmage. Be prepared to take away a pinching defensive end now. Be smart enough to handle the tackle/end mix with the guard. Blocking misses on draws is a different task. Proper sets and communication with teammates can eliminate some of the pain caused by movements. Quick set the guards for one count, then run your feet. The center sets with the proper guard, based on protection rules. Work together on the defensive tackle, then climb to the appropriate linebacker. If we're outnumbered, we check out of the play.

We added the draw fake in the backfield on some five step routes. By doing this we sufficiently tie the inside linebackers in a knot. The new two-deep coverages put such a strain on this position, the draw pass is quite effective.

The running back aligns on the 3 technique side out of the shotgun formation. Under center, he slide-shuffles to the 3-technique side. He must attack the line of scrimmage. The play is designed to bend behind a shade and split the defensive tackle versus a G and 3 technique.

Quick Game (Three-Step Drop)

When it comes to throwing the football, we like the three-step drop passing game, our 90 series, as our base. Some programs tend to lean on five- and seven-step passes. We evolved our quick game into four different routes. The number one pattern we run is a decision route by the inside-most receiver and a fade by the outside wide receiver. We call this route combination 99 (figure 5.5).

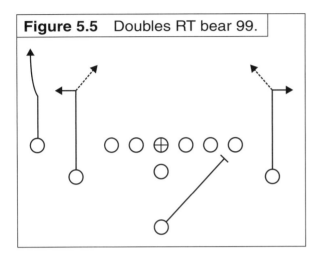

Figure 5.5 Doubles RT bear 99.

Within our 90 series, receivers and the tight end must understand protections. Routes are ruled by the inside-most receiver, middle receiver, and outside-most receiver. For example, in doubles formation if we call the tight end to stay in protection, Z then assumes the inside-most receiver rules. All our athletes learn how to run the decision route. Based on formation or protection, all could be called on to execute the route.

The decision route is a three-step diagonally stemmed route by the inside-most receiver. He keeps the inside foot up. On the plant of the third step, he must make a decision—do I run a speed-out or a slant? Wide receivers and the tight end always anticipate the out cut and adjust if the slant is made available. When the defender covering down is inside, he chooses speedout. When the defender is outside the alignment, he chooses to run a quick slant. For years we called speedout only to find outside leverage on the receiver, or we called a slant only to find inside leverage. This decision route has allowed us to be correct as play callers.

The offensive line firmly blocks the protection we called on the line of scrimmage. If we get a chance to cut block, we will. All other receivers are running either seams or fades. Seldom do they get the ball. The quarterback must set on his third step and wait a split second for the decision to be made; 95 percent of the time, the ball is delivered on time. Occasionally, the quarterback must wait to see the decision the wide receiver has made. I like this play on third and short to third and medium. Our players believe in the play. Out of Normal grouping, we have three or four different formations to run 99 in every game plan.

As with most routes that have some ambiguity, this concept is difficult for some players to grasp. Since installing 99, we have completed it at a 70 percent rate. In certain games, it becomes run offense. Yards after catch have increased remarkably since we installed the 99. It will always be a part of the Purdue offense. We continue to look for ways to quickly deliver the ball to the receivers. Take what they give you. Our quarterbacks have always had the green light to take the quick game if it's available. The 99 play has only helped our cause.

Play-Action Pass

The play-action pass is critical in any offense. Using Normal grouping affords us many different schemes to choose from. We mentioned earlier the success we've had with the draw fake play action. Our number one structure over the years has been our bootleg series. We refer to the play as naked right (figure 5.6) or naked left. In both of these plays the offensive line runs the run called. We'll always be faking our

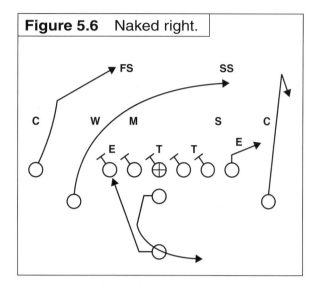

Figure 5.6   Naked right.

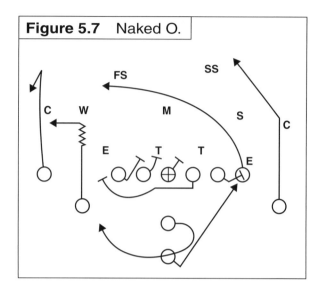

Figure 5.7   Naked O.

inside zone play. Our quarterback will fake, then bootleg away. A hard sell in the backfield is important on this play. Not pulling a guard in the series helps in the sell of the run.

The routes are driven by rules. Our best formation has been doubles. The inside receiver to the bootleg side has a slam-flat route, 4 to 6 yards after selling the run. The backside receiver has a drag route 10 to 12 yards deep. This route must get in front of the quarterback. In doubles, the backside widest receiver (X or Z) runs a post. The frontside widest receiver runs an 18- to 16-yard comeback. The quarterback's progression is simple—read slam-flat to drag to comeback. We never bring the post into the progression on this series.

The technical part of the quarterback getting square to his targets is always an issue. What happens when the defensive end doesn't take the cheese? Our answer has been to incorporate a pulling guard into the scheme. We retitle the play naked O (figure 5.7). When running the play out of the shotgun, we prefer naked O. Also, when our number two quarterback is not where he needs to be, we'll always protect our starter with an O call.

The flexibility of this series can be seen in many ways. We talked about our

O call. Now by adding "pin" to the O call, we invent another play (figure 5.8). Pin tells the inside receiver responsible for the slam-flat route to stay in and pin the defensive end inside. This changes the quarterback's progression and allows us to bring the backside post into play. The quarterback reads drag, post, and comeback. We'll touch on a gadget play we like out of the naked pin O series a little later. As you can see, our naked series affords us more play-action possibilities than we can ever call. We enjoy the flexibility and production. Over the years we've completed this series at 65 percent.

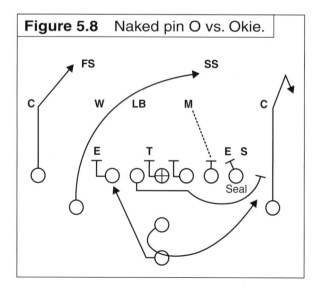

Figure 5.8   Naked pin O vs. Okie.

Drop-Back Pass

When people think of Purdue, they think pass-happy five-step patterns, throwing the ball 60 times a game. In eight years at Purdue we have averaged 40 passes a game. Just under half of these throws were five-step drops. Our base play is a four vertical route we call 73 (figure 5.9).

Everyone throws some version of four verticals; once again, Normal grouping out of doubles formation is our preference. Our landmarks are consistent with the rest of the world. The inside receivers (A and Y) are landmarked 1 yard outside the hash. The outside receivers are landmarked on the numbers. Receivers are allowed to get creative with their releases as long as they're where they need to be 15 yards downfield. Running backs are always involved in six-man protection on 73. Their rule is to check over the ball after their blocking responsibilities have been executed.

The quarterback progression is based on coverage. Against man-to-man coverage teams, we'll always take the best matchup, which often is the tight end on a linebacker. Against two-deep shell coverages, we read the field-side inside receiver to the check down. The receiver route changes if after 12 yards his path is obstructed by a secondary player.

He then bends into the middle of the field and is identified as the bender. Against cover-3 teams, we read the middle safety. The quarterback tries to move the safety with his eyes, reads his movement, and delivers the ball to the appropriate inside receiver.

We use four verticals to set up many different concepts in our offense. We have generated many big plays with 73. We use the concept of four verticals out of every formation we keep in the game plan.

Protections

We encourage everyone who's sold on throwing the football and using Normal grouping to first consider protections. The two formations we discussed earlier mandate two distinctly different protections. Obviously, in the empty formation you have to adjust a five-man protection to fit (figure 5.10). In doubles, a five-, six-, or seven-man protection can be used.

We start implementing protections with five man. This is our base protection, and everything grows from it. Philosophically, the center is the brains of our operation, and the tackles are our eyes. Simply put, the tackles must identify a blitz threat, and the center must

---

Figure 5.9 Doubles RT 73.

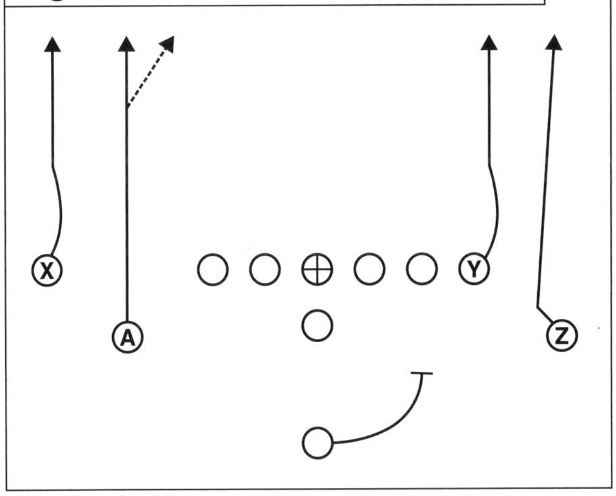

Figure 5.10 Five-man protection.

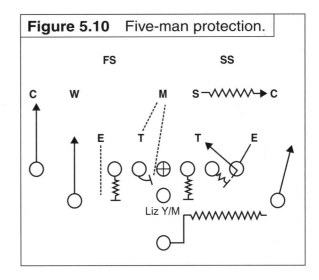

make changes to accommodate these threats. The center is the only player allowed to slide the offensive line. Some programs predetermine slides, but we do not. Our philosophy is to base everything we can and slide when we must. Our base is man-on when covered, man over when uncovered.

In five-man protection, both tackles are to alert blitz looks. The task that falls on the center is to block the five most dangerous defenders. Predetermining slides in five-man protection allows the defense to rush just one man and have the offense outnumbered. Bad strategy! The center needs to have a way of sliding two, three, four, or five offensive linemen to the right or left. Eight different words to fit those needs

make up the total vocabulary for all our protections.

Situations arise that force you to have a plan. Crowded linebackers in the A and B gaps force you to use communication to gap down your offensive line. We always try to let the widest man go free. Throwing out of the shotgun is more forgiving for the crowded linebacker.

How to handle pressure is the next step in the evolution of five-man protection. What do you do when six defenders blitz? We have two answers: throw hot and maximize the protection. Over the years, these have been the most simple to execute (figure 5.11).

Implementing six-man protections is simple after five-man has been taught. We use the running back as the sixth

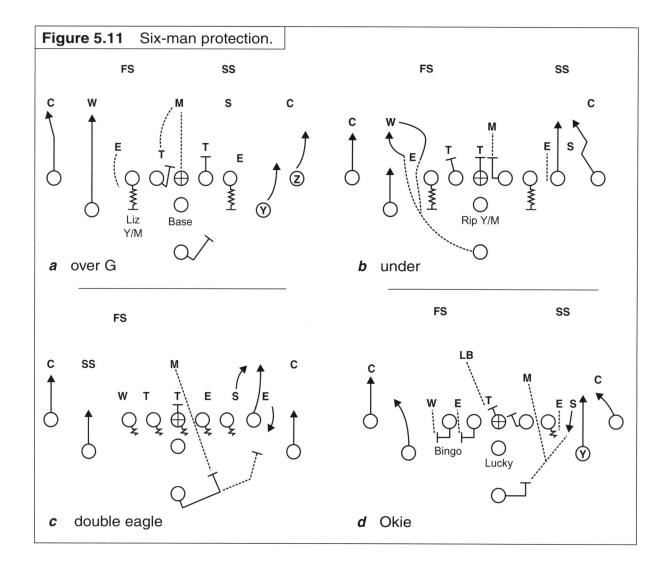

Figure 5.11 Six-man protection.

a over G

b under

c double eagle

d Okie

man. The offensive tackle to the side of the running back doesn't need to be alert for blitz. The running back is responsible for understanding the offensive line scheme. His responsibility is a dual read of linebackers. His count starts with the first defender off the line of scrimmage that the offensive line has not accounted for. This takes some time. They are 6-1/2 yards deep and can adjust the alignment as needed.

Running backs align in different areas to execute their assignments. We can't afford to let the defense understand our protection by the mere alignment of the running back. It's essential that you free-release the running back occasionally. What appears to the defense as a six-man protection is actually a five-man. Stay offensive! More games are lost with protection problems than won. Put the needed time in so your players are comfortable with your chosen weapons. We adhere to the KISS (keep it simple, stupid) theory when talking protection.

Auxiliary Plays

Every offense has plays that would not be considered a staple of the offense but nonetheless are important to the team's success. We chose years ago not to invest the time needed on the counter play. Misdirection has always been an issue in Normal groupings, doubles formation. We chose to slow down the linebackers by freezing them with the Tom play (figure 5.12). This has become a popular play of the new millennium. We stole it also.

The playside is blocked exactly like a lead play. The backside offensive guard has base cutoff rules. The backside offensive tackle is to pull around the double-team block of the center and guard to the first linebacker in the box. Basically, we exchange our offensive tackle for a fullback in a two-back offense. You can get as creative as you

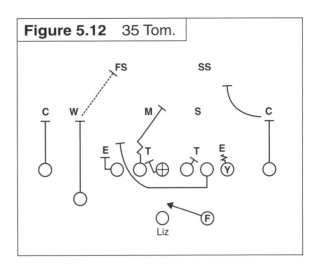

Figure 5.12   35 Tom.

want in the backfield. We call the play two different ways—the running back is aligned on the playside, or the running back is aligned on the backside of the play. We predominately run out of the shotgun, but Tom also has been good to us in short yardage under center.

Many teams are running this scheme while running the quarterback with the ball. We primarily give the ball to the running back. It's not a particularly good play into pressure. We allow the quarterback to change this play as needed, usually to base inside zone. We have struggled finding a play-action pass off this action, mainly because of protection problems. Tom allows us to double-team a defensive tackle, which we need to do from time to time. We usually run away from the 3 technique. The shade-side guard and center double-team a lot. Lead and Tom are the same for them. We're always looking for carryover in our running game.

A wise old coach once said that a simple hitch is a good way to jump-start a drive. He was right. When evaluating our offense in the off-season, we consistently agree that we need to throw more hitches. As mentioned earlier, the quick game is a great substitute for the run game when things are tough.

Whatever formations we have in the game plan, hitches are always available to the quarterback. Simple route, firm protection, and nonmoving targets are made for success. For years, we counted steps by the wide receivers on hitches. We have changed. Coming up short on third and four changed our minds. Tight ends, wide receivers, and running backs all run hitch routes the same. We refer to this as 90. The depth of the route is 7 yards from the line of scrimmage. Our favorite formation is to throw it out of fox (figure 5.13). Most of the time, the tight end or A will get the ball.

We convert the hitch (90) by an outside wide receiver to a fade. We haven't thrown a converted 90 in years. If we want a fade, we call it. On 90, inside receivers have permission to stem the route away from the defender covering them down. This is a little gray. We try not to overdo this. We have thrown hitches at 65 percent over a 10-year

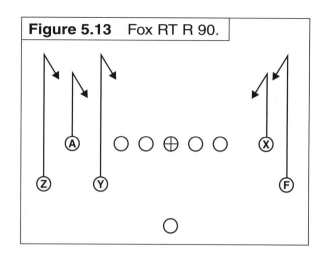

Figure 5.13   Fox RT R 90.

period. It's a great first-down call. Listen to those wise old coaches.

Gadgets

We have a couple of plays that we don't use much except in specific situations. The first is a keep play off the bootleg series. We've discussed our naked play-action pass. Adding the words "pin keep" to the play changes the play to a quarterback sweep with a pulling offensive guard (figure 5.14). A short-yardage situation is an ideal time to call the naked pass series or an occasional naked keep.

Most teams use their inside linebackers to jump the drag routes in our naked series. When this happens, we call the "keep" play.

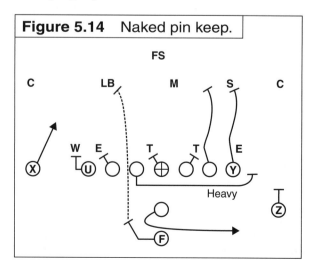

Figure 5.14   Naked pin keep.

The tight end must pin the defensive end to the inside. The decision you need to make is how to handle a wide 9 technique. As mentioned earlier, we use this play on short yardage. We see very little wide 9 technique in this situation. If it occurs, we send the tight end through to first inside and let the guard handle the defensive end. The running back must tighten his track or mesh with the quarterback. His responsibility is to take the fake and find a way to get to the backside linebacker.

After the mesh with the running back, the quarterback has to find the guard and follow him through the hole. Blocking support on the strong side, the Z receiver blocks man-on. Depending on how many times you plan to call the keep, you can get more complicated with your scheme chores.

Other than short yardage, the four-minute drill at the end of the game to secure victory is a perfect time for the keep. You expect man coverage in the four-minute drill. The defense can't let you run the ball. Slipping in a quarterback run is a perfect change-up in this situation.

Keep has some inherit problems. By pulling the backside guard, you create a hole inside your protection. Some zone pressure or man blitzes can cause trouble. You must decide if you want to take your chances on a big play or err on the conservative side and check out of these blitzes.

The second special play is our F-go play. Very similar to the keep play, we fake the inside zone, then bootleg. Similar to the keep play, the playside tight end pins the defensive end. The quarterback follows the pulling guard, selling naked O or the keep play. Once the quarterback breaks contain, he plants and throws back side.

After the fake of the inside zone, the running back (F) passes and then accelerates to the flat area, turning downfield on the numbers. We run out of Normal

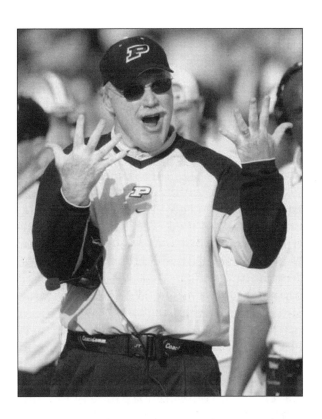

grouping, doubles formation a lot. The X receiver runs a deep post route. He must attract the cornerback while staying away from the free safety. The A receiver runs a drag, trying to take the free safety out of the quarterback's vision with his route. The quarterback's read is similar to a postwheel pattern in the drop-back game—key the corner. Versus man-to-man coverage, the quarterback is allowed to throw whatever ball needed to attack the linebacker covering the running back. Some of our best success stories with F-go have come when the running backs tell us they're uncovered. Listen to them.

The situations we look for on F-go vary. It's a perfect play after a big turnover near midfield. We like F-go from the 50- to the +35-yard line. Versus man-to-man coverage teams, we're constantly checking to make sure the defense covers the faking running back. Young linebackers tend to fall victim to this play regularly. Remember, as in the keep play, there are some flaws to the protections. Make sure you have addressed and practiced your plan versus pressure before calling F-go.

For nearly 20 years, we've been using Normal groupings within the spread to be productive. We believe in the system, and so do our players. Proper evaluation of players is essential in determining the proper groupings to use. We're constantly tweaking our offense. Year to year, we have some fluctuation in what the number-two grouping will be, but the constant has been Normal. Using multiple formations makes it difficult for the defense. Conversely, you find time to practice them. This seems to be the single biggest issue we face. Practice time is precious. By using Normal most of the time, we can get efficient at several formations and plays. Players can learn a lot. We continue to throw a lot at them, and they continue to impress us. Don't be scared to try new plays and concepts. Your players will love you for it. Their brains need to be fed. We have been blessed with some talented football players. Tight ends and wide receivers come in all sizes and shapes, but they all seem to fit into this system. There's a spot for quick kids, fast kids, possession receivers, blocking tight ends, and receiving tight ends. They are all pieces to a beautiful puzzle that you get to put together.

Go out of your way to make it hard to defend your offense. Always think offensively. Never allow the defense to dictate your approach. Normal grouping is the way to answer most questions that arise in the spread. Find three solid wide receivers, one good tight end, and go for it. Get creative. Shift, motion, shotgun—try it all. You'll love it.

We're very proud of our offensive product at Purdue University. Using three wide receivers and one tight end is just our "normal" way of life.

CHAPTER 6

Four Receivers

Gregg Brandon
Bowling Green State University

Greg Studrawa
Bowling Green State University

The Bowling Green State University football program is proud to be one of the contributors to this book. In recent years, we have used four wide receivers as the base set of our offense. The base formation that we'll focus on here is a two-by-two set in which there are two wide receivers on each side of the ball and one back in the backfield.

Generally, the quarterback is in the shotgun position with the back offset to the strength of the formation. It's not imperative for the quarterback to be in the shotgun position, but in our offense it gives us the best advantage against the opposition. Being in the shotgun position eliminates unnecessary steps that must be taken by the quarterback. He has the freedom to make his reads without focusing on dropping back into the pocket.

The single running back is in an optimal position to protect or receive the football. Solo is the term we use for this formation. It has been one of our top formations since we adopted the spread offense. Our intent in adopting the spread offense was to force the defense to defend the entire field on any given play. As a staff, we feel that putting skilled athletes in positions to make plays gives us an advantage over running the traditional I formation. Running this type of offense allows us

to take advantage of how the defense aligns on a given play. Ultimately, this enables the offense to attack the area of the field that the opposition is not defending.

In running this type of offense, we take best advantage of our personnel. It's not easy to recruit tight ends or fullbacks to run the I formation attack, but we're able to recruit skilled athletes who have the ability to make things happen when they touch the ball. Using these athletes gives us the chance to make every play a big play.

Two other key items are necessary to make this formation a success. One is that we don't huddle between plays. This allows us to run plays rapidly, which can create confusion and fatigue for the defense. The opposition has to line up immediately after each play and be ready to defend the next play. We aim to create a tempo that causes the defense to substitute more often than they would like to. If we can get the second-tier players in the game more often, this creates a greater opportunity for us to make big plays. If the starters stay in the game, we try to physically wear them down by coming at them with a fast tempo. We have also found that our tempo makes it difficult for defenses to signal in multiple blitzes, coverages, fronts, and other changes that the opposing team might have prepared for us. The faster we can get to the line of scrimmage and line up to run a play, the faster the defense has to get in position to execute their defensive call. Whether we run the play quickly or not, the defense has the illusion that we're going to snap the ball and they have to get ready. You don't have to be a no-huddle team to run this offense, but we've found that the no-huddle offers many potential advantages and makes the spread offense more difficult to defend.

The other feature of our four wide-receiver set that has worked to our benefit is, as I have already mentioned, the shotgun alignment. You don't *have* to move the quarterback from under center to run this offense, but that works best for us. We believe the shotgun benefits our running game, and it's easier for the quarterback to read pass keys from this position. But the offense can be executed with the quarterback under center, if you choose. The same plays can be run with only a few adjustments to the running game.

As I've stated, the formation we're going to focus on is called *solo* (figure 6.1). This formation is difficult to defend because it balances up the defense. It also gives us the ability to attack all areas of the field with the run or the pass. We want to be able to run the ball and throw the ball with equal effectiveness.

One of the mistakes often made in the spread offense is creating a wide-open offense that is reckless and throwing the ball with no concern for the running game. This is not a good idea. This offense can be a ball-control offense with the potential to create big plays at any time. The running game is critical in this offense, and the quarterback is the secret ingredient in the running game. The defense has to be accountable for the tailback as well as the quarterback at all times.

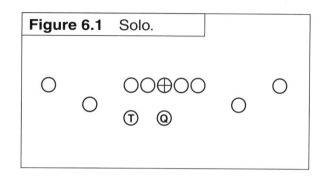

Figure 6.1 Solo.

For this offense to be most effective, you need a balanced run-to-pass ratio. We have been balanced in our attack for the past four seasons, passing more than running in only one of those seasons. That's the key to managing this offense—the defense can either take away the run or the pass, but not both. If you strive to perfect the running and passing games, you can be successful in any game situation.

From here on in this chapter you'll see how we move the football in this formation. We'll analyze the best runs and passes we have out of this set. We'll also examine pass protection used out of this set.

We'll describe a few of our basic plays and concepts, starting with the three-step quick-passing game, and we'll discuss a couple of those concepts. We'll then take a look at the five-step passing game, which allows us to attack the defense further downfield. Finally, we'll present our protection schemes and our best running plays out of the solo formation. We've also included a trick play that has been successful for us.

Three-Step Doubles Concepts

This package is designed to give the quarterback two different sides of the field to work with and to give the quarterback some short throws in a blitz situation.

We name each concept individually. The first concept is called to the strength of the formation, for example, solo RT 360 lite/lion (figure 6.2). The right side of the formation runs the lite, and the left side runs the lion.

Each concept is designed to beat a certain coverage presented by the defense. The quarterback looks at the defense to get a presnap read, which helps him decide where he wants to go with the football. The quarterback's read might change postsnap if the defense rolls or shifts their coverage.

The offensive line understands that this is a three-step concept based on the protection call. The protection has the number 3 in front of it, so the offensive line is keyed in on aggressive pass protection. That aggressive pass protection is usually cut blocks to get the defenders' hands down.

The lite concept has double hitches run at 6 yards. At Bowling Green State University, we run routes based on steps. To get 6 yards, the player has his inside foot up and runs five steps. Double hitch is a one-safety beater. The quarterback is going to read the hitches outside-in. If the outside hitch has press coverage, the player running the route converts his route to a fade. The inside hitch will not convert.

The lion concept has double slants. This concept is designed to beat two-safety coverage. Both receivers run three-step slants. The inside receiver's

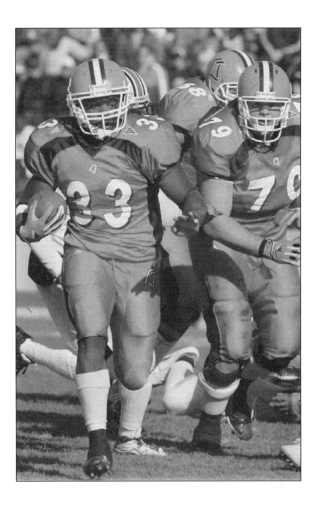

job is to shave the inside shoulder of the outside linebacker and then get back skinny upfield. The outside receiver's job is to run his slant no deeper than 9 yards. He wants to keep his route flat and less than 9 yards because he wants to stay away from the safety. The quarterback's read is the outside linebacker. If the outside linebacker caves in with the inside slant, the quarterback throws the outside slant. If the outside linebacker runs under the outside slant to expand the field, the quarterback throws the inside slant.

The majority of the time we package our two-safety beater with our favorite one-safety beater, which is the lite concept described previously. Our Ohio concept is a two-safety beater designed to stress the corner (figure 6.3). In Ohio, the inside receiver runs a four-step speedout. This can't be stopped if run

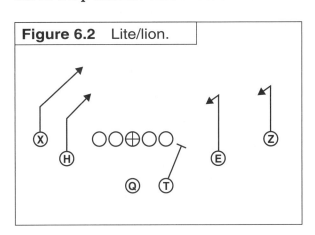

Figure 6.2 Lite/lion.

Figure 6.3   Lite/Ohio.

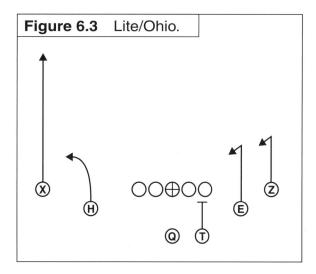

the correct way. The outside receiver runs a protection release fade. He must protect the speedout by releasing outside the corner. He takes his inside arm and rips it through the defender's outside shoulder, running and settling in the vacuum between the safety and the corner. The quarterback's read is the flat defender. If the corner is taken away by the protection release and the speedout has leverage on the outside linebacker, the quarterback throws the speedout. If the corner peaks and is not affected by the protection release, the quarterback throws the fade in the vacuum between the safety and the corner.

Five-Step Concept

Building off the three-step is the five-step passing game. The five-step passing game gives receivers more time to run longer routes. It also gives the quarterback more time to read the coverage and go through his progressions. This ultimately helps to open up the three-step passing game because the defense has to prepare for the deep passing game. The deep threat helps prevent defenses from sitting on three-step routes because they must be ready to turn and run if we decide to throw the ball deep.

One of our favorite five-step pass plays is four verticals, which we call "all go." We also like the smash because if the defense relies too heavily on stopping the four verticals, we simply come back and throw to a receiver sitting in the curl flat zone while the other receivers run deeper routes.

All Go

All go is our four vertical concept in the five-step passing game. All four wide receivers space evenly across the field and get vertical as quickly as they can. We want to stress the defense down the field and make them defend the entire field. The outside wide receivers run a go route with a landmark 2 yards outside the numbers (figure 6.4a). They come off to beat the defender over the top of them. If they can't beat the man over the top of them by 12 yards, they run a dropout at 15 yards (figure 6.4b) to give the quarterback a throw he can complete if his read takes him to the outside. The inside wide receivers also run go routes, trying to take an outside release to create a lane for the quarterback to throw the ball. Their landmark on the field is 2 yards outside the hashmark on their side.

The inside wide receiver on the strong side of the formation must read the middle of the field. If it's open, he runs a bender and takes what the defense gives him. He breaks at 10 to 12 yards. The tailback will check release and run a dump route over the ball at 4 yards.

The quarterback takes a full three-step drop in the shotgun and reads whether we have a 1-hi look or a 2-hi look from the defense. His movement key is the free safety in a 1-hi look. His progression is the seam away from the free safety to the outside vertical/dropout, to the dump at 4 yards. If the quarterback sees a 2-hi look, he looks to the bender, to the outside vertical on that side, then to the dump.

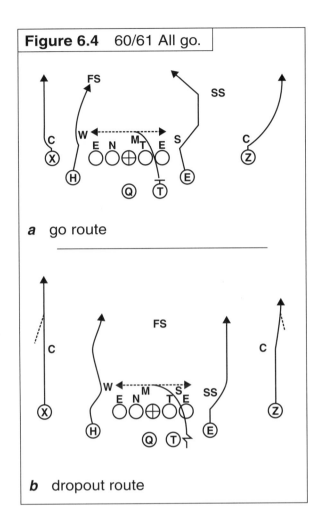

Figure 6.4 60/61 All go.

a go route

b dropout route

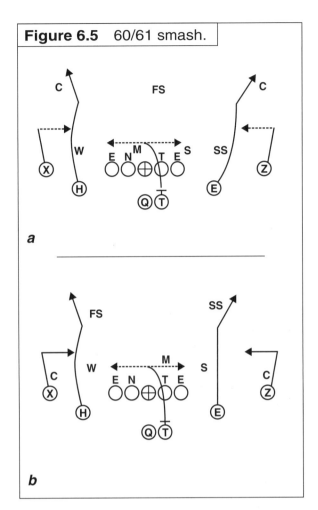

Figure 6.5 60/61 smash.

a

b

Smash

The 60/61 smash concept (figure 6.5) is a sideline stretch concept in the five-step passing game. The outside wide receivers on each side run a width hitch. They align in a normal alignment and run a 6-yard stem with 2 yards width. They should stand almost 2 yards from the boundary. The inside receivers take an outside release on the defenders to protect the hitch throw by the quarterback. If they're covered in any way by the flat defender or in man to man, they run flat back inside and sit in the void of the zone or continue to run versus man coverage. They must get that outside release because it helps the picture for the quarterback. They'll continue on a vertical stem of 10 to 12 yards and break

25 yards deep on a corner route 25 yards deep on the sideline. The tailback will check release and run a dump route over the ball at 4 yards.

The quarterback determines which side of the field is the best side to throw the hitch to. If the sides are equal, he looks to the width of the safeties. His movement key is the corner to the side of the throw. His progression is the width hitch to the corner route to the dump. Any time we're able to take a hitch throw, we'll take it.

60/61 Protection

This is our fundamental protection—part man and part zone. It's a six-man slide protection that includes the back and five linemen, allowing four receivers to free-release. The fundamental rule is quite simple—slide the line away from the call, starting at the first uncovered lineman, and give the back a dual read to the front side of the protection. Sounds easy, but we want to pick up the six most dangerous defenders, so the offensive unit must know who the six defenders are and who's responsible for getting to them. These intricacies are what make this protection solid versus blitz, which is where teaching and play calling can keep the quarterback on his feet and the chains moving.

Our terminology is as follows. The 6 in 60/61 stands for six-man protection,

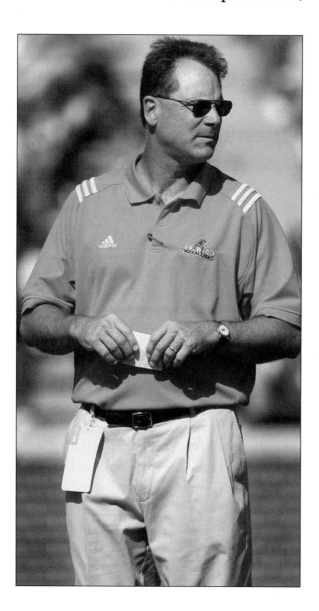

the 0 and 1 tell us which way the back will start and which side of the line is the man side (the playside). T is the tailback; PS is the playside; BS is the back side; T, G, and C are the tackle, guard, and center. PS and BS precede the T and G so the rules cover both tackles and guards whichever way we call the protection. S, M, and W are the Sam, Mike, and Will linebackers, starting from the offensive strength call. B is the backside linebacker in an odd front. F is the backside free safety. *Covered* is the term used if a defender is aligned on the line of scrimmage immediately to the call side or heads-up to an offensive lineman (also termed man-on). *Uncovered* is the term used if a defender is not aligned on the line of scrimmage immediately to the call side or heads-up to an offensive lineman. Gus means the guard starts the slide; cat means the center starts the slide. Fan means that two are coming outside the backside tackle.

The four base fronts for protection purposes are 41 stack (figure 6.6a), 42 (figure 6.6b), 42 under (figure 6.6c), and odd (figure 6.6d).

The rules are as follows:

PST: If covered, block man-on. If uncovered, block man outside.

PSG: If covered, block man-on. If a defender times his blitz through the A gap, take him; the back will adjust. If uncovered, make Gus call and start slide (block backside gap).

C: If covered, block man-on and listen for Gus call. If Gus call, turn back to protect backside gap. If uncovered and no Gus call, give cat call and start slide (block backside gap).

BSG: If covered, block man-on and listen for Gus or cat call. If Gus or cat, protect backside gap. If uncovered, turn back and protect backside gap. Set hard to backside gap if BST gives fan call.

BST: Turn back in protection and block outside. Set to widest defender. If there are two defenders, head up to

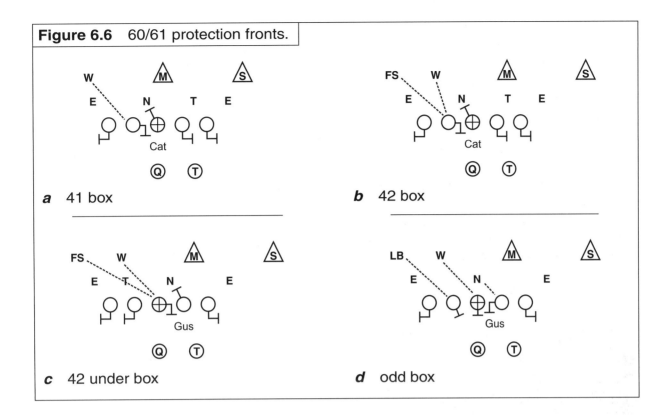

Figure 6.6   60/61 protection fronts.

a   41 box

b   42 box

c   42 under box

d   odd box

outside and give fan call to ensure slide comes all the way out.

T: Read Mike to Sam. Work inside to outside. If a defender times his blitz through the playside A gap, the PSG takes him. Adjust and cut the defensive lineman for which the PSG was responsible. If fan call, check one more man to the back side before releasing.

QB: If two come front side, you are hot. If they come back side, you must be aware so you can buy some time to get rid of the ball.

A few coaching points can make the protection easier than six guys all being in man protection. If on the playside of the protection, you're in a man scheme; take your guy. Stop the penetrator and chase the looper. If on the back side, trade off twists—you're on the zone side. Don't come off until you're knocked off. Stop the penetrator and bump to the looper. Don't slide to air. Turn your eyes back to the gap for which you're responsible while helping with the playside defender.

Inside Zone and Trap

Now we'll look at two of our base running plays out of solo formation in the shotgun alignment. Inside zone (read) and trap are two plays we carry into every game. They are productive and efficient plays in the spread one-back offense. We show them against two base defensive looks that we've faced in this offense: 4-3 and odd defense.

Inside zone, or the read play, is a running play that uses a zone blocking scheme and technique with the offensive line, man blocking with the wide receivers, and a read by the quarterback. The running back reads the blocking of the offensive line, which tells him where the ball should be run. When we run this play versus a base 4-3 defensive look, we block the inside zone play, as shown in figure 6.7.

The playside tackle blocks man-on the defensive end. The playside guard and center double-team the defensive tackle to the frontside linebacker. The backside guard and tackle double-team

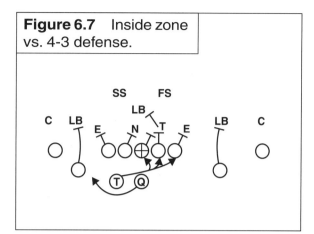

Figure 6.7 Inside zone vs. 4-3 defense.

Figure 6.8 Inside zone vs. odd defense.

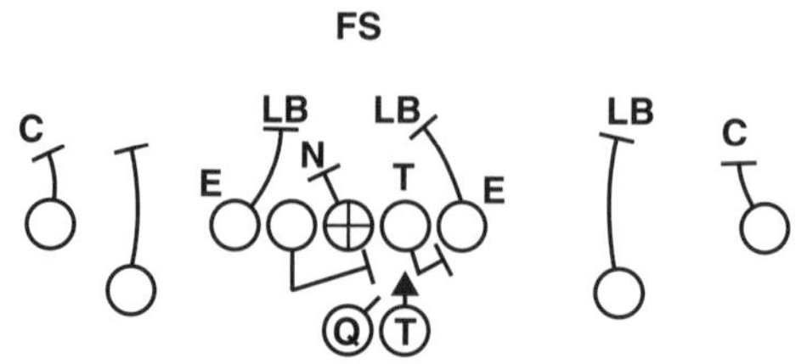

the nose tackle to the backside linebacker. If he's outside the tackle box, the backside tackle man blocks the defensive end, and the wide receiver (H) blocks the outside linebacker. The other receivers block support to man over.

The quarterback reads the backside defensive end. If he's not in position to make the tackle on the back, the quarterback hands the ball off to the back (give read). On a give read, the back takes two steps past the mesh point and reads the first down lineman past the center. He bounces it outside, bangs it inside, or bends it backside. If he's in position to make the tackle, he pulls the ball and runs to daylight (keep read). The important block on a keep read is that of the inside receiver on the linebacker.

When running the inside zone play versus an odd defensive front, we block the inside zone play, as shown in figure 6.8. The rules for the receivers, quarterback, and running back are the same as versus a 4-3 defense. For the offensive line, the playside tackle and guard double-team the defensive end to the playside inside linebacker. The center and backside guard combo the nose tackle to the backside linebacker. The backside tackle steps to block the B-gap defender.

The next play is trap, which is a quick-hitting, downhill play. Trap is a

gap-blocking scheme by the offensive line. We show trap versus a 4-2 defensive front and odd front. If running trap versus a 4-2 front, we like to run it to the 3 technique.

Rules for the receivers are that they'll block man over. The playside tackle inside releases to the near linebacker. The playside guard influence kicks out on the defensive end. The center blocks back on the nose tackle, replacing the pulling guard. The backside guard pulls and traps the 3 technique. The backside tackle inside releases and blocks the near linebacker. The quarterback catches the snap and extends the ball to the back. The back lead steps downhill to the center's playside leg and reads the block of the pulling guard. Depending on how the defensive tackle plays the block, the guard either traps the 3 technique or logs him. It's the back's job to read that block.

If running trap versus an odd defensive front (figure 6.9), the trap block by the pulling guard takes place on the defensive end. The playside tackle will still inside release to the near linebacker. The playside guard and center double-team the nose to the middle linebacker. The backside tackle inside releases to the near linebacker. The rules for the quarterback, receivers, and running back remain the same.

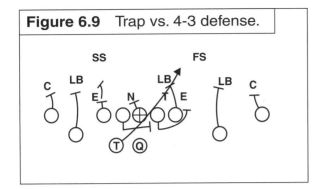

Figure 6.9   Trap vs. 4-3 defense.

Switch-Up or Gadget Play

We use a reverse play (figure 6.10) to keep the defense honest, one that complements the inside zone and all-go packages described previously. Though the quarterback has the option to keep the ball in the inside zone, which keeps the backside defensive end honest, we've developed a gadget play to keep all of the backside defenders honest.

First, the playside outside receiver is in motion toward the heart of the formation. On the snap of the ball, he bellies out around the backside of the formation. The other three receivers initially show as if they're running the all go, then they break 10 to 15 yards downfield to block the man-on defenders. All of the offensive line, except for the backside tackle, block zone to the playside. The backside tackle blocks the defensive end down for a count and

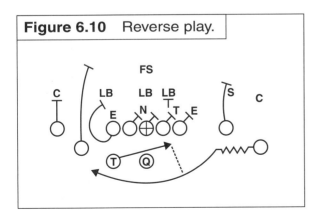

Figure 6.10   Reverse play.

then wheels around backside to block the most dangerous defender backside. The quarterback hands the ball to the back as if we're running zone. The running back pitches the ball to the bellying receiver on the reverse. The receiver continues around to the backside and plays off the backside tackle's block to get as many yards as possible.

We ran this play in the spring game this year at the beginning of the fourth quarter, and it worked like a charm. The reversing receiver received the ball from the tailback, came around the corner of the defense, and followed the backside tackle upfield. The backside tackle and receivers made some great blocks, and the receiver on the reverse went the distance for a 65-yard touchdown. The entire defense bit on the fake. By the time the defenders could redirect, the receiver was too far downfield to catch. This gave us the lead, which ultimately led to the win.

Summary

In this chapter, we've provided information on how we execute a few of our offensive plays out of the solo formation. Obviously, the spread offense we run has many more formations and plays incorporated in it, but the plays and concepts described here are the bread and butter of our offense.

The ideas are expanded on in different formations with the same general rules applied. We have switched up personnel groupings to get our best players in position to make plays. We suggest that any coaching staff do the same, no matter what type of offense is run, because you need to put the best 11 players on the field. As far as we're concerned, this is our most advantageous personnel grouping (one back and four receivers) and formation (solo).

The solo formation puts our 11 best athletes on the field, but your optimal personnel grouping may be different. This formation can be achieved with almost any personnel grouping. In 11 personnel (one back, one tight end, and three receivers), the tight end is split out in a receiver position. In 12 personnel (one back, two tight ends, and two receivers), the tight ends are split out away from the line in receiver slots. In 20 personnel (two backs, three receivers), the fullback is set out in a receiver slot or, transversely, the running back is put into a receiver slot and the fullback is set in the back field. In 21 personnel (two backs, one tight end, and two receivers), the tight end and fullback are set in receiver slots, or the tight end and running back are set in the receiver slots with the fullback set in the back field. Solo formation can be created by setting any particular position in motion in any of the aforementioned personnel groupings. The fullback, running back,

or tight end can be set at any of the receiver positions in this formation, either inside or outside, as long as you end up in a two-by-two receiver set. It doesn't matter how the solo formation is accomplished. The same schemes mentioned in this chapter can be executed out of any type of personnel grouping you choose to use.

Coaches who run the spread or any type of offense could benefit from some or all the schemes out of the solo formation. Whether you have a great formula for success with or without the spread offense, these ideas could definitely benefit your running and passing games to make your offense more successful. We worked for four years in developing this offense, looking for the best formula for victory on Saturdays. We're not there yet, but we're working rigorously to achieve the best schemes out of this formation for any situation.

PART III

Shotgun Formations

CHAPTER 7

Three Receivers, One Tight End

Randy Walker
Northwestern University

Mike Dunbar
Northwestern University

We came to Northwestern in 1999 with a conventional prostyle offense. However, we found that we lacked the personnel to create impact depth at the tight-end and fullback positions. Our challenge was twofold. First, how could we find a niche that could give us success in the Big Ten? Second, how could we be productive on offense with the personnel already on our team?

We visited Clemson University in the spring of 2000 to investigate their no-huddle attack. Head coach Tommy Bowden and offensive coordinator Rich Rodriguez were extremely helpful in developing this element for our offense. We had always thrown out of a shotgun set, but we found Clemson's running game out of the shotgun very intriguing.

What began as mostly a four wide-receiver set has developed over the past few years to expand the role of the tight end. With this personnel set we can spread the defense with three wide receivers and still have an extremely effective running game.

This personnel group offers several advantages. In addition to giving the offense diversity, it allowed us to expand our arsenal of both run and pass offense. Obviously, the addition of a tight end to the offense helped both at the point of attack and in cutting off backside defensive ends, a common nuisance for the shotgun running game. This has allowed us to expand the zone running game and enhanced the option attack we believe in so strongly. In the passing game, the tight end gives us a big body to throw to and a more effective play-action fake if we need it.

Another advantage of the offense is that it should be easy to learn. The system fits the concepts of all the basic schemes we had used in our prostyle offense, one back or two back. We'll explain later how we use the concept of the two-back zone play when we run the one-back zone with a wide receiver as a lead blocker at the point of attack. A commitment to this personnel set enhances all aspects of offense and gives us the weapons we need to attack defenses successfully.

Strengths and Weaknesses of the Shotgun Formation

Before discussing sets and plays in detail, let's discuss some factors that must be taken into account when considering this offensive package. We hope that our experience in learning from these problems in the past can help others avoid them in the future.

The first consideration for any shotgun offense is the extreme importance placed on the consistency of the gun snaps. The accuracy is crucial to the timing of the play. A quarterback must be able to receive the snap and see the field. If the quarterback must be concerned with receiving the snap, he'll be late getting into his postsnap read progression. Going one step further, if the snap is inaccurate, the quarterback might have difficulty finding the handle or getting a clean grip on the ball. Lack of a clean grip

can affect a handoff in the running game or the timing of the passing game.

A drawback of any shotgun offense is the predictability of the back set. Much of the base running game takes the back from one side of the quarterback to the other, allowing the defense to key the back for play direction. In the offensive staff room every week, we make a conscious decision to remove keys from the back. To do this, we use backfield motion, have the back cross the quarterback's face to pass protect, or use the tailback as an overload to the side on which he lines up, using a speed option or free-releasing him in the passing game.

Another weakness is having only one edge secured. By having three wide receivers in the game, we forfeit the ability to protect the point of attack on both sides of the formation. We attempt to turn this weakness into a strength by using a number of techniques in both the running and passing games.

The first pressure answer we have in the running game is the bubble-adjust rules. The defense can always outnumber us at the point of attack away from the tight end. If the defense tries to pressure at the point of attack away from the tight end, the receivers must recognize the pressure and respond accordingly. The inside receiver will bubble, allowing the quarterback a sight adjustment in the running game, while the outside one or two receivers, depending on the set, will block as if the play were a toss sweep.

The next method in the running game is motioning a wide receiver to be used as a lead back. This wide receiver replaces the fullback in two-back schemes, allowing us to secure the point of attack. If a team overloads to the tight end and we run a play to the tight end, especially outside, we must zone out. To secure the point of attack, the tight end and tackle combo to an outside linebacker or strong safety instead of to the inside linebacker, as they normally would.

In the passing game, the first problem is the same as in the running game—the defense can always outnumber the protection. Our base protection is a six-man protection in which the tight end releases, so we can protect only three to a side. We protect against pressure by keeping both the tight end and running back in to block, using a seven-man protection that can protect both edges if the calls are made correctly. However, we do prefer to use the six-man protection, so we must have answers for both man and zone pressure. Typically, we see four to a side zone pressure, usually away from the tight end. The most common man pressure we see is four across, often with some defensive lineman bailing out inside. We'll plan each week how to handle the various pressures, but our typical response is to build hots for zone pressure and check versus man pressure.

For this personnel set to be successful, certain concerns need to be addressed. The most difficult concern to satisfy is the tight end. It's uncommon to find a tight end who's both athletic enough to stretch the field in the passing game and physical enough to block at the point of attack in the running game. Normally, you must accept some compromise at this position, which will limit your package. It's also sometimes difficult to find the right personnel to play slot receiver in this personnel group. We ask the slot receiver to be quick enough to defeat safeties and linebackers in the passing game and physical enough to block them in the running game at the point of attack; we also want them to be able to react to the bubble-adjust rules.

Any shotgun offense usually uses the quarterback run. This can be a tremendous asset or can be a liability. As a positive, we view quarterback run as having a 12th man on the field. We're able to run a two-back offense with only one back in the backfield. The running back becomes the lead blocker when the quarterback is the ball carrier. In addition, spreading the defense with three wide receivers means the quarterback won't have to run against eight or nine men in the box, creating bigger seams and running lanes. Because of this, we ask the quarterback to gain 50 yards a game on the ground. The negative to all this is that the quarterback takes more hits than normal during the course of a game. As a coach, you must make a difficult decision between playing with reckless abandon and protecting your quarterback, keeping him healthy for the next snap.

These concerns are valid, but if practiced diligently and packaged correctly, this personnel group can help you avoid many of the problems and remove keys by exploiting these concepts from multiple formations. We use three main formations in this personnel group.

Basic Formations

The first formation is the 2-×-2 set (figure 7.1). In this set, Y (the tight end) is aligned on the ball tight to the formation to create the running strength mentioned earlier. The Z receiver takes his split, depending on the play. If he's running a route across the middle of the field, he might tighten his split a yard or two to get into the quarterback's vision more quickly. If the play is an inside running play that could cut back to his side, Z might widen his split to take the cornerback further out of the play. On the other side of the formation, the X receiver lines up on the ball. In our offense, X runs deeper routes than H, so we prefer to have X on the ball. In addition, for the bubble-adjust rules mentioned earlier, we prefer to have the inside receiver off the ball so that he has an easier course to bubble. The running back also aligns according to the play; his width and depth are critical to each play we call. The quarterback stands with his toes at 5 yards. The relationship between the quarterback alignment and running back alignment is crucial on certain plays, such as zone and option.

In this set, we typically set the tight end into the boundary, for several reasons. Because it's a balanced formation, the defense must decide where they will set their strength—to the passing strength to the field or to the running strength to the boundary.

To keep the defense honest in this offense, you must have a boundary run-

ning game. This forces the defense to defend the entire field. Because only one edge is secured by a tight end, the defense will be able to create pressure at the point of attack if you allow them to overplay one side. If the defense rolls their coverage to the field, they will be a man short in the boundary running game. If they keep an extra defender to the boundary, we should be able to take advantage of the field. Having two receivers to the field spreading the defense creates exploitable seams for both run and pass. We also can exploit the run by assuring that the backside end is cut off by our tight end. In the passing game, we use a large number of two-man patterns built for different coverages.

If the defense chooses to play truly balanced with only one safety high and one in the flat, we have an advantage because we forced the defense to decide to stop the run. They have created open seams down the field and in the flat for the passing game.

The next formation is the 3-×-1 set with the tight end set to the field (figure 7.2). In this set, Y is aligned on the ball tight to the formation to create a running strength again. The Z receiver again takes his split depending on the play; typically, he's going to be at the top or bottom of the numbers. The H receiver, who's now between Y and Z, aligns according to the play, most often splitting the difference between them. Although he's still the slot receiver, he no longer has bubble-adjust rules because he's set to the tight-end side. In our offense, any wide receiver set to the tight end doesn't have bubble-adjust rules because the tight end can protect the edge. Alone now on the other side of the formation, the X receiver is again lined up on the ball. The running back and quarterback follow the same rules as before—running back to the play and quarterback's toes at 5 yards.

In this set, the tight end is set to the field, for a number of reasons. This

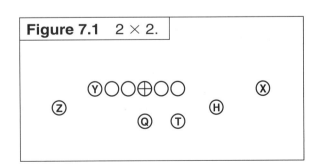

Figure 7.1   2 × 2.

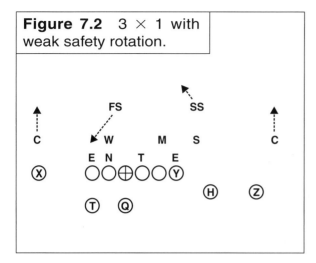

Figure 7.2 3 × 1 with weak safety rotation.

set usually forces the defense into a safety rotation. Both our running and passing strengths are to the field, so the defense must respond accordingly. In our 2-×-2 set we attempt to get the defense to show their plan—we force them to defend one side. If they rotate to the tight end and two wide-receiver side, they are one alley player short on the back side, opening our boundary running and passing games. In a strongly rotated defense, the flat player to the boundary must be the weakside linebacker. We try to put pressure on him to defend both the run and the pass. The tailback aligns to the field and runs back to the boundary side. In the passing game, we design routes with individual calls to the X receiver on the back side. If the flat defender is in the box playing run, we take short throws to the X. If the flat defender walks out of the box, we come back to our running game at him.

Because of our weakside game, many defenses have begun to defend this formation by rotating their safeties weak (figure 7.2). This does slow our weakside game, but the defense is now one man short to our passing and running strength in a large area to the field. When we force the defense to defend the boundary in this formation, we have a great deal of offense we can run to

the field and have at least a one-man advantage.

The least common defense against this formation has zero rotation by the safeties, keeping two of them high. Against this defense, we feel we must run the football to force them to bring a safety down and then respond accordingly.

The final formation we use out of this personnel set is the 3-×-1 set with the tight end to the boundary and all three receivers to the field (figure 7.3). In the last two years, we used this formation the least of the three mentioned here, but it definitely has its purposes.

In this formation, Y is aligned tight to the formation to create a running strength. To the field, the outside receiver is now the X, similar to the 2-×-2 formation. He aligns according to the play call, typically at the top or bottom of the numbers. Also similar to the 2-×-2 formation, H is the inside receiver, aligning to the play call, usually 6 yards away from the tackle off the line of scrimmage. Because the tight end is away from him again, his bubble-adjust rules come back into play. This is another reason he's aligned as the inside-most receiver.

We prefer to have the same wide receiver doing the bubble adjust for two reasons. First, we have selected him to play H because he has the best ability to run a bubble-adjust route and gain yardage after the catch. Second, we prefer to keep the concept as simple as possible for players to execute. One small problem with simplicity in this formation

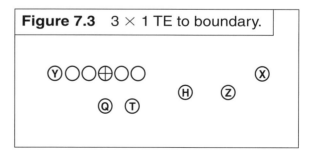

Figure 7.3 3 × 1 TE to boundary.

concerns the Z receiver. Z is again off the line of scrimmage, but now he's an inside receiver instead of an outside receiver. This move inside requires the intelligent young men we have at Northwestern. Because our passing system is based on inside and outside receivers, Z must learn the rules for both to get in this formation. For his alignment, he splits the difference between H and X.

We use this formation to again separate our running and passing strengths. However, in this formation, our passing strength is more pronounced than our running strength, so the defense is forced to commit to defend either the pass or the run. Most teams will put the extra safety to the field and force us to account for a cornerback to the boundary.

This formation is least used for running but does allow us an easy way to get in seven-man protection while retaining a three-man route combination. We can protect the quarterback for an extended period of time while three receivers stress the defense to one side. If we used seven-man protection in the previous 3-X-1 formation, we could not focus the stress on the defense to the same side, as we do in this formation.

Motion

A great way to make the most of the multiplicity of this personnel group is through motion. We use simple motions or shifts to take us quickly from one formation to another (figure 7.4). The example in figure 7.4b shows us motioning H to go from a 3 × 1 to 2 × 2 formation. The H back is the most common motion man we use. The motion helps him get in position to make the difficult blocks he must make.

We are extremely conscious of packaging motion run plays with complementary pass plays so that the defense can't use motion as a run/pass key. These

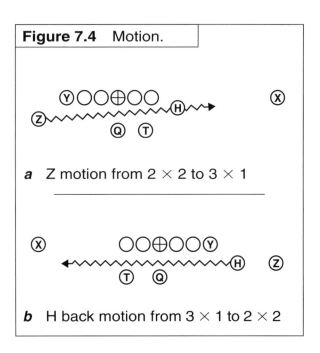

Figure 7.4   Motion.

a   Z motion from 2 × 2 to 3 × 1

b   H back motion from 3 × 1 to 2 × 2

motions also help make our offense less predictable by formation and back set, one of the challenges with the shotgun game. If we line up in a formation with a particular back set, such as 3 × 1 with the tight end to the field and the back to the field (figure 7.2), the defenders on the field will immediately try to predict the package of plays we run from that set. However, as soon as we motion or shift to another formation, defenders must think not only of plays in which we run with motion but also of plays that we run out of the new formation. We force the defensive players to think on the run.

Plays

The first running play is the outside chase zone play (figure 7.5). For simplicity's sake, in the running game we focus on the 3-X-1 formation with the tight end to the field because it's our preferred running formation. We prefer to check the zone play to the closest technique or A-gap player. This allows the offensive linemen to get outside number aiming points and stretch the defense. We generally call the play to the split-end side, predicting where the A-gap player will be. If we check to the tight end, the tailback shifts to the other side.

This play is based on playside zone combination blocks in the D, C, B, and A gaps. The backside blockers are responsible for reach blocks inside with the backside defensive end being accounted for by the quarterback read. We plan this play based on the number of defenders in the box. The blocking rules for the interior line and tight end are as follow:

X: Stalk and crack. Block overhang or rotating safety first. If none, block man over.

H: Man over to next level. Block man over. If none, look to help inside to safety.

Z: Block man over.

Receivers are an integral part of the blocking as well, but their rules are simpler and apply to all plays.

On all running plays from the gun, we specify the quarterback and tailback rules for alignment and mesh responsibility. In this play, the quarterback is responsible for the mesh. He opens to the tailback, rides through the handoff, and nakeds away. The tailback aligns behind the tackle, slides open, and chases the playside tackle's outside leg.

Versus 43 defense, run to SE to shade technique (figure 7.5a)

PST: Zone drive C gap; zone combination with PSG to Will LB.

PSG: Zone drive B gap; zone combination with PST to Will LB.

OC: Zone drive A gap.

BSG: Reach backside A gap to Mike LB.

BST: Reach backside B gap.

BSTE: Reach backside C gap to Sam LB.

TB: Press PST's outside leg.

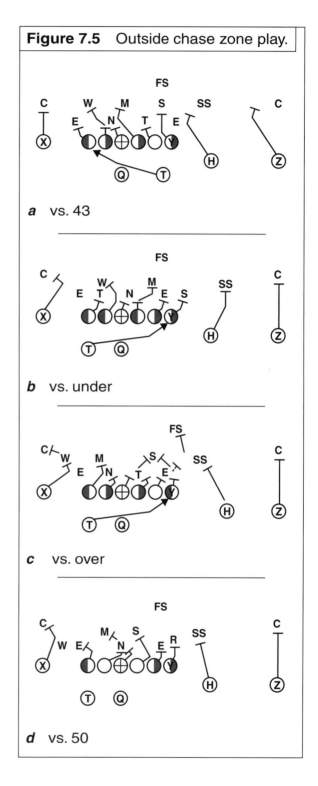

Figure 7.5 Outside chase zone play.

a vs. 43

b vs. under

c vs. over

d vs. 50

The toughest block is for the backside guard to get the middle linebacker. We choose to run the play to the closest technique, which is to the split-end side. If we run the ball to the tight end, the 3 technique could give us problems.

Versus under defense, run to TE to shade tech (figure 7.5b)

PSTE: Zone drive D gap; man-on to Sam LB.

PST: Zone drive C gap; zone combination with PSG to Mike LB.

PSG: Zone drive B gap; zone combination with PST to Mike LB.

OC: Zone drive A gap.

BSG: Reach backside A gap to Will LB.

BST: Reach backside B gap.

Versus over defense, check to TE away from overload weak (figure 7.5c)

PSTE: Zone drive D gap; zone combination with PST to number 4. If number 4 is covered up by H, TE works back up inside.

PST: Zone drive C gap; zone combination with PSTE to overhang SS.

PSG: Zone drive B gap; zone combination with OC to Will LB.

OC: Zone drive A gap; zone combination with PSG to Will LB.

BSG: Reach backside A gap.

BST: Reach backside B gap to Mike LB.

Versus 50 defense, run to TE, D gap blocker (figure 7.5d)

PSTE: Zone drive D gap; rover support.

PST: Zone drive C gap; zone combination with PSG.

PSG: Zone drive B gap; zone combination with PST to Sam LB.

OC: Zone drive A gap; reach combination with BSG to Mike LB.

BSG: Reach backside A gap; reach combination with OC to Mike LB.

BST: Reach backside B gap; sift technique to overhang Will LB.

The next running play out of this personnel group is the speed option to the tight end and split end (figure 7.6). The speed option is a great play to get outside and attack the edge of the defense. It's also a great blitz check to keep defenses honest. It has big play potential in a critical situation.

The speed option play is based off zone-blocking rules comparable to the outside zone play except that the outside lineman zones up instead of zoning out. The quarterback is responsible for pitching off the end man on the line of scrimmage. For the option, the tailback again aligns behind the tackle. His steps are bucket step, crossover, and eye the quarterback's pitch hand. The tailback is responsible for maintaining the pitch relationship. This play can be called to a tight-end side or split-end side. Check it based on overhang defenders and play-side linebacker alignments in the box.

Versus 43 defense, to TE (figure 7.6a)

PSTE: Versus 9 technique, dip and rip for SLB; versus 7 technique, zone hook C gap to SLB; zone combination inside.

PST: Zone hook C gap to MLB; zone combination inside; dent the edge.

PSG: Zone hook B gap to WLB.

OC: Zone hook A gap.

BSG: Bubble cutoff backside A gap.

BST: Bubble cutoff backside B gap.

Versus under defense, to TE (figure 7.6b)

PSTE: Zone hook C gap to MLB.

PST: Zone hook C gap to MLB; zone combination inside; dent the edge.

PSG: Zone hook A gap to WLB.

OC: Zone hook A gap.

BSG: Bubble cutoff backside A gap.

BST: Bubble cutoff backside B gap.

Versus over defense, to TE, SS becomes EMOL (end man on line) for quarterback read (figure 7.6c)

PSTE: Zone hook C gap to WLB; zone combination inside; dent the edge.

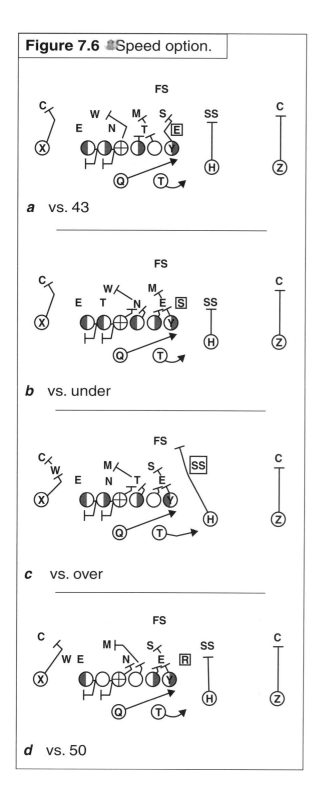

Figure 7.6 Speed option.

a vs. 43

b vs. under

c vs. over

d vs. 50

PST: Zone hook C gap to WLB; zone combination inside; dent the edge.

PSG: Zone hook B gap to MLB.

OC: Zone hook A gap.

BSG: Bubble cutoff backside A gap.

BST: Bubble cutoff backside B gap.

Versus 50 defense, to TE (figure 7.6d)

PSTE: Zone hook C gap to SLB.

PST: Zone hook C gap to SLB; alert triple call.

PSG: Zone hook B gap to MLB; alert triple call.

OC: Zone hook A gap to MLB.

BSG: Reach backside A gap.

BST: Bubble cutoff backside B gap.

The third running play is the tackle pull play series in the one-back offense (figure 7.7). The tackle pull play is a man-blocking scheme that dents the defense inside with guard and center combos. It's a slow developing play with similar timing to a draw play and still involves a quarterback read on the backside defensive end. This play could turn into a track scheme and tackle trap versus inside linebacker pressure.

This play involves full-flow action by the tailback and counter back action as a complement. The counter back action allows the tailback to get downhill more than the full-flow course. This play is best to an A-gap player, which is how the counter back action is called without moving the tailback when the quarterback checks the play.

In this play, the tailback is responsible for the mesh. The quarterback sits down to read the defensive end. If the play is full-flow counter, the tailback jabs away and turns and runs, following the offensive tackle. If the play is the counter back action, the tailback opens to the quarterback, crosses over, plants, and follows the offensive tackle into the hole.

Versus 43 defense, to SE, A-gap defender (figure 7.7a)

PST: Control drive man-on. If wide technique, pass set and throw defender up field.

PSG: Combo A-gap player with OC to MLB.

OC: Combo A-gap player with PSG to MLB, alert for backside A-gap run-through.

BSG: Cut off covered technique.

BST: Open pull for WLB, pull into the line of scrimmage on third step, alert for trap block versus WLB outside blitz.

BSTE: Reach backside C gap to SLB.

QB: Read backside DE for pull read.

Versus under defense, check A gap to TE, TB uses counter back footwork and doesn't shift to full flow (figure 7.7b)

PSTE: Control drive man-on, D gap.

PST: Control drive man-on, C gap.

PSG: Combo A-gap player with OC to WLB.

OC: Combo A-gap player with OC to WLB, alert for backside A-gap run-through.

BSG: Cut off covered technique.

BST: Open pull for MLB; pull into the line of scrimmage on third step, alert for trap block versus hard fill LB.

Versus over defense, check to TE away from overload weak; TB uses counter back action to get downhill versus B-gap defender, becomes A-gap play (figure 7.7c)

PSTE: Control drive D gap to number 4 (SS). If H has SS covered, help secure 7 technique.

PST: Control drive C gap DE.

PSG: Control drive man-on B-gap player, give a call to tell pulling OT it will be tighter.

OC: Combo backside A-gap player with BSG to MLB.

BSG: Combo backside A-gap player with OC to MLB.

BST: Open pull for WLB, tight course (A gap) versus 3 technique.

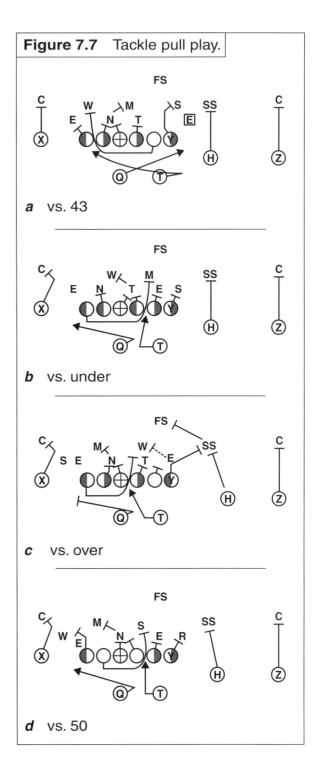

Figure 7.7 Tackle pull play.

a vs. 43

b vs. under

c vs. over

d vs. 50

QB: Read backside DE for pull.

Versus 50 defense, check to TE with overload weak (figure 7.7d)

PSTE: Control drive D gap to number 4.

PST: Control drive C gap, man-on.

PSG: Odd call, combo nose with OC to MLB.

OC: Odd call, combo nose with PSG to MLB, alert for backside A-gap run-through.

BSG: Odd call, open pull for SLB, alert for trap block versus hard fill LB.

BST: BSG pulls, sift through DE to overhang WLB.

QB: If DE crosses BST's face, pull read is overhang WLB.

The natural complement to our running game is our play-action pass off our best running play, the zone play described earlier. The most common boots we run are X boot (figure 7.8a) and Z boot (figure 7.8b).

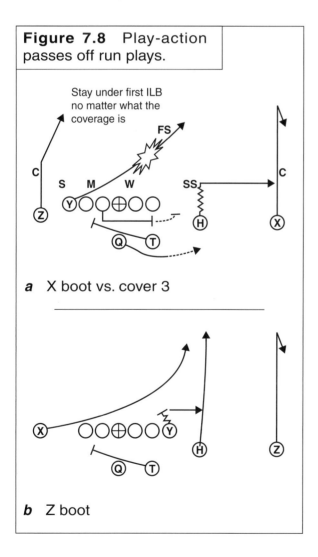

Figure 7.8 Play-action passes off run plays.

a X boot vs. cover 3

b Z boot

The protection used for the boot game is a typical out-of-the-pocket protection. The center, guard, and tackle away from the fake direction sell the zone fake. The guard to the side of the fake pulls to the opposite edge to protect the quarterback by logging or kicking out the defensive end. The tackle to the side of the fake stays big on big. The quarterback sits and rides the tailback's hip, allowing the guard to get in front, trying to leverage the defensive end so the quarterback can get outside the pocket. The tailback accelerates through the mesh to chase the tackle, selling the run and protecting against pressure from the other edge.

Shifting to the pattern itself, the X receiver must understand the coverage because his route technique will change based on the coverage the defense is showing. Versus a cover-3 look (figure 7.8a), X will execute a vertical release comeback at 18 yards. Versus the cover-2 look (figure 7.9), he'll execute a positive outside release stop route. Positive outside release means that the wide receiver must outside release the corner regardless of the corner's alignment or how he reacts. The positive outside release protects H by holding or widening the corner as much as possible so that he won't come off and defend H's route immediately.

We call the route for the H back a late shoot. The late shoot means he'll come off the ball as if he's blocking the run-

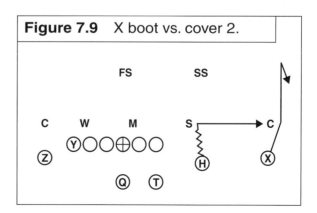

Figure 7.9 X boot vs. cover 2.

ning play. He comes off and runs the route off the man over him (in cover 3, that's the strong safety; in cover 2, that's the Sam linebacker). Once the ball is snapped, H reads the man over him. If the defender reacts to the run fake, H pushes to his outside shoulder as if he can't get into position to block him, reverse pivots, and bursts to the sideline. If the defender is in man coverage, and his demeanor says he has H man to man, H executes a man route by pushing into the defender's chest as if he's going to block the run. H then plants off the inside foot and bursts to the sideline.

Note that once H bursts to the sideline, he can't drift upfield. Drifting gives the quarterback a bad angle to make the throw and gives the defender the opportunity to run under and defend the play.

In the next piece of the play, Y executes an over route (figure 7.8a). The rules for a boot over route stem from the protection. In this protection, we pull the backside guard to block the defensive end. If the defensive end gets upfield and the guard is forced to kick him out, the quarterback will have to pull up in the pocket and look to quickly throw the ball to the over route. We call this the step-under spot. However, if the guard is able to log the defensive end or seal him inside, the quarterback breaks contain and attacks the perimeter. If Y sees the quarterback get outside, he bursts into the next window 17 yards deep and in phase with the quarterback.

Teaching the over route can be tricky, so we have developed some simple rules. First, protect the quarterback by being in position for the step-under. Second, if you don't get the step-under throw, gain depth immediately to get to 17 yards across the field. Finally, give the quarterback a realistic throw. In other words, stay in phase with the quarterback—don't force him to throw back across his body.

The final route in the boot pattern is the clear route by the Z receiver. The clear is essentially a deep post route. On the back side of a boot play, the chances of the Z getting the ball are extremely low. However, if a coach in the box notices that the free safety is not aware of Z on this play, he'll recommend alerting the quarterback to stop and read the play Y to Z (figure 7.10). This is more of a down-the-field shot (big-yardage play). If this alert is made in the play call, Y would abandon his step-under responsibilities and alter his route to attract the near safety so the quarterback can launch the clear to the Z.

The next play is the boot in the 3-×-1 formation with the tight end to the field. Figure 7.11 shows the play against cover 3 (figure 7.11a) and cover 2 (figure 7.11b). The base assignments are

Z: Comeback.

H: Blow out.

Y: Shoot.

X: Step under/over.

The Z receiver, now the outside receiver to the play call, has the same assignment X had in the previous play. Versus a soft corner (cover 3), he has a 16- to 18-yard comeback route. Versus a hard corner (cover 2), he must positive outside release and stop on the sideline.

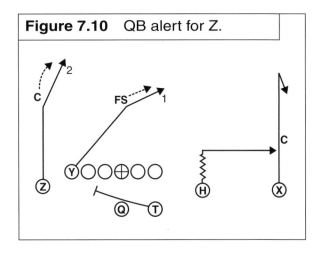

Figure 7.10   QB alert for Z.

Figure 7.11 Boot from 3-×-1 formation: TE to the field.

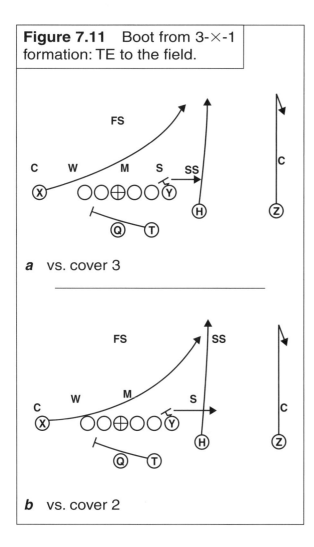

a vs. cover 3

b vs. cover 2

Figure 7.12 Z boot wheel.

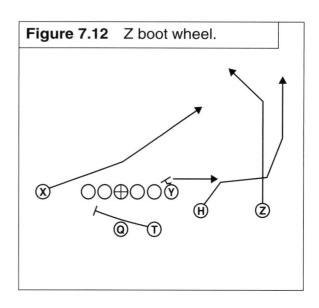

The H receiver now has a blow-out route. Versus cover 3, he outside releases the flat defender and bursts down the seam to attract the attention of the corner and the free safety. Versus cover 2, he runs through the near safety.

In this formation, Y now has the late-shoot route. However, this route is slightly different than the late shoot by the slot wide receiver. The timing of this route is critical to the success of the play. If Y releases too quickly, the quarterback won't be ready to throw him the ball, and the defense will react to cover him. More often than not, Y takes too long to release, allowing the quarterback to get out in front of him and be forced to make a throw back across

his body. We teach the tight end to take three hard steps, slam the defensive end, reverse pivot, and release straight down the line of scrimmage. If the tight end is in doubt, he should reach down inside to make a better sell for the running play.

The X receiver in the 3-×-1 formation now has the step under/over route. X will alter his split according to the play. In this particular play, to be able to get in position for the step-under, X must cut his split to 5 yards from the tackle. He should go flat under the first inside linebacker and work to the spot 8 yards over the guard/tackle area for the step-under. If he doesn't receive the step-under, he must accelerate to a spot 17 yards deep in phase with the quarterback.

We have many variations of these two routes to make it more difficult for secondary players to read our patterns. Figure 7.12 shows one of our most common variations, the Z boot wheel. In our system, we call these variations by making individual calls to the H or creating tag words.

The final piece to this puzzle is a play we use to complete this package—a reverse. Our reverse comes off zone action and is primarily a 3-×-1 play. We

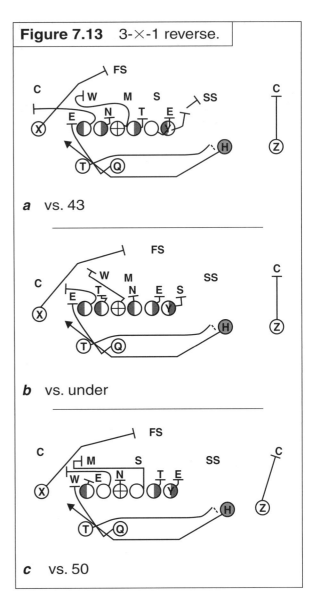

Figure 7.13 3-×-1 reverse.

a vs. 43

b vs. under

c vs. 50

use it in 3 × 1 again because we prefer to run from this formation and because we hope it eliminates a weakside overhang. Figure 7.13 shows the reverse against 43, under, and 50 defenses. We audible out of the play versus the over front because of the overhang defender.

In this play, the frontside guard, tackle, and tight end block zone. From the center back, the two uncovered linemen block down for two counts and release for the backside inside linebacker and the corner, respectively. The only exception to this rule is with a 50 front. Against a 50 front, both uncovered guards release.

We have used this play to great success against teams that overpursue the running game. A couple of years ago, we called this play on fourth and long in the red zone against a fast-flowing defensive team. Our players executed very well, allowing us to score on the play.

Our offensive staff does an excellent job of integrating base concepts with multiple personnel groups and a variety of formations. Their creative implementation of these concepts and formations have been vital to our offensive flexibility and maintaining unpredictability in calling plays. If the defense has to defend the entire field, and the offense has balance between run and pass, you have a great chance for success.

CHAPTER 8

Four Receivers

Rich Rodriguez

West Virginia University

When people think about the spread offense, they think of a no-huddle, fast-tempo, high-finesse style of play. While the spread *is* a fast-tempo, no-huddle offense, we don't really view it as high finesse. We see the spread as an offense that continuously applies pressure to the defense, while allowing us to play with a distinctly physical style.

Every coach attempts to create an advantage for his football team. The spread offense gives us a number of advantages. It forces a defense to align quickly and reduces defensive substitutions, which can directly dictate the tempo of the game. Because of the lack of defensive substitutions, conditioning becomes a major factor. Other major advantages associated with the spread are that it forces a defense to cover the entire football field, thus creating space in which our athletes can work. Along with creating space, the spread also helps create clear pictures for the quarterback, making it a quarterback-friendly offense.

The basic elements of running an effective shotgun spread offense are listed here:

1. Make the defense defend the entire field.
2. Play with multiple tempos.
3. Make the quarterback a dual threat—run and pass.
4. Make the execution of the offense simple but not predictable.
5. Execute base plays. Practice repetitions. Get good at something.

The base formations used in the four-receiver shotgun spread offense are doubles (2-×-2 set, figure 8.1a) and trips (3-×-1 set, figure 8.1b). When using these two formations, recognizing and reading safety alignments becomes very important.

The first safety alignment is what we call single-hi, meaning that there's one safety in the middle of the field (figures 8.1a and 8.1b). With a single-hi look, no more than six defenders can be in the box unless a receiver is uncovered.

The next safety alignment is the double-hi, meaning there are two safeties high (figure 8.2). With double-hi safeties, no more than five defenders can be in the box unless receivers are uncovered.

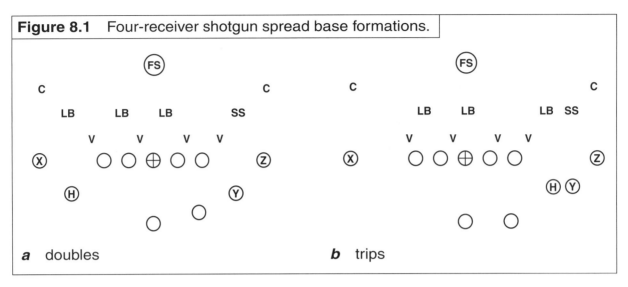

Figure 8.1   Four-receiver shotgun spread base formations.

a   doubles   *b*   trips

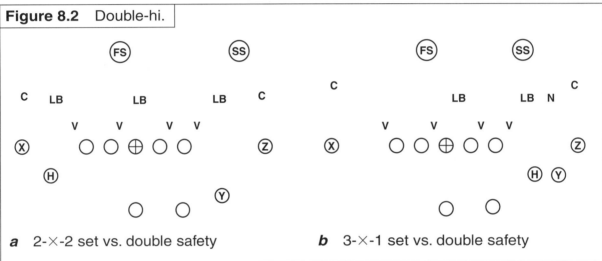

Figure 8.2   Double-hi.

a   2-X-2 set vs. double safety   *b*   3-X-1 set vs. double safety

Based off these two safety alignments, double-hi or single-hi, the scheme allows the offense to choose which plays to run, creating numbers or angle advantages for the offense to run or pass.

Before installing base offensive plays, understand and teach the basic formations and fundamentals associated with the procedure of running an effective no-huddle, spread offensive attack. As in any offensive attack, the execution of base plays still depends on having an effective system that can be easily communicated to players, allowing them to concentrate on the fundamentals associated with the running and passing schemes and not the procedure itself.

In our running-game system, we concentrate on three schemes: zone schemes (zone), man schemes (draw), and pull schemes (trap and dart). In our passing game, we throw five base concepts, based on areas on the field: quick game, intermediate, deep, sprint, and run-action passes (nakeds).

As the spread offense has evolved and become more popular, defenses have devised different schemes to defend the spread. Defenses try to give multiple looks by stemming and disguising, looking to confuse the quarterback and play caller. Stemming defensive line techniques (for example, three techniques become one technique and vice versa) is often an attempt to slow the tempo of the offense and clutter the picture. Other defensive line movements include angling and slanting the line once the ball is snapped.

Disguising occurs through showing a double-hi safety look and rotating to a single-hi safety look, seeking to gain an extra defender in the box for run support. A defense can also attempt to disrupt the picture by using the alley defenders as gray-area defenders (outside linebackers or strong safeties), again looking to gain an advantage in the running game and quick passing or perimeter throws. To counter this, the offense must have a thorough package to attack the stemming and disguising defenses, such as quick screens, quarterback runs, and run-action passes consisting of drop-backs and nakeds.

Running Game

Because of the various ways that defenses are now defending the spread, the first run scheme that we install in our running attack is the zone scheme.

Zone

The zone scheme (figure 8.3) helps us against teams that are slanting or angling, stemming and disguising. The zone forces a defense to play disciplined. Including the quarterback as a run threat allows us to even the numbers versus a six-man box by allowing the quarterback to read the extra number.

To be an effective zone team, every offensive position must be on the same page, and all must be accountable for their roles. The five offensive linemen must handle the five most immediate threats in the box. The running back must make correct reads, thus making the offensive line correct. The running back must demonstrate great patience *to* the hole, but not *through* the hole. The running back is responsible for placing the linemen on their blocks. For the running back to be able to do this, the back's course must be consistent with each back carrying the football. The quarterback must be disciplined and correct in reading the extra defender. The receivers must be able to block the gray-area defenders by using proper landmarks and taking the correct paths to their blocking assignments.

All covered offensive linemen must take a directional zone step at the defensive lineman's outside-arm breast plate. Uncovered offensive linemen must take the proper landmark to block second-level defenders. All linemen must stay

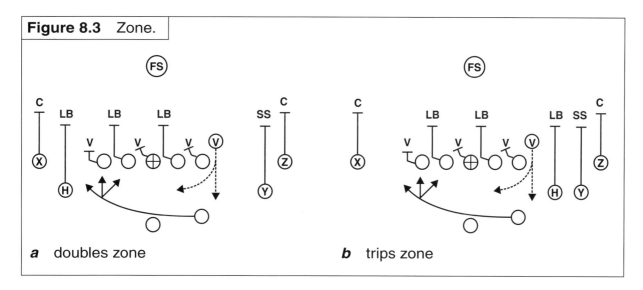

Figure 8.3 Zone.

a doubles zone

b trips zone

on their tracks (not a man scheme). The guard to the bubble side (1 technique or 5 technique) must be alert for the 1 technique nose to chip him before taking his track to the second-level defender (figure 8.4).

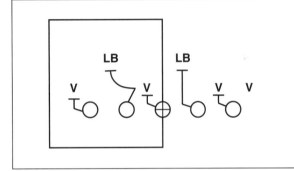

Figure 8.4 Guard waits for nose to chip-block him before taking his track to the second-level defender.

The running back's steps in the zone scheme consist of an open step and a crossover before meshing with the quarterback. After the handoff, the running back takes two steps past the quarterback, rolling downhill, aiming at the butt of the offensive tackle. The running back reads the first down defensive lineman to second down defensive lineman. The back has three options after his read of the down defensive linemen: bang, bend, or bounce.

The quarterback secures the snap and stays flat-footed for the mesh, making sure to keep his eyes on his read defender. He executes the handoff or keep, based on his reads.

The inside receivers take the proper path to block the alley defenders. They must work to a position in which they can dig the defenders out and get them displaced vertically up the field. The outside receivers block base, blocking the man over.

This is our base running play; we can run many plays off the zone concept, including nakeds, play-action passes, screens, and reverses.

Draw

The first man scheme in our run game is the draw play (figure 8.5). This scheme allows us to attack the defense downhill, while the defense is displaced covering the formations. The draw play is used to slow down a defensive team's pass rush, to take advantage of alley defenders expanding in the passing game, and to continue to keep the defense off balance between run and pass. The draw play has been very effective in passing situations, whether the running back or the quarterback carries the ball.

The offensive linemen must show pass, allowing the defensive linemen to get up the field to rush the passer. The linemen must transition from

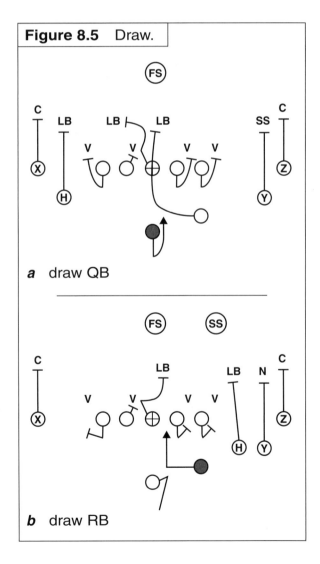

Figure 8.5 Draw.

a draw QB

b draw RB

being pass setters to run blockers. The center and guard to the nose side must be ready to set together and combo the backside linebacker.

The running back takes a natural pass set action while sliding in for the mesh with the quarterback to receive the ball. The running back's aiming point is downhill at the bubble.

The quarterback secures the snap, taking a small-rhythm, three-step drop. The quarterback must focus his eyes downfield, giving the illusion that a drop-back pass is occurring.

The receivers must have great get-off on the snap, selling as if a pass is occurring. The outside receivers block man over, while the inside receivers are responsible for the alley defenders. Just as in the zone play, the inside receivers must take a great path to blocking their assignments.

The draw scheme is a great comple-ment to a passing game as well as a run-ning game. The draw can slow down a good pass rushing defense, making the pass rushers hesitate.

Trap

When putting together a running game package, a coach needs a quick-hitting, downhill running play. The play we use most is the influence trap (figure 8.6), which allows us to package the zone play with the trap play. Packaging the two together creates stress on a defen-sive unit's run fits. In the trap game, either the running back or the quarter-back can carry the ball.

The tackles apex in to the near-side linebacker. The center blocks back. The playside guard influences out to the defensive end. The backside guard pulls and traps the playside 3 technique. (Note that on occasion, if numbers allow, we trap the 5 technique, as shown in figure 8.6b.)

The running back takes a directional downhill 45-degree angle step toward

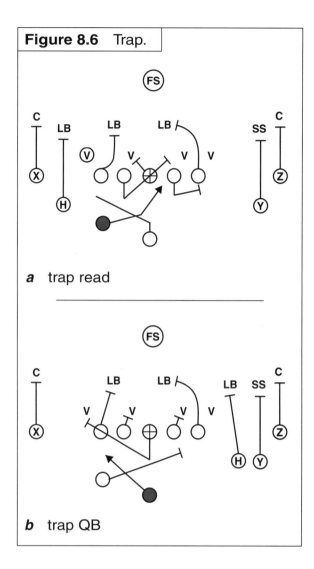

Figure 8.6 Trap.

a trap read

b trap QB

the aiming point of the center's playside hip. The back reads the playside apex linebacker.

The quarterback secures the snap and works the downhill action, stepping with the foot opposite the running back (for mesh purposes). On QB trap, the quarterback's reads are the same as the running back's.

The outside receivers block man over. The inside receivers are responsible for the alley defenders. They'll use the same technique as used with the zone play.

Running the trap play allows us to take advantage of angle blocking and force the defense to defend another run scheme.

Dart

The dart play (offensive tackle pull play, figure 8.7) is a staple of the spread offense and can be a very productive football play. Because of the backfield action, the dart gives the appearance of the zone play but allows you to attack the bubble with a difference scheme. The quarterback must read the extra defender in the box and may also run the play himself, if needed (figure 8.7b). The dart is a great misdirection to add as one of your base plays to successfully run your spread offense.

The playside tackle must attempt to reach the defensive end to sell the zone action. The playside guard and center ace block to the Mike or backside linebacker. The backside guard blocks man-on, and the backside tackle pulls and blocks the playside linebacker.

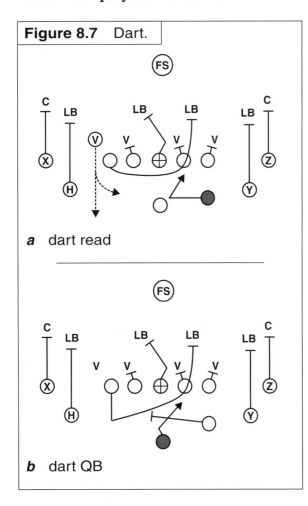

Figure 8.7   Dart.

a   dart read

b   dart QB

The running back takes an open, crossover plant step, selling the zone action, which causes the defense to flow. At the mesh point with the quarterback, the running back pivots out and picks up the pulling tackle for his read on the leverage of the playside linebacker. It's imperative that the back doesn't rush out of the pivot, which allows the tackle to get position on his block.

The quarterback secures the snap, then puts his eyes on his read, which is the backside defensive end. The quarterback must stay flat and allow the running back to stay flat, because this helps prevent starting downhill too quickly. The quarterback must read correctly for the give or keep. If the ball is given, the quarterback will fake boot action.

Receiver blocking is the same as for all the base running plays. The inside receivers are responsible for the alley players, and the outside receivers are responsible for man over. At times, we'll game plan the receivers' blocking responsibilities to include blocking safeties.

The dart play is a great change-up to combat fast-flow defenses. If executed correctly, the dart can complement the zone play by slowing the flow of second-level defenders. Based off the game plan, we'll also change the playside tackle's assignment by pass setting the playside defensive end, which might create a bigger bubble for the run lane.

Passing Game

To throw the football effectively in the spread offense, a team must plan what exactly it wants to accomplish. We want to make sure that our passing game complements our running game. Whether we run or pass, we want to play fast tempo. We achieve this with a passing system that consists of a quick, intermediate, and a deep passing game, coupled with sprint-outs and play-action passes coming off our base running plays. We want to change up the quarterback's launch points.

Quick Game or Hitches

When we refer to our quick game (figure 8.8), we mean a three-step drop by the quarterback or, if we're in the gun, the quarterback is in catch-and-throw mode. The breaking points of the routes are at five yards. To be successful with the quick game, we must have great rhythm and timing.

The offensive line blocks aggressive turn-back gap protection, not allowing any penetration. Again, the linemen must be aggressive and come off the football. We want to create clear vision for the quarterback.

The running back aggressively blocks the edge away from the turn-back protection, protecting inside-out. The run-

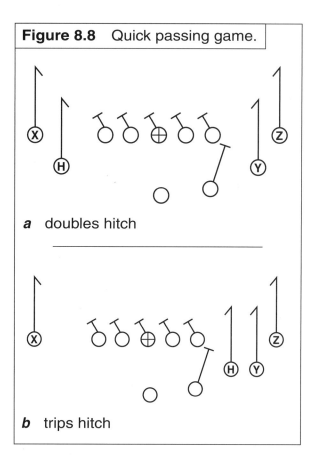

Figure 8.8   Quick passing game.

a   doubles hitch

b   trips hitch

ning back must take a great path off the tackle's hip to get the edge secured.

From the gun, once the quarterback secures the snap he drops, catches, and throws. If we go under center, the quarterback takes a three-step drop. We really stress rhythm and timing with the hitch game. In terms of the quarterback's reads and progressions, he'll think shortest throw, softest coverage. He wants to take the easiest throw—we want completions! With the progression of the route, once the quarterback has determined which side to attack, he'll work inside-out, working off the flat defender.

The receivers must explode off the ball. We want to create a deep feeling in our routes. The receivers will sell the vertical. The outside receivers run three-step hitches, while the inside receivers run five-step hitches. We do this for spacing and to create clear pictures for the quarterback. Once the receivers get to their routes, they square their numbers to the quarterback and make themselves big. Again this is a rhythm- and timing-oriented throw. We really stress the run after the catch.

Smash

The next passing package we use in the spread offense is what we call the smash or hitch-corner concept (figure 8.9). This concept qualifies as an intermediate to deep throwing play—we have a deep throw with the corner route and an intermediate throw with the hitch route. We want to put a high–low stress on the flat player or the corner versus rolled coverages. We run this concept from drop-back and also from sprint-out; either way, the mechanics of the route package stay the same. Only the protection and the quarterback's mechanics are adjusted.

The offensive line works with the running back in a six-man drop-back protection scheme. The offensive line is

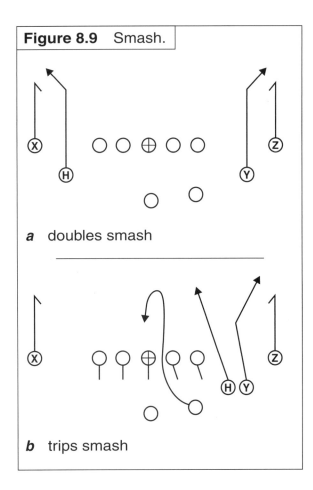

Figure 8.9 Smash.

a doubles smash

b trips smash

a 10- to 12-yard corner route, initially taking a high angle. Spacing on this play is critical to its success. Versus an alley presence on the corner route, we prefer the inside receiver to take an outside release, getting back vertical, and running the route off the double high safety. When we run smash from a 3-×-1 set, the number three receiver runs a vertical seam.

Sprint Crease

The crease package (figure 8.10) is based on our sprint game. We flood the outside area of the field while putting stress on the defense by changing the quarterback's launch point. We put a high–low stress on the flat defender, while keeping a built-in shot or opportunity for an explosive play with the vertical clear route.

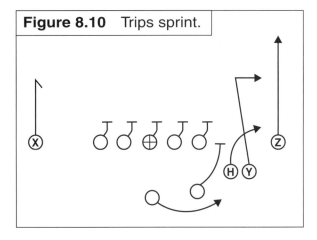

Figure 8.10 Trips sprint.

responsible for the four down linemen and the backside linebacker.

The running back works with the offensive line to block the six defenders in the box. The running back protects inside-out to a route of choice. We game plan the running back's route from week to week, based on the coverages we're seeing.

From the gun, the quarterback secures the snap and takes a three-step drop with a hitch. He takes his reads off the flat defender, reading it high to low or from corner to hitch. If we're in a 2-×-2 set with a single high safety alignment, we work opposite the alignment of the free safety. We constantly remind our quarterback not to forget his running back.

The outside receivers run a five-step hitch with a landmark at the bottom of the numbers. The inside receivers run

The offensive line protects with a reach technique. The line works in unison, aggressively reaching to the point of attack.

The running back protects the front-side edge of the sprint-out protection, working outside-in. The running back must be aggressive and in an attacking, downhill mode. We want to get the edge for the quarterback.

The quarterback works his sprint mechanics. Once the snap is secured, he laterally attacks the defense, looking to break contain. We want the quarterback to be a dual threat, able to run or throw the football. He looks to throw off his fifth or seventh step, throwing no later than his ninth step. His thought process is the same as in a drop-back—we really stress rhythm and timing of the play. The quarterback reads and bursts with a slight bubble when reading the flat defender. He throws the flat route off his fifth step or the crease off his seventh step. He also takes a peek to the vertical clear for the homerun shot. The quarterback must really work to get his shoulders, hips, and feet in proper throwing position to execute the throw.

The outside receiver runs a vertical clear, with a mandatory outside release. Versus rolled coverages, we take a mandatory outside release to get the corner's eyes off the number-two receiver and allow the quarterback to throw the hole shot. The number-two receiver runs a 12- to 15-yard roll-out. We don't want any signs of breaking down on the route. If the flat defender has expanded with width, the receiver throttles in the opening as he will not run to get covered. The number-three receiver runs a 3-yard flat route, looking to stretch the coverage immediately. When number three reaches the top of the numbers, he throttles down. If he gets 5 yards from the sideline, he sits down and shows his numbers to the quarterback.

Screen Plays

You need to be able to use and execute screen plays in the spread. We want to be able to throw multiple screens to different players and positions. We want to get the running backs and receivers involved in the screen game.

Dual Read Screen

A screen that has been effective for us is what we call a dual screen (figure 8.11). We call it a dual screen because two different screens occur at the same time. A running back screen or a swing screen occurs on the front side of the formation, while a receiver screen or jailbreak screen occurs on the back side of the formation. Sometimes we put the running back screen on the back side of the formation and the receiver screen on the front side of the formation. The dual screen has developed into a universal screen that's good versus man or zone coverage teams.

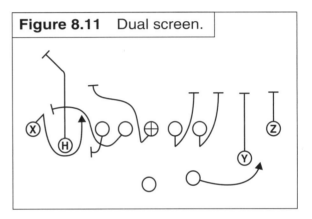

Figure 8.11   Dual screen.

The backside offensive tackle pass sets the defensive end. The backside guard sets, punches, and releases out to the flat area. The center sets, punches, and releases down the line of scrimmage to the alley. The playside guard sets, punches, and releases down the line of scrimmage to the inside. The playside tackle pass sets, flashes, and releases down the line of scrimmage to the alley. It's important that the offensive line works flat to their landmarks on the field.

The running back opens quick and fast, looking to get an immediate stretch to clear the defensive end. The running back executes a swing route, or what some people call a flare. The running back doesn't want to lose any ground. After the catch, he finds the alley and gets vertical upfield, reading the blocks of the pulling offensive linemen.

numbers of the receiver, right through his chest.

The receivers opposite the running back or swing side of the screen run the receiver or jail-break screen. The inside receiver (number two) executes what we call a trap block, blocking the defender over the number-one receiver (the receiver who's catching the football). The receiver performing the trap block must force the defender to work underneath and not over the top of the block. The outside receiver (number one) pushes upfield for three steps, then retraces his steps to get in position to be 1 yard behind the line of scrimmage. The tighter the coverage, the wider the receiver will work upfield with his three steps. We push up the field for three steps for timing purposes. This gives the quarterback time to read the back-side defensive end. If the ball is thrown to the receiver, he reads the alley and the blocks occurring on his side of the screen. Once he makes his read, he wants to get vertical up the field.

The receivers on the running back's side of the formation swing side, block base, or man over. They must do a great job of putting themselves in the proper body position to sustain their blocks on the perimeter. As a change-up versus man coverage teams, we employ a crack scheme to the running back's side of the screen, in which the inside receiver (number two) cracks the frontside inside linebacker, and the offensive tackle still runs the alley (figure 8.12).

After securing the snap, the quarterback takes a quick three-step drop with his eyes on the rushing defensive end to the running back's side or the swing side of the screen. If the defensive end bends or the quarterback has a clear picture of the running back, he throws it to the running back. Ball positioning is critical because we want the ball to skim the running back's breast plate, turning him into a runner. We don't want the running back to have to reach back for the football. If the defensive end hugs or peels to cover the running back, the quarterback stops and throws back to the other side, where we're executing the receiver screen or jail-break portion of the dual screen. Again, ball positioning is very important to the play. The quarterback needs to put the ball in the

Figure 8.12   Dual screen with crack.

Bubble Screen

In the screen family, the staple of the spread offense is what's commonly called a bubble screen, or an uncovered screen (figure 8.13). The bubble screen is thrown to the slot or inside receivers. The bubble screen is given, not taken. It's thrown against a defense that wants to cheat their alley players into a gray area, looking to be able to play both the run and the pass. They're trying to cheat their alignments over the slot receivers. The bubble screen takes away the defense's ability to cheat the run lanes. The key to running the bubble is having the right mindset and patience to throw the bubble. The bubble is nothing more than a toss sweep. You can think of it more as a running play than a traditional screen pass.

The mechanics of the play are simple. The inside or slot receiver pushes off his inside foot, looking to push toward the sideline. The receiver doesn't want to lose much ground. We're looking to get the ball outside. We want to out-leverage the defense by running away from the alley defenders. The receiver wants to keep his shoulders square to the line of scrimmage so he can advance the ball upfield.

The quarterback's accuracy is a critical element in executing the bubble. Just as if he were throwing the dual screen to the running back, the quar-

terback wants to skim the receiver's breast plate, turning him into a runner. We don't want the receiver to have to reach for the football. The outside receiver (number one) must be in stalk-block mode, blocking the defender over himself. He must have the mentality to maintain the block in space, and the understanding that we're trying to out-leverage the defense.

Another version of the bubble screen is to arc-block the perimeter, meaning that the outside receiver (number one) blocks the defender over the slot receiver (number two). This adjustment is used versus a deep-playing corner. The arc scheme allows the slot receiver to be in a one-on-one situation with the corner once he catches the ball (figure 8.14).

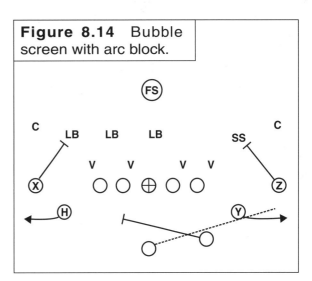

Figure 8.14 Bubble screen with arc block.

The bubble screen can be packaged with the running and passing games in many ways. The bubble screen can be protected in numerous ways. Because the quarterback is in catch-and-throw mode, you can leave a certain running play on with the offensive line or use the aggressive gap protection used with the quick-passing game. The bubble screen is very versatile and can fit the protection scheme that you use in your offense.

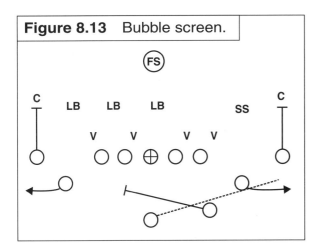

Figure 8.13 Bubble screen.

The plays discussed in this chapter are the base plays to our spread offensive attack. We want to be able to execute these plays against any defensive looks. Combining the execution of these schemes with a fast-tempo attack has given us an advantage over our opponents.

The spread offense has produced great numbers and success over the years, regardless of level of play or area of the country. The spread allows you to put the ball in your best player's hands. It's a multiple attack that makes the most of your players' skills.

An effective spread offensive football team needs a great plan of attack. The spread offense isn't just a set of plays but rather a system designed to take advantage of a defense. You must have answers for disguises, stems, and pressures or blitzes. Remember that an offensive tempo can be a weapon. It's easier to slow down the tempo than it is to speed it up. Attacking a defense comes down to numbers, angles, and grass.

There are no magical answers or solutions. Offensive football requires fundamentals, attention to detail, and execution. When installing the spread offense, you must have a strong belief in the system. You can't minor in it—you must major in it. If your players can execute the schemes, and the entire offensive team—players and coaches—understands the system, you can have a lot of fun and success with the spread.

PART IV

Wing-T Formations and Option Game

CHAPTER 9

Delaware Wing-T

Tubby Raymond

It's with concern that I write this chapter about the Delaware Wing-T. That's what we called our offense for the past 50 years, although our offense was under constant revision, and the version of the wing-T we used in 2000 had little resemblance to the wing-T of the early 1950s. For sentiment and because we still had books to sell, we kept the name. And there was one aspect of the offense that did remain the same over the years—it always allowed us to move the ball. As our wing-T developed over time, we did try to maintain some basic principles, and we always enjoyed the warmth of applause and the compliment of imitation.

Forest Evesheski at Iowa used the wing-T in 1957 to win the Big 10 championship and Rose Bowl. Paul Dietzel's LSU version of the wing-T won the national championship in 1959, and Ara Parseghian, who contributed significantly to the modernizing of the wing-T, won the national championship with Notre Dame in 1973. By the early 1980s, the wing-T was the offense of choice in high school football.

Not knowing were to start—early, middle, or late—I've decided to write an anthology of the growth and evolution of the wing-T.

The Early Wing-T

The original wing-T of 1951 was a hybrid, a mix of Fritz Crisler's single wing, Clark Shaughnessy's straight-T, and Rip Engles' unbalanced wing-T. Its beginnings were simple, but the principles it was founded on remain sound. Myriad factors created change. Defensive trends certainly had an impact, but rule changes that permitted the use of hands when blocking and the movement of the hashmarks toward the center of the field were also catalysts. The increasing skill of players later demanded that we spread out and throw more.

The original version of the wing-T was stark in comparison to the offense we ran in 2000. In the 1950s, we used two tight ends, a dive back, and a wing (figure 9.1). The linemen were referred to by number—two through eight, from right to left. We were a four-back running attack that used sequence or series football to threaten several points of attack at the snap with the flow of the backs. Counter and misdirection became our trademark; we threw the ball rarely, and when we did, it was from play action.

We didn't count on having great athletes, so the skill responsibilities were

Figure 9.1 1950's wing-T: two TEs, a dive back, and a wing.

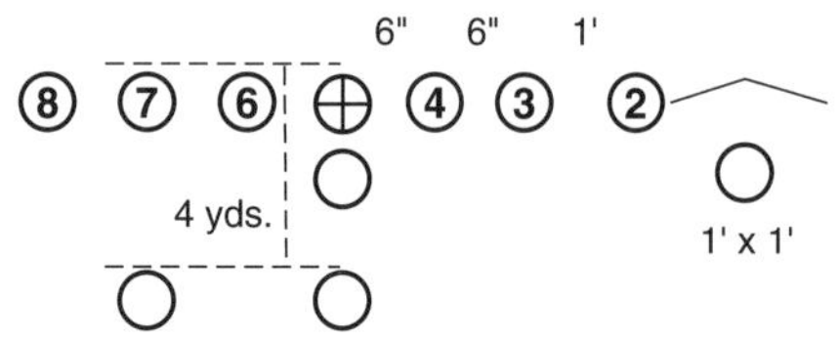

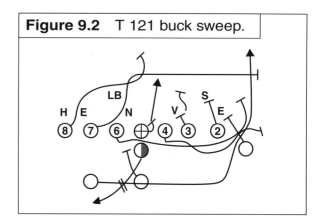

shared. The quarterback handled the ball and sometimes passed, and the halfbacks and fullbacks shared carries. The linemen used shoulder blocks, and no one was asked to block someone he didn't have an angle on. We avoided single blocking as much as possible. I think these were the reasons so many people pilfered the early wing-T.

In 1951, we focused on two passes and four running plays: buck sweep, guard trap, belly cross-block, and tackle trap counter. We occasionally ran a half-back-to-halfback reverse that we called the criss-cross counter. We threw from the bootleg off the buck sweep and the keep pass from belly action.

Buck Sweep

The trademark of the Delaware Wing-T was the buck sweep (figure 9.2), which we used through the 2000 season and employed many formations. The right halfback blocks the first free man to his inside, the first man he has an angle on. We never asked a player to do something he might not be able to do. The tight end and tackle both gap block the down linebacker. The right guard pulls and blocks the first man outside the right halfback's block. The center checks the attack-side gap and then goes man-on. The left guard pulls and blocks through the hole and in, while the left tackle blocks at the cutoff and out. The quarterback reverse pivots and hands off to the left halfback, then bootlegs away from the sweep. The fullback fakes up

the middle. If a defense rotated to the wing, we would run the same sweep away from the wing using motion.

Figure 9.2 T 121 buck sweep.

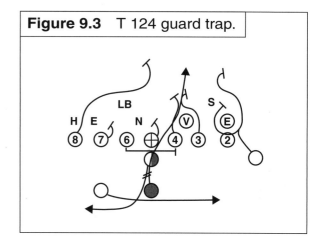

Guard Trap

If the defensive tackle came upfield, we would guard-trap him and give the ball to the fullback (figure 9.3). The center blocked either on or left. The right guard blocked down on a man on the center, a linebacker, or, if a man was in the gap, the guard would pull away as on the sweep. The left guard trapped. The right tackle blocked the first linebacker from the center. The right half faked a down block, then went to the cutoff. Recognize the conflict of both the defensive tackle and the end. Both are out, flanked for the sweep, yet if they come upfield they'll be trapped.

Figure 9.3 T 124 guard trap.

Cross Block

Our third staple at the time was the cross block to the dive man (figure 9.4). The left tackle blocks a man on or down. The left guard pulls and traps. The center reaches to protect the gap. The left end blocks the nearest linebacker. The dive man steps out and then blocks through the hole. The quarterback reverse pivots, gets some depth, and rides the handoff to the fullback, who circles his path to the opening. If the defense overpursues, the fullback winds back. The right half leaves in motion and circles the handoff, blocking outside-in to create the illusion of a keep pass.

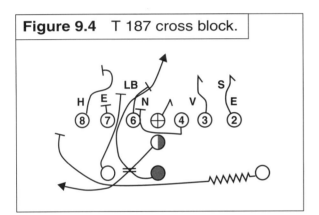

Figure 9.4   T 187 cross block.

Tackle Trap Counter

The fourth play was the tackle trap counter (figure 9.5). The right guard leads, blocks a linebacker if he can, gets, or pulls away. The center posts man-on or leads left. The left guard posts or blocks his area. The left tackle pulls and traps. The right tackle blocks the first linebacker from the center, and the right end blocks the next linebacker. The right halfback is in motion. He fakes around the handoff and then walls off at the flank. The fullback dives for the outside left of the left guard and checks for the pulling left tackle. The quarterback reverse pivots. On the third step, he hands off inside to the left halfback, then continues faking a bootleg.

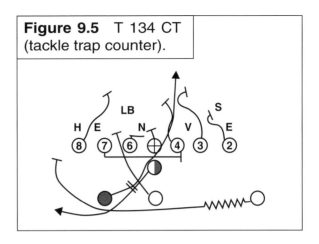

Figure 9.5   T 134 CT (tackle trap counter).

Keep Pass

When throwing the keep pass (figure 9.6), the quarterback makes a distinct ride to the fullback, then keeps the ball. The left halfback dives, then slides into the flat. The left end runs a seam pattern. The left tackle blocks gap on down. The left guard pulls and walls off. The center and right side of the line step toward the action, then cup away from the action. The right end also steps and cups, then runs a delayed crossing pattern.

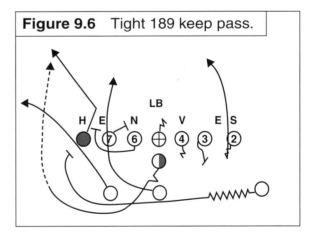

Figure 9.6   Tight 189 keep pass.

Buck Sweep Bootleg

The bootleg off the buck sweep (figure 9.7) was the forerunner of the waggle, which we'll discuss in detail later. The buck sweep bootleg was as simple as that—everyone ran the sweep, and the quarterback kept the ball away from the action. The receiver ran the pattern shown in figure 9.7.

Figure 9.7   T 121 bootleg.

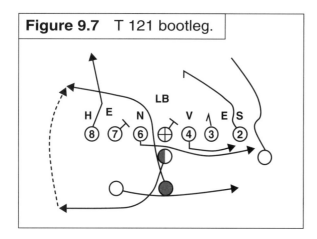

Spread End and Unbalanced Front

By the mid 1960s, we began to spread an end both to the wing and away. The obvious advantage of bringing both ends to one side to create an unbalanced front was impressive. We could run our basic offense unbalanced without changing assignments.

Spread Trap Option

Now we needed a play to the spread flank as effective as the buck sweep to a tight end. By the mid 1970s, we were running a trap option (figure 9.8). The

Figure 9.8   Spread 121 trap option.

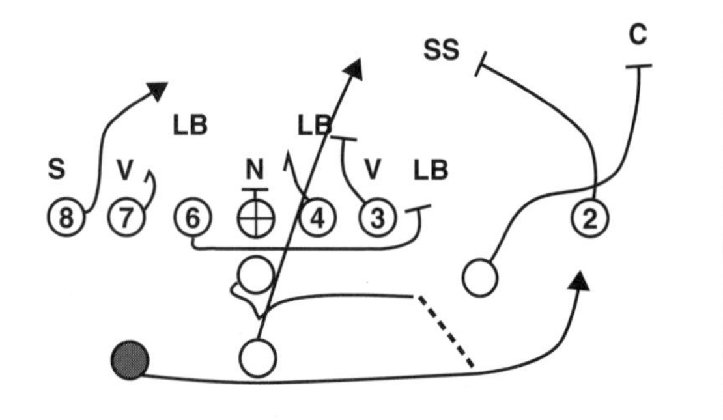

right tackle blocked gap, bump, lead, and up to the linebacker. The right guard blocked gap, post, lead linebacker. The center blocked post or left linebacker.

2: If spread, crack 2, stalk 1.

3: Gap, bump, lead LB; block LB with gap call.

4: Gap, on, lead.

5. Reach, on backer; post versus 55.

6. Pull, block first man on or outside of 3.

7: Reach, on backer.

8: Cut off.

QB: Reverse pivot, two-step depth, sprint to flank, execute option.

Left HB: Be in position to receive pitch.

Right HB: Check 2, stalk 1; if three men are outside of 3 man, wall with two.

FB: Fake 24 gut.

The left guard pulled and blocked the first man on or outside the right tackle. The left tackle blocked his gap then on or away. The tight end blocked at the cutoff. The quarterback reverse pivoted to the midline for two steps, allowing the left guard to pass, then sprinted to option off the third defensive man at the flank and pitched it or kept it. The spread end cracked a second defensive man, if possible; if not, he blocked number one. The right half flared and blocked the remaining man. The fullback faked the guard trap, and the left half sprinted to a pitch relationship.

The trap option was immediately successful. True to our nature, we wanted a pass from this action. By the early 1980s, the trap option pass was a staple (figure 9.9). The spread end faked a crack block and then slid into an opening behind the strong safety. The right half flared and ran upfield. The inverted safety had to support or cover the flat. If he waited, the spread end blocked him on the trap option. If he supported the action, he gave up his coverage.

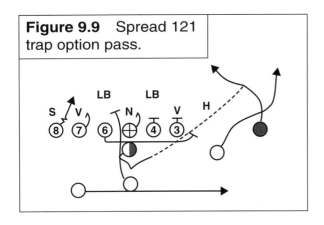

Figure 9.9 Spread 121 trap option pass.

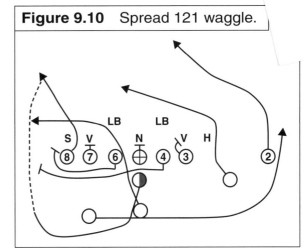

Figure 9.10 Spread 121 waggle.

2: Fake crack, look for pass.

3: Gap on area.

4: Gap on area.

5: On left.

6: Pull; block first man outside of 3.

7: Pull check.

8: On release.

QB: Reverse pivot, two-step depth, turn, pass to HB.

Left HB: Sprint for pitch position.

Right HB: Flare upfield.

FB: Fill for 6 man.

The exceptional thing about the play is the number of options available. The quarterback can throw to either the spread end or the wing. He can pitch the ball to the left half if the defense drops with the pass threat.

Waggle

The problem with the spread trap option pass came when the offside free safety quickly pursued and filled at the flank. This scenario suggests the waggle (figure 9.10), which would put the free safety in conflict. The waggle has been one of our most used plays, and at one time we felt it was almost an offense within itself. While at Notre Dame, Ara Parseghian thought the waggle was the best play in football.

2: If tight, crossing pattern; read safety.

3: Gap on area; pull check versus eagle.

4: Pull, read 6 man's block, clean up chase, block out; don't pull versus eagle.

5: Reach right.

6: Pull; hook second man from 5.

7: Gap down on.

8: If tight, release inside; run seam pattern.

QB: Reverse pivot, fake to left HB, option run or pass.

Left HB: Fake 21; block first man outside 3 man's block.

Right HB: Fake 121; key middle safety; run crossing pattern.

FB: Dive for 6 man's inside foot; block 6 man's area; delayed slide into flat.

Virtually, every play has its companion pass. The waggle comes off buck-sweep action. The waggle to the tight end begins with back-sweep action or, in this case, the beginning of the trap option. The quarterback reverse pivots and moves away from the line, faking to the left halfback. The fullback dives and runs between the pulling guards, then slips out into the flat. The tight end releases inside, then runs a corner pattern. The right halfback runs a crossing pattern, and the wide-out runs a post. The left tackle blocks gap down on. The left guard pulls and hooks the first man outside of the tight end. The right guard pulls, avoids the fullback, then blocks out at the flank. The center blocks on or away. The right tackle pulls down to the center and then blocks back. The left halfback fakes a sweep and then flares upfield. All five eligible receivers are upfield. The quarterback reads the free safety. If the free safety flows with the original action, the quarterback directs his attention to the tight end or fullback in the flat. If the free safety doesn't flow, the quarterback considers throwing back to the wide-out running the post or the right halfback. Remember that the left halfback is flaring upfield and becomes another receiver. The quarterback may choose to run using his guards' blocking.

In the late 1980s, we started to run a belly play to the tight end and wing with the guard kicking out. This became an important play because it created conflict as a companion play to the buck sweep.

Right Down

The tight end blocks gap read down backer (figure 9.11). The right tackle blocks gap down, and the right guard pulls to kick out. The right halfback fakes his buck sweep block, then walls off a linebacker. The offside lineman reaches. The fullback drives for the inside left of the right end, receives

the ball, and stays tight to his block. From his dive spot or a wing, the left halfback leaves in motion to create a pitch relationship. The quarterback reverse pivots flat and fast, meshes a ride handoff to the fullback, and then fakes the option.

2: Gap down backer.

3: Gap down backer.

4: Pull, block out.

5: Reach on backer.

6: Reach on backer.

7: Reach on backer.

8: Release through 1.

QB: Reverse pivot, hand off to FB, fake option.

Left HB: Leave in motion, fake pitch at 1.

Right HB: Influence first man on or outside of 2 man, block area.

FB: Carrier; run for 2 man's inside foot.

This action naturally creates an opportunity for the quarterback to keep the ball or pitch to the left half. Figure 9.12 shows the quarterback pitching off the strong safety. The line assignments are the same as when running down, with the exception that the guard logs his block.

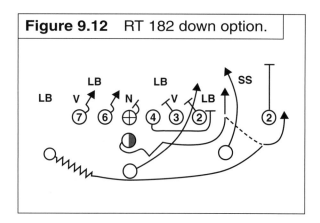

Figure 9.12 RT 182 down option.

2: Gap down backer.

3: Gap down backer.

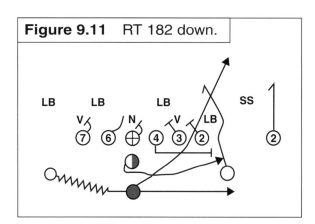

Figure 9.11 RT 182 down.

4: Pull, block out.

5: Reach on backer.

6: Reach on backer.

7: Reach on backer.

8: Out cut.

QB: Reverse pivot, fake to FB, run option.

Left HB: Leave in motion, fake pitch at 1.

Right HB: Influence first man on or outside of 2 man, wall off.

FB: Fake 82 down.

Triple and Drop-Back Passing

We had two quarterbacks in the late 1970s who would become successful starters in the National Football League: Jeff Komlo and Scott Brunner. Rich Gannon, the MVP who took Oakland to the Super Bowl, came five years later. Matt Magy was our quarterback in 2000, and he went on to throw well in the Arena Football League. Although we threw the ball more in one game in the 1970s than we did in an entire year in the 1950s, we still hadn't taken advantage of the skills of our quarterbacks. In the 1990s, we had two fine running quarterbacks, Bill Vergantino and Leo Hamlet, and it became imperative that we seriously consider the triple and drop-back passing options.

By 1990, we recognized the need to accommodate the ever-increasing skill of modern players. We had quarterbacks who could both run and pass, and spread receivers who needed space to do their thing. We wanted to retain the advantage of three backs yet employ a formation that would enhance our passing game. Above all, we didn't want to succumb like the avalanche of coaches going to the one-back concept. We didn't feel we could depend on having linemen good enough for zone blocking or one

back talented enough to run successfully without deception. But, above all, we wanted to be different. Everyone was going to a one-back spread, and we wanted the advantage of uniqueness. Thus, the final stage of the Delaware offense employed the addition of multiple spread formations to enhance the passing game and retain three-back running. Like its grandfather in the 1950s, this offense became a combination of wing-T, triple option, Oakland Raiders three-step passing, and some run-and-shoot principles.

Our first move was to replace the tight end at times with a spread end and move the dive back to a wing, creating a double wing formation (figure 9.13). Next, we used the same end over techniques with one of the spread ends (figure 9.14). This, of course, eliminates the eligibility of the inside receiver, referred to as X, a situation recognized by many of our opponents and some of the officials. We called the formation TRA. Despite the change in eligibility, the play required the defense to make last-second adjustments. Stepping the short side wing up and the widest receiver off creates trips (figure 9.15). We used a step-to technique at the last second to change eligibility.

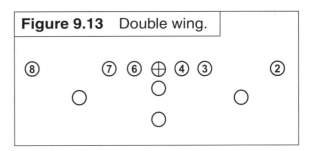

Figure 9.13   Double wing.

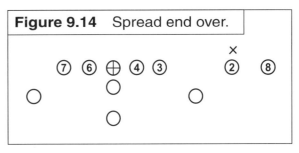

Figure 9.14   Spread end over.

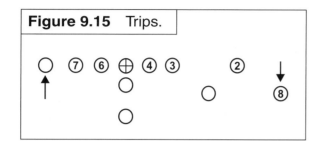

Figure 9.15   Trips.

The speed sweep (figure 9.16) is a fine example of creating a three-back running threat from spread formations via motion. The quarterback initiates motion with his heal. The left wing sprints in motion across the formation and receives the handoff at controlled full speed. It's advantageous to use sound for the snap to facilitate timing as the quarterback pivots to hand off. The 3 man reaches on the 1S man off his shoulder. He doesn't have to knock him down, just tie him up. The 4 man pulls and runs for the flank to pick up pursuit. The assignment at the flank begins with the right halfback's decision to block the first man outside the tackle's block. He will call his attention to X, who in turn will call to the spread end. The fullback fakes up the middle, and the quarterback fakes the bootleg, creating the three identical fakes of the original buck sweep.

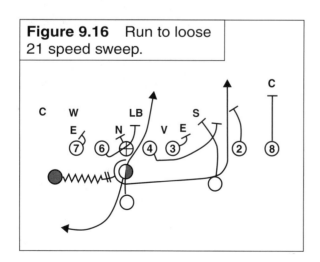

Figure 9.16   Run to loose 21 speed sweep.

2: If spread, stalk 1 (2 count) or crack 2 (3 count).

3: Reach on backer; pull and wall off if uncovered.

4: Pull and wall off; escape to backer if tackle is uncovered.

5: On, left.

6: Pull, wall off 5 man's tail.

7: Cut off.

8: Out cut.

QB: Reverse pivot, handoff to left HB, fake 24 gut, bootleg.

Left HB: Carrier; run to motion, receive handoff.

Right HB: Block first man outside 3 man.

FB: Fake 24 gut.

Give the ball to the fullback after faking the speed sweep is blocked guard trap on or gut (figure 9.17). Some success with the sweep (sequence football) and the defensive tackle chases suggests gut blocking. The 3 man blocks as on the speed sweep, and the 4 man pulls. The center blocks on or left as the 6 man pulls around 5 to block the middle linebacker. The fullback reads the 5 man's block and cuts behind him if the nose chases the play action. It may be blocked on.

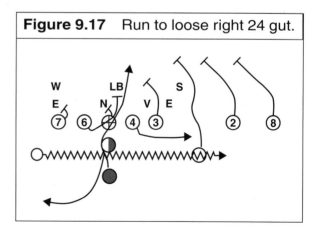

Figure 9.17   Run to loose right 24 gut.

2: If spread, out cut.

3: First backer from 5 man.

4: Pull, fake 21.

5: On, left.

6: Pull, block through the hole.

7: Gap backer on.

8: Cut off.

QB: Reverse pivot, handoff to FB, bootleg left.

Left HB: Fake 21.

Right HB: Fake 21, cut off.

FB: Carrier; dive for 5 man's left foot.

Triple Option (40s)

Similar to the offense in the beginning, a hybrid of several concepts, the addition of the triple option was a natural for our latest version of the wing-T. Over time, we had been impressed by its effectiveness, an attractive concept of three-back football. We were blessed with talented running quarterbacks in the early 1990s, so the triple was a natural addition. We were told that you couldn't use it unless you made a complete commitment to it.

We began by calling the options. We would call the fullback play or the option behind it. We soon learned that reading it was rather simple if it was modified. The quarterback would step back and jab the ball to the fullback, initiating a ride step. The ride was neither as long nor as far into the line as those we had borrowed. The quarterback simply made his decision to pull before the ride step was completed. If the fullback could still feel the ball late in the ride, he would expect to keep it.

We were now using many formations that required defensive adjustments. We didn't want the triple as a staple but only to a flank we felt was neglected.

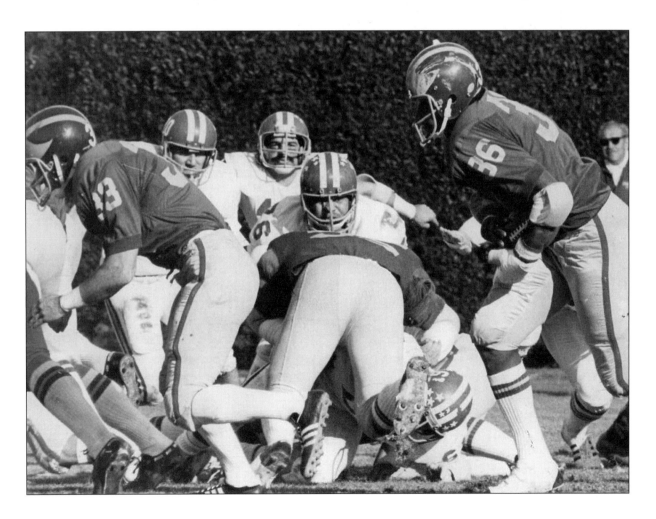

Figure 9.18 shows the 40 option to the short side away from trips. Now on the line, the wing will release if two defenders are outside his tackle or wall off a linebacker if there's only one, as in figure 9.18 (he walls off). The quarterback and fullback execute the ride, and the right halfback leaves in motion to become the pitch man.

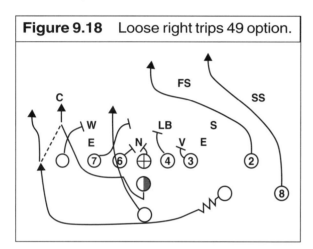

Figure 9.18   Loose right trips 49 option.

2: Cut off.

3: Reach on backer.

4: Reach on backer.

5: Reach on backer; post versus 55.

6: Gap on lead.

7: Gap bump lead backer; block LB with gap call.

8: Cut off.

QB: Step back, ride ball to FB, execute triple option.

Left HB: Wall with 2.

Right HB: Leave in one-step motion; be in position to receive pitch.

FB: Dive for 6 man's outside hip; accept handoff or fake and block area.

Now, don't tell me you would aggressively attack this action by forcing with the cornerback and filling with the safety. Since I have the chalk, let's look at the pass from this action from the same formation.

For the loose right trips 49 option throw back (figure 9.19), the option play is faked. The quarterback gives ground and reads the area vacated by the safety. The left halfback flies, and X runs through the safety; the wide-out runs a cross route underneath him.

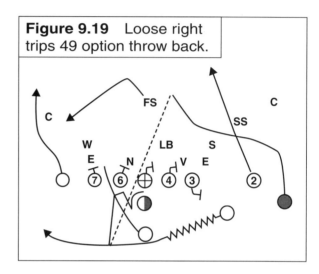

Figure 9.19   Loose right trips 49 option throw back.

According to wing-T lore, every play must have a counter (figure 9.20). The right halfback begins with short motion but reverses and walls off at the right flank. The fullback and quarterback fake the weakside option. The quarterback abbreviates his ride, then steps back toward the opposite flank. The left halfback leaves on the snap and sprints to a pitch relationship at the right flank. The right tackle and guard block option at their flanks. The center posts, then blocks left. The left guard

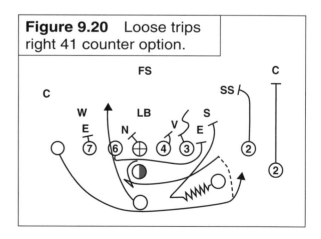

Figure 9.20   Loose trips right 41 counter option.

pulls and logs or blocks out on the first man who shows.

Y: Block 2.

2: Block 1.

3: Bump lead backer.

4: Post backer.

5: On, left.

6: Pull wall off or log.

7: On, outside.

Left HB: On line. Sprint for pitch.

Right HB: Leave with motion; reverse or wall off.

FB: Fake 49 option.

Every play has a counter. The Sally is an inside counter. The right halfback, fullback, and quarterback execute the 49 option (figure 9.21). After faking to the fullback, the quarterback takes two steps deep, then hands off inside to the left halfback, who runs to daylight on the strong side. The fullback aborts his fake and blocks chase. The attack-side center, guard, and tackle all step and cup, as in pass protection. They move defenders in the direction they choose to go. One or more may be able to release on a linebacker.

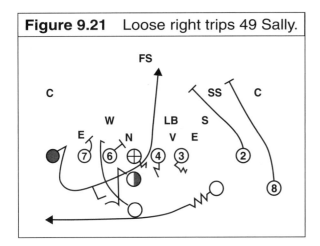

Figure 9.21   Loose right trips 49 Sally.

3: Step and cup, block on, outside, delayed backer.

4: Step and cup, block on, outside, delayed backer.

5: Step and cup, block on, outside, delayed backer.

6: Gap on backer.

7: Gap on outside, gap backer.

8: Release.

QB: Fake ball to FB, hand off inside to left HB.

Left HB: Carrier; counter step, receive ball from QB, head for 4 man's tail.

Right HB: Leave in early motion, fake 49 option keep pass.

FB: 40 option ride at 6 man's tail.

The tackle trap (figure 9.22) is an example of combining a basic wing-T play with a spread formation. It provides a strong post lead, a solid block adjacent to the post block, which controls all of the gap problems presented by modern defense and a trap. We continued to use it from many formations (see also figure 9.5).

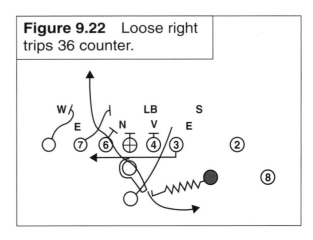

Figure 9.22   Loose right trips 36 counter.

2: If spread, out cut. If tight, cut off, go inside 3 man.

3: Pull, inside-out.

4: Area post.

5: Post lead backer.

6: Gap lead backer.

7: First backer from 5 man; block safety.

8: Gap backer.

QB: Reverse pivot, hand off to right HB, bootleg at right.

Left HB: Leave in early motion, block first man outside 2 man.

Right HB: Carrier; rock weight on right foot, receive inside handoff.

FB: Dive for 3-4 seam, block first man in area.

The left guard blocks gap leader backer influence. If he can't lead or get to a linebacker, he'll fake pass protection or pull away. The center posts a man on him or leads in the direction of the lead. The right guard blocks area post as the right tackle pulls and traps. The left tackle blocks the first linebacker from the center. The left halfback blocks downfield. The right halfback, who is the carrier, leaves in motion, which is timed to place him at his original 5 position. The fullback dives to block the first man off the right guard. The right halfback should receive the ball just as he clears the fullback.

May I say, with a smile, while week after week the defense is playing against linemen who are standing up and pushing, shoulder blocking is received like a pail of cold water in the face.

Drop-Back Passing

We added the spread formations, devised a three-back running attack, and now we wanted to raise the level of sophistication of our passing game. Our first venture into drop-back passing began with the three-step series. These steps began with the right foot (assuming the quarterback throws right-handed), then left, and finally his right, where he's prepared to throw immediately. He must get the passing grip as he takes the ball from the center and turn his hips and shoulders in the direction of the first read, prepared to deliver.

These three steps give the wide-out time to run 6 yards and make his cut. The base route calls for him to loop out at 6 yards (figure 9.23). The wing to the call looks in as a hot receiver, then pro-

ceeds to 12 yards, where he hooks out. Naturally, a presnap read may give the quarterback a suggestion, but he reads the wide-out first before considering the wing, unless he sees heat and the wing is uncovered. The opening must be anticipated and delivered as the cut is made.

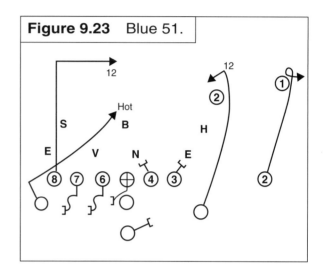

Figure 9.23 Blue 51.

2: Run loop out pattern at 6 yards (signals).

3: Gap on, outside.

4: Gap on, inside.

5: Step and cup.

6: Step and cup.

7: Step and cup.

8: If tight, look in.

QB: Three steps then SE, right HB, and TE.

Left HB: Flare and hook at 3 yards.

Right HB: Hook at 12 yards; turn upfield and look over inside shoulder; run companion route if pattern is called.

FB: Read inside backer; if he drops, read 3 and block if he drives; gap call, block 3.

We developed many pattern variations. We also added the opportunity for the wide-out to signal alternative routes. Trips may be added by bringing the left half in extended motion (figure 9.24). The letter M brings the left halfback into motion, suggesting sweep. He then moves to his place in the pattern (figure 9.25).

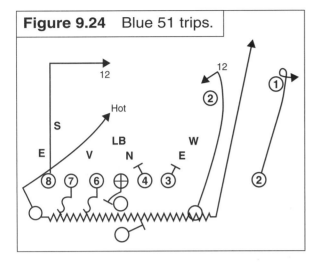

Figure 9.24   Blue 51 trips.

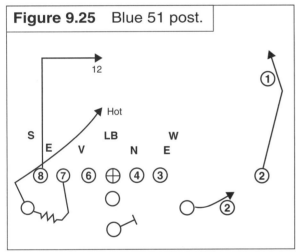

Figure 9.25   Blue 51 post.

The 50 play series required blocking technique adjustments because the ball was thrown so quickly. If the call of the pass is to the right, the 3 man begins showing pass protection (for 1 count), then aggressively blocks his opponent low so the defensive man cannot stand up and block the pass. The 4 man aggressively blocks his assignment as he would on a running play. The 5, 6, and 7 men all step and cup away from the call. The fullback checks the 3-4 seam to pick up a firing linebacker, then checks outside the 3 man's block. If called, he will flare control and the outside backer to clear the passing lane.

In 60 protection for the five-step drop-back pass, the line assignments are identical to those used for 50 protection but require technical adjustments. The linemen retreat, taking the inside seam away and riding their opponents back and out of the throwing cup. The fullback's assignment is the same as 50 protection, but he will fake a draw when a deep pattern is called or will flare for some patterns.

The basic pattern 61 (figure 9.26) is directed to the right and is nicknamed Harry. We used nicknames to facilitate audibles, if necessary. Here, the wide-out to that side runs 12 yards, where he hooks on the hash. The right wing runs a crossing pattern at 5 yards, while the left halfback crosses under him. The fullback flares to provide an immediate hot man or draw underneath coverage away from the throwing lane. The left end (8) curls at 12 yards.

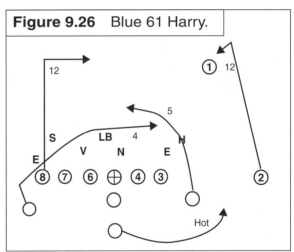

Figure 9.26   Blue 61 Harry.

3: Gap on, outside.

4: Gap on, inside.

5: Step and cup left.

6: Step and cup left.

7: Step and cup left.

QB: Take five steps quickly; read through flat coverage.

Left HB: Pattern.

Right HB: Pattern.

FB: Flare control.

It has been a pleasure to reminisce about the history of the Delaware Wing-T and the talented young men who gave us such success. We won some and lost some but, in retrospect, the victories and losses were insignificant compared to the relationships built among players and coaches. Above all, we made a great effort to be ourselves even when defenses forced some conformity to the latest trends.

CHAPTER 10

Air Force Flexbone

Fisher DeBerry
Air Force Academy

Chuck Petersen
Air Force Academy

Although we take great pride in what we do, we can't claim any of it as our own. We owe a great deal to those coaches who came before us for the development of the system we use today. This chapter is dedicated to these great option coaches and the players who make the system work.

Triple Option

The triple option has been the bread-and-butter option for Air Force's attack since 1980. It has remained relatively unchanged since its inception and is our starting point for all game plan discussions. This is the first option we must make defenses defend, and all other options serve to complement this series.

The triple option gives us many advantages in attacking defenses. While we acknowledge that there are many ways to skin a cat, this option gives us a competitive advantage in most areas:

1. Very few offenses run this series. As a result, a defense has only a short time to prepare to defend the option. It's very difficult for defensive coaches to game plan and teach their players in two to three days to play assignment football.

2. The triple option forces defenses to balance based on the offensive formation. In every instance, there are three immediate threats to both sides of the defense. Defenses must defend all areas of the field.

3. The triple option takes advantage of defensive mistakes. Because there are three options prior to the snap, defenders must play assignment football, and one defender who fails allows a big play.

4. You can recruit or fit your personnel to make this series successful. There's no prerequisite height for offensive linemen. A shorter, quicker kid is generally more effective. While everyone else is looking for a tall, strong-armed quarterback, we prefer a shorter, quicker athletic quarterback. Our backs and receivers are multitalented (good pass receivers, quick and tough) but don't need to be extremely big.

5. It's a versatile series, effective in all areas of the field and at all downs and distances. Throughout the years, many of our best third-and-long plays have been triple options.

6. The triple option develops a mental and physical toughness within the

football team. A team can't practice the triple option half-speed or with a thud tempo.

7. The system ensures single coverage on the four immediate receiver threats, enhancing the opportunity for big plays in the passing game. We see very few blitzes because we're ready and able to run the triple option.

Multiple Formations in the Triple Option

One of the biggest changes we've made to our basic offense is the use of multiple formations. Since 1980, we have lived with the triple option as our base play.

From 1980 until 1993, our base formation was the wishbone, with one tight end and one split end or two split ends. During that time, we had a tremendous amount of success. We beat Notre

Dame four consecutive years (1983 to 1986) and played in nine bowl games, including victories over Vanderbilt, Ole Miss, Virginia Tech, Texas, Ohio State, and Mississippi State. We also shared a Western Athletic Conference championship in 1985, finishing the year 12 and 1 and ranked number five in the country.

Although we had great success, we found it increasingly difficult to move the football from the traditional wishbone set. At the same time, Hawaii and Georgia Southern exploded onto the scene with an option-based attack from a double-slot formation. We made a difficult but fortunate decision in the off-season of 1993 to break the bone.

Our reasons for breaking the bone were threefold. First, we felt that our basic offense could remain unchanged by moving the halfbacks to the slot, but that it would immediately put four downfield threats at or near the line of scrimmage (figure 10.1). Second, we felt that our pitch relationship would be enhanced. Instead of our halfbacks catching the pitch 3 to 4 yards behind the line of scrimmage (as was the case from the wishbone), the double slot demanded a flatter pitch, and the back received the pitch near the line of scrimmage (figure 10.2). Third, moving the halfbacks to the slot helped them execute their blocking assignments because they were closer to their targets.

Since 1993, we have grown more multiple by moving our slots to flanker positions and introducing multiple motions to our attack. As defenses continue to adjust, we must continue to adjust. Figure 10.3 shows our basic formations, and figure 10.4 illustrates our motions.

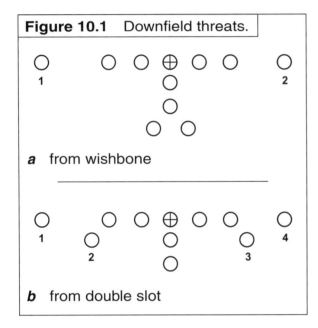

Figure 10.1   Downfield threats.

a from wishbone

b from double slot

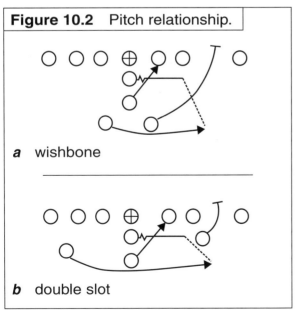

Figure 10.2   Pitch relationship.

a wishbone

b double slot

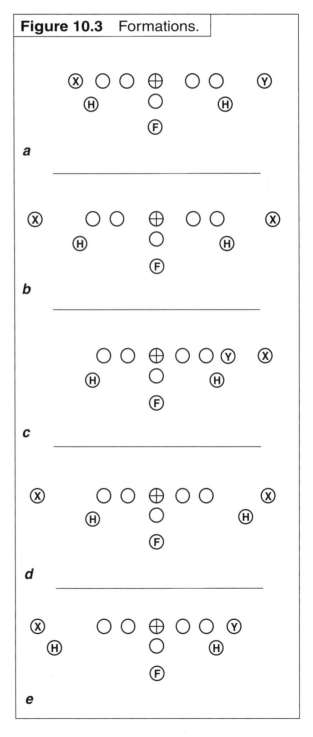

Figure 10.3   Formations.

a

b

c

d

e

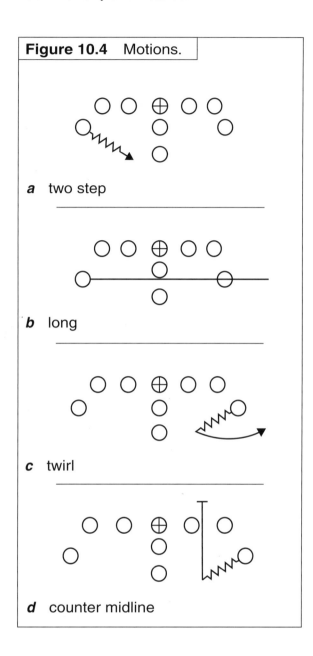

Figure 10.4   Motions.

a   two step

b   long

c   twirl

d   counter midline

Basic Triple-Option Attack

Our use of formations and motions has changed a great deal over the years, but the mechanics of the triple option has been consistent since 1980. The basic premise behind the play is to assign two people to the inside linebacker, read the first down lineman from the B gap out, and pitch off the next defender. We have two schemes to accomplish this, and the scheme is based on the defensive front we're facing. The first scheme is the zone-arc scheme, which is run against seven-man fronts. The second scheme is the veer-load scheme, which is run primarily against eight-man fronts. We'll discuss our primary attack shortly, but first we need to define seven- and eight-man fronts.

We try to make it as easy as possible for the quarterback to determine the particular front we're facing. As a rule, the center makes calls, and the quarterback reacts off the center's call. Any time the defense has a zero technique nose guard or a middle linebacker, the quarterback sees the defense as a seven-man front. Some examples of these defenses are 50, 4-3, and 6-1. Anything else—eagle defense, shade, and G defense—are considered eight-man fronts.

Zone-Arc Scheme

As stated earlier, we'll run the zone-arc scheme against seven-man fronts (figure 10.5). The two men assigned to the playside halfback are the playside guard and the playside tackle. The playside halfback is responsible to arc block the primary run support defender—hence the term zone-arc. The playside receiver is responsible for the first threat in the secondary zone. The center, backside guard, tackle, and tight end are in a scoop-hinge blocking scheme.

For the quarterback footwork, we use a clock system with 12 o'clock at the quarterback's nose. Six o'clock is at his back, and 3 and 9 o'clock are to his right and left hip, respectively. His first step is at 4 o'clock if the play is to his right and at 8 o'clock if it's to his left. We emphasize two things to help the quarterback accomplish his first step correctly: prior to the snap his weight is on the foot opposite to the play, and his toe must point to the direction on the clock. Over the years those two points have helped tremendously. The second step is with the foot opposite the play and puts the quarterback per-

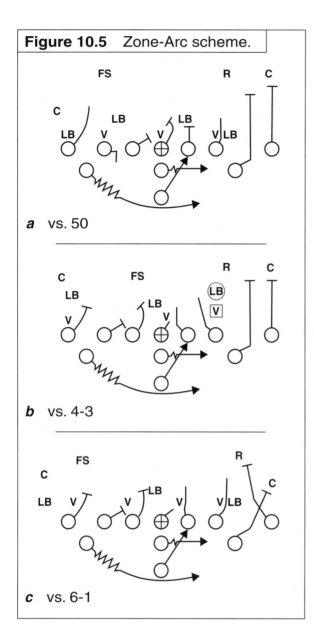

Figure 10.5   Zone-Arc scheme.

a vs. 50

b vs. 4-3

c vs. 6-1

with the benefit of two angles of game video and slow motion, but the 21-year-old kid with a split-second to make a decision needs to have confidence. His confidence comes from his coach's belief in him, repetitions, and certain presnap thoughts.

The key to a successful mesh is repetition, repetition, and more repetition. Repetition gives the mesh the consistency necessary to be successful. The fullback is as critical to a consistent mesh as the quarterback is; I will discuss the fullback's part later on. Besides the quarterback footwork already discussed, the ball placement is also important. From the snap, the quarterback should take the ball back with his chin on his front shoulder pad. His playside elbow should be seated into his rib cage. We teach the fullback to soft squeeze the ball in the mesh. If the quarterback is to give the ball to the fullback, he will pressure the ball with his front hand. If the quarterback pulls, we want the fullback to feel the quarterback's back hand sliding across his stomach. This concept is rather esoteric, but the main point to all of this is repetition.

The quarterback's read can be as easy or as difficult as the coach makes it. We try to give the quarterback a presnap thought and then ask him to react from that thought. It is similar to the process a baseball hitter goes through on a 3-0 count. Barry Bonds has a green light to swing on 3-0, but he's looking for one pitch and one location. If he gets what he's looking for, he'll rip it; anything else he'll let go because he has two other strikes. Similarly, we tell the quarterback that four things can happen in the read and three of them tell him to give the ball to the fullback. His presnap thought then is to give. We read the near shoulder of the read key.

The four things that can happen in the read and the reactions are squat (give), up charge (give), Q stunt (give),

pendicular to the line of scrimmage. The quarterback's third step is a weight shift through the mesh to the front foot. His fourth step is to accelerate off the mesh to his pitch key.

The quarterback's read and mesh are the bread and butter to any triple-option attack. The quarterback must be proficient to put maximum pressure on the defense. We try to make this process as simple as possible and in any situation give the quarterback the benefit of the doubt in his decision-making process. It's very easy to be critical on Sunday

and mesh charge (pull). A read key that squats is playing the quarterback but trying to tackle the fullback with an arm tackle. The quarterback must give, and the fullback must run through the arm tackle. An up charge is easy. The read key works up or out playing the quarterback. The Q stunt is the most difficult read. The read key starts down for the fullback but works up for the quarterback. The quarterback must be patient in the mesh and give. The mesh charge is where the read key crashes for the fullback, and the quarterback must pull.

The other factor to the read is the position of the read key. If the read key is in the B gap cocked toward the mesh, the quarterback thinks pull presnap. If the read key is a wide and loose technique, he continues to think give. Once the ball is snapped, all the quarterback has to do is react off his presnap thought. If his presnap thought is to give, he gives unless the read key reacts differently than he is anticipating.

In all situations, the quarterback must make his decision prior to the fullback getting to his front hip. He must live with his decision by that point. Most mesh fumbles occur because of doubt in the decision-making process. A great rule of thumb we use is *when in doubt, give.* It may be the wrong decision, but at least we avoid a bad play.

Once the mesh is complete, the quarterback must attack the pitch key. First, we emphasize the importance of not being in a hurry getting through the mesh but accelerating to the pitch key once the mesh is complete. Young quarterbacks have a tendency to run through the mesh, which can get them into trouble. Our greatest quarterbacks (Dee Dowis, Beau Morgan, Blane Morgan, Chance Harridge) had the God-given ability to accelerate from the mesh to the pitch key faster than most.

We teach quarterbacks to attack the inside shoulder of the pitch key. The quarterback has to deal with three things when attacking the pitch key: hot, slow play, and pitch. If the pitch key comes hot, the quarterback stops, drops his tail, pitches, and gives with the hit. In effect, he becomes a shock absorber. When the pitch key goes to the pitch, the quarterback turns up and looks to stretch the field. When the pitch key slow plays, he's in effect playing the quarterback but trying to string the play to allow for inside-out pursuit. Once the ball is pitched, he tries to tackle the pitch back. The quarterback can do a couple of things, but he can't let the pitch key string it for long. As he attacks the inside shoulder, he should dip to his inside, pitch, and eliminate the pitch key by crossing his face. The other thing the quarterback can do is stop and fake a pitch with a naked hand and then turn up under the pitch key.

The pitch itself requires repetition. We teach the basketball toss (hand under the ball, shoot the ball end over end), but we don't try to change a quarterback who pitches thumb under if he's successful. The key to either technique is to pitch the ball from chest to chest. The quarterback must step to the pitch back and look the ball in to the pitch back.

The playside halfback is responsible to arc-block the primary run support defender. He must presnap read the coverage and react from his presnap read. We define the blocking zones as load, primary, and secondary (figure 10.6).

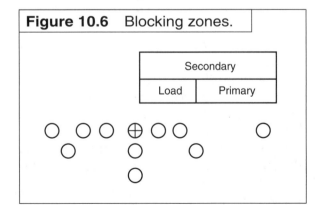

Figure 10.6   Blocking zones.

Most coverages, with the exception of a four-across look, have already defined the primary run support area. The halfback will block an inverted strong safety (cover 3) or rolled-up hard corner (cover 2). From his base alignment, the halfback opens up and attacks the hip away from him. He must attack, not wait, and take up the space of the defender. He will try to punch the near hip with his eyes up. If the defender works upfield or feathers, the halfback works the breast plate of the defender and kicks him out. He must show the pitch back what he's doing because the pitch back will work off his block.

The wide receiver is responsible for the first threat in the secondary zone. As shown in figure 10.6, he may have two threats presnap and should block the defender who is the most dangerous after the snap. In a traditional cover 3, the wide receiver will push to 5 yards, looking at the corner. If the corner has backed off, he'll plant off his outside foot and accelerate at a negative angle toward the line of scrimmage and block the safety. He'll build a fence on the free safety's near shoulder and collapse him down. If the free safety tries to work across the wide receiver's face, he'll drop his tail, move his feet, and prevent the free safety from crossing his face. If the corner squats, he's the most immediate threat, and the wide receiver stalks him. The wide receiver drops his tail, moves his feet, and builds a fence. He punches the defender's numbers with his thumbs up and elbows in.

The first and most important thing for the fullback is his alignment. The most consistent element in his alignment is his depth from the quarterback's heels. Some people align the fullback from the tip of the ball, but it's not always easy for the fullback to see the tip of the ball. He can always see the quarterback's heels. The fullback's hand is 6 feet from the quarterback's heel.

The next thing is the fullback's first step. He takes a 6-inch lead step with his playside foot to the guard's outside hip. We use a fire hose in drill work to ensure his first step is consistent.

The fullback should be in a three-point balanced stance, with his weight slightly back. As he explodes from his stance, his inside arm is on top, and he gives the quarterback a soft squeeze pocket. We don't want him to clamp down until he feels the quarterback's pressure with his front hand.

Another key point in the mesh is that the fullback must stay on his pathway if he doesn't get the ball. If he cuts back as the quarterback is pulling the ball, he might hit the ball with his hip and the ball might go on the ground.

Last, low man wins! It's critical that the fullback comes out of his stance with his shoulders down. We use the chutes to drill the fullbacks in the importance of keeping the pad level down.

As stated earlier, the frontside guard and tackle are responsible for the playside linebacker. Our basic horizontal splits are 3 to 4 feet from center to guard, 4 to 5 feet from guard to tackle, and 5 feet from tackle to tight end. The rule of thumb we use is linemen should take a split that allows them to get their jobs done. If that means they need to bring their splits down, they have the flexibility to do that. Our vertical splits are as deep as we can be. Their helmets will be slightly in front of the center's belt plane. This unique alignment helps the line to adjust to defensive movement and in the backside scoop. The guard and tackle attack the playside linebacker with an over-and-up combination step. They're in a balanced stance, with playside hands down. Most of their weight is back. The first step is a short lateral step with their playside feet, and the second step is a vertical step. The target is the near hip of the playside linebacker. If the playside linebacker runs, they attack the backside linebacker.

We use a scoop-hinge blocking pattern for the center, backside guard, backside tackle, and tight end. The center and backside guard are responsible for the nose guard to the backside guard. The backside tackle is usually in a hinge technique if he's without a tight end. If he's to the tight end, he can switch with the backside guard, depending on the guard's technique. The tight end's technique is a stay cutoff. He releases through the inside shoulder of the technique on him and releases downfield to block the backside corner. The scoop block by the center and backside guard is important to the overall success of the play. The center snaps and steps with his playside foot to the nose guard's playside hip. He stays with the nose guard until the backside guard engages the nose guard. Generally, the center tries to get off to the backside linebacker. The backside

guard steps with his playside foot to the nose guard's near hip, working to get his head across. If the nose guard disappears, the backside guard works up to the backside linebacker.

The backside tackle uses a hinge technique to eliminate backside pressure. He steps with his playside foot and drops his opposite foot in a hinge position. If he receives pressure, he stays in a hinge. If he feels no pressure, he releases to the next level and blocks the first opposite-colored jersey.

The pitch back's alignment is foot to foot with the offensive tackle and 1 yard deep. Our snap count is down, set, hike, and he'll come on the "s" of "set" as he aims for the heels of the fullback's alignment. The pitch back is responsible for establishing and maintaining pitch relationship. Ideally, he would like to be 4 yards outside the quarterback and 1 yard deep. As the quarterback works downfield, the halfback should stay in that 4-and-1 relationship. When the quarterback pitches the ball, it's important for the halfback to look the ball into his hands first. Once the pitch is secured, his eyes go to the arc block to set up and work off that block.

Veer-Load Scheme

As discussed previously, the veer-load scheme is used against eight-man fronts (figure 10.7). The two players assigned to the playside linebacker are the playside tackle and the playside halfback or the playside tackle and tight end. The quarterback's read is the same as in the zone-arc scheme. He always pitches off the next man outside. In the veer-load scheme, it's the primary run support defender. In this scheme, the quarterback's mechanics are the same as in the zone-arc scheme, so I won't repeat what has already been written. The blocking for the fullback, wide receiver, pitch back, and backside offensive line is the same as in the zone-arc as well. The veer-load system differs from the

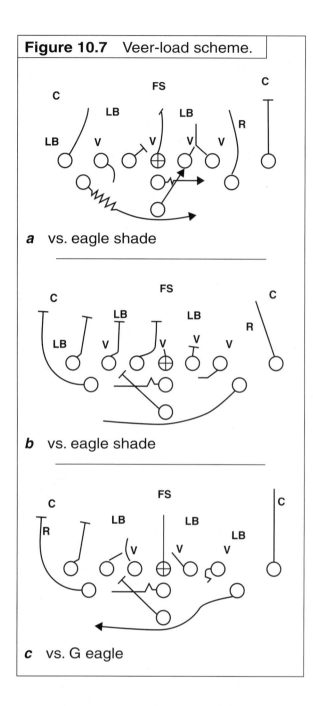

Figure 10.7 Veer-load scheme.

a vs. eagle shade

b vs. eagle shade

c vs. G eagle

zone-arc system in the blocking of the frontside guard, frontside tackle, and frontside halfback or tight end.

The playside halfback is responsible for the playside linebacker when he's away from the tight end. Any linebacker who is head up to the inside by alignment is defined as the playside linebacker. When the halfback is to the tight-end side, the tight end is responsible for the playside linebacker, and the halfback is responsible for the primary run-support defender.

The playside halfback attacks the playside linebacker's near hip. His eyes must be up and on his target. One of the key points we coach is that the halfback must be tight on his pathway. He can't get beat underneath. As he attacks the near hip, he adjusts to the pathway of the linebacker. If the linebacker works over the top, the halfback works with him, staying between the linebacker and the quarterback. It's similar to the wide receiver's block on the free safety. If the linebacker attacks the line of scrimmage, the halfback punches through the near hip with his eyes up. He's always looking to get extension on his block upfield.

When the play is to the tight-end side, he's responsible for the playside linebacker. His release is based on the technique aligned on him. As a rule, he releases inside with a 9 or 6 technique and outside with a 7 technique. He has the flexibility to change his release based on how the technique is playing him. The release technique the tight end uses is a dip-and-rip technique. On the snap, he takes a short step with his inside foot. He then brings his outside foot up as he dips his outside shoulder. His third step is a vertical step with his inside foot as he rips his outside shoulder through. His target is the playside linebacker's near hip, but he tries to anticipate where the linebacker will be. If he attacks the linebacker's near hip where he is, he might not accomplish his assignment. From that point, he should attack the linebacker as the halfback does on his load block.

The frontside guard, tackle, and center block the veer-load scheme based on the techniques aligned from the center out. In this system, we always double-team combo block with two linemen. If the center is uncovered, the combo block is accomplished by the playside guard and playside tackle. In that case, the center is in a backside scoop position. If the center is covered or the guard has an inside technique, the combo block is accomplished by the center and playside guard. The playside tackle, in this case, uses the same dip-and-rip technique the tight end does on his way to the playside linebacker.

We teach the center-guard combo a little different from the guard-tackle combo. With the center-guard combo, the center steps to the crotch of the defender, and the guard steps with his inside foot to the near hip. It's a read combo with the guard working off to the backside linebacker. On the guard-tackle combo, the guard's target is the crotch of the defender, and the tackle's target is the near hip. They come together and maintain the double team. It's more of a true double team. If the defender tries to work hard inside or outside, the lineman not opposed works to the playside linebacker to backside linebacker.

Midline Triple Option

With the exception of our multiple uses of formations, the introduction of the midline option has had the greatest impact on our offensive success. Prior to the 1995 season, we were paid a visit by Mike Summers, the offensive coordinator at Oregon State. He came to talk to us about some of the things we were doing. As is usually the case, we asked him if they were doing some different things. He then proceeded to show us their midline option, and as they say, "The rest is history." We'll never know if OSU benefited from Mike's visit, but I can tell you we benefited a great deal. We believe that Lake Highlands High School in Texas started the midline craze, but regardless of where it started, even nonoption teams have inquired about it, and it has probably been one of the biggest new option plays in the last 15 years.

The midline option offers many advantages:

1. It controls the 3-technique defender. With the success of the University of Miami and Dallas Cowboys attacking style 4-3, it became more difficult to attack the 3-technique area with the inside veer. The midline option takes advantage of upfield pressure 3 techniques and forces them to play read-technique football.

2. It allows you to read the defense's best player instead of having to block him. As with most option teams, we would prefer to read down linemen instead of trying to block them for 80 plays a game. The midline option allows the offense to read a 3 technique, which means he must be coached in a different way.

3. It gives the offense different blocking angles from what the triple option allows and forces defenses to defend areas on the field they never had to defend before.

4. Combined with double and triple options, the midline option gives us an option in every defensive gap. In a two- to three-day period, it's difficult for defensive coaches to adequately prepare for all options.

The midline load scheme is by design a fullback-quarterback play (figure 10.8). The quarterback takes the play to the largest technique, usually a 3 technique. The midline has been called a *quarterback duck play* by coaches and television analysts alike because there's a great likelihood the quarterback will carry the ball in the C-gap area. In 1996, Beau Morgan made a name for himself when we beat Notre Dame in South Bend using this play exclusively. This scheme had as much to do with our victory that day as anything else did.

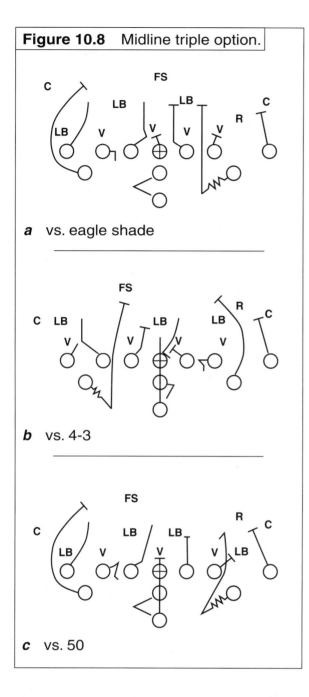

Figure 10.8   Midline triple option.

a   vs. eagle shade

b   vs. 4-3

c   vs. 50

The quarterback footwork is again a four-step process. Prior to the snap, his weight should be on his playside foot. His first step is a heel-to-toe clear step with his opposite foot. This step on the clock should be at 4 o'clock on a play to his left or 8 o'clock on a play to his right. He should open on his second step so that he becomes perpendicular to the line of scrimmage. His third and fourth steps are identical to the third

and fourth steps of the inside veer. He should shift his weight to the front foot and accelerate from the mesh on his fourth step.

Although the read and mesh are different from with the inside veer, the mechanics are taught in the same way. The fullback's pathway is obviously different, but the ball placement and soft squeeze previously discussed remain unchanged.

The quarterback reads the first down lineman from the guard out. This read is a quicker read than the B-gap read of the triple option, so the quarterback's presnap thought is different. We teach him to have a presnap thought to pull. Although the read key can react in the same ways as the B-gap read, he must declare quicker, which makes it an easier read for the quarterback. On average, we spend 25 percent less time on this read in practice.

The fullback's base alignment is 6 feet from the quarterback's heels. His first step is a 6-inch vertical lead step with his playside foot. His pathway is the crack of the quarterback, and he should stay on his pathway through the mesh. It's extremely critical that he comes out of his stance with his pads down. He soft-squeezes the ball and works off the center's block.

From his base alignment, the halfback is responsible for the playside linebacker. Depending on the play call, he can do this with or without motion. If motion is called, he'll go on the quarterback's heel in counter motion away from the call. On the snap, he plants and attacks the playside linebacker's near hip. He must always expect the linebacker to attack him tight off the 3 technique and adjust his pathway from there. If no motion is called, he attacks the linebacker with the same target but has to realize he has a greater distance to cover. In some cases, he might need to cheat his alignment to get his job done. He must also be aware of the playside tackle's block. If the playside tackle washes his technique inside, the halfback bounces outside to get to his linebacker.

The wide receiver is responsible for first by alignment in the secondary zone. This is a different rule for him than his triple-option rule. He blocks the first defender aligned in the secondary zone and won't be responsible for the free safety. In a cover-three alignment, he stalks the inside half of the corner. In a cover-two alignment, he blocks the inside half of the near safety.

The frontside blocking pattern changes based on if the play is being run to or away from the tight end. In either case, the frontside guard's rule remains the same. He's responsible for the playside linebacker to backside linebacker. He always releases inside the read key. If he's covered, his first step is with his inside foot, and he dips and rips to his linebacker. If the read key crosses his face, he may wash him down. If he's uncovered, he uses an over-and-up zone step to the playside linebacker.

The playside tackle must know if he's to a tight end or away from a tight end. If he's away from the tight end, he's responsible for the first defender outside the read key. His first step is to the near hip with his outside foot. He'll try to create space for the quarterback inside of him. If the defender tries to cross his face, he'll wash him down inside. In that case, the quarterback and halfback will bounce outside. If the playside tackle is to the tight-end side, they'll combo block the technique on the tight end to the stack linebacker or rover (in this case the playside tackle is usually uncovered). This combo block is a slow developing block. They'll both stay with the tight-end's technique until the stack or rover declares inside or outside. Both the tight end and playside tackle must have their eyes on those defenders as they are double-teaming the tight end's technique. If the stack

works inside, the playside tackle comes off and attacks his inside half. If the stack stays outside, the tight end comes off and blocks the stack.

The center and backside guard are responsible for the first down lineman from the center back to the backside linebacker. There are many combinations that can occur. As a general rule, if the center has a zero technique or shade, he blocks that technique, and the backside guard blocks the backside linebacker. As that technique works to a 1 technique on the guard, they exchange responsibilities. Regardless of what technique is on the backside, the fullback's pathway must be kept clear. Sometimes that technique will try to cross the center's face. In this case, he'll work him to the front side, and the fullback will cut back behind the center's block. The backside tackle and backside tight end have the same hinge and stay cutoff rules as previously described.

Counter Running Game Off the Triple Option

The next component of our running game that's critical to our success is our counter running game off the triple option. One way defenses try to stop the option game is to run their linebackers and secondary with our motion to try to outnumber us on the perimeter. The counter game helps us control their aggressiveness. It also gives us a predetermined running play, which allows our players a greater degree of aggressiveness and takes some pressure off the quarterback by allowing him to hand the ball off and not have to make a decision.

We have a variety of different counter plays that allow us to change our motion, ball carrier, and lead blocker without changing our blocking up front.

This gives us a great deal of flexibility and diversity without confusing our players. I'll talk about each backfield action first and then discuss the line blocking rules.

Counter Fullback Isolation With Backside Halfback as Ball Carrier

On this play, the fullback is the lead back, and the backside halfback is the ball carrier (figure 10.9). The playside halfback motions to decoy the playside linebacker. He'll come in his normal pitch motion and continue on his pitch pathway. The fullback takes a jab step away from the call, turning his head and shoulders away as well. Off his jab step, he'll find the playside linebacker. In a 4-3, he'll block the stack. He'll accelerate to his target and drop his tail, punch through the breast plate, roll his hips, and run his feet. We don't allow him to cut in the hole because this clutters the hole for the ball carrier.

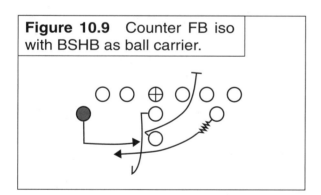

Figure 10.9   Counter FB iso with BSHB as ball carrier.

The quarterback takes a 4 o'clock or 8 o'clock first step away from the call, ball flashes to the fullback while shifting his weight to his front foot, and steps straight back, handing the ball as deep as possible to the ball carrier. On the snap, the backside halfback backpedals three steps and aims into the B gap away. He has his inside arm up and follows the fullback to daylight.

Counter Halfback Isolation

On this play, the quarterback and backside halfback have identical mechanics as in the play previously discussed. The difference is that the playside halfback is the lead blocker, and the fullback is the decoy away (figure 10.10).

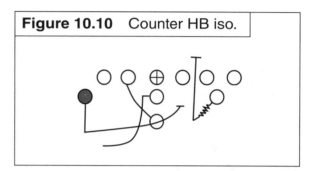

Figure 10.10   Counter HB iso.

On the snap, the fullback runs his triple-option pathway away from the call and either gets tackled or blocks level on his pathway. The playside halfback comes in two-step counter motion away from the call and blocks the playside linebacker. He must plant hard on his second step and find the linebacker. He uses the same rules and technique as the fullback did for the previously discussed play.

Counter Fullback Isolation With Playside Halfback as the Ball Carrier

This play is the same as the fullback isolation but has the other back carrying the ball. The quarterback snaps the ball after the playside halfback motions to a spot 6 yards deep in the I formation (figure 10.11). The fullback blocks as he did on the other fullback isolation play. The playside halfback, after he passes the fullback on his motion, plants his foot away from the play on the snap, opens up to the line of scrimmage

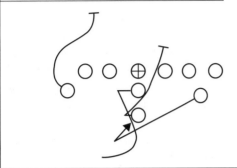

Figure 10.11 Counter FB iso with PSHB as ball carrier.

with his inside arm up, and follows the fullback into the hole. The backside halfback releases to the free safety and blocks downfield.

Offensive Line Blocking for Counter Plays

The beauty in this series is that we have three plays with different backfield actions but the same offensive line rules. This allows us to change things very easily as the game unfolds if one action gives us a better chance of success. The rules for our offensive line can generally be categorized as covered tackle or uncovered tackle on the playside.

In most cases, when the playside tackle is uncovered, the playside guard is covered (figure 10.12a). The rule for the playside guard and playside tackle is to double-team combo block the technique over the guard and create movement. Once that movement occurs, the lineman who has the easiest time getting off proceeds to the playside linebacker or middle linebacker. The motion used in the backfield gets the linebacker to work with it and buys time for them to be patient. The tight end base-blocks the technique on him. The center and backside guard block the technique on them to the backside linebacker—the same combo block as in the midline. The center usually stays with a tech-

nique on or near him (zero, shade), and the guard usually stays with the technique on or near him (A gap, 1, 2). The backside tackle will always base.

When the playside tackle is covered, he and the tight end will base-block (figure 10.12b). They try to get movement and take the defender where he wants to go. The center and playside guard combo block the technique on the center if the playside guard is uncovered (zero or shade). They try to get movement, and one, usually the center, will get off to the backside linebacker. If the playside guard is covered, he'll base, and the center will work to the playside linebacker. The backside guard and backside tackle will base the technique on them.

Figure 10.12 Offensive line blocking on counter iso.

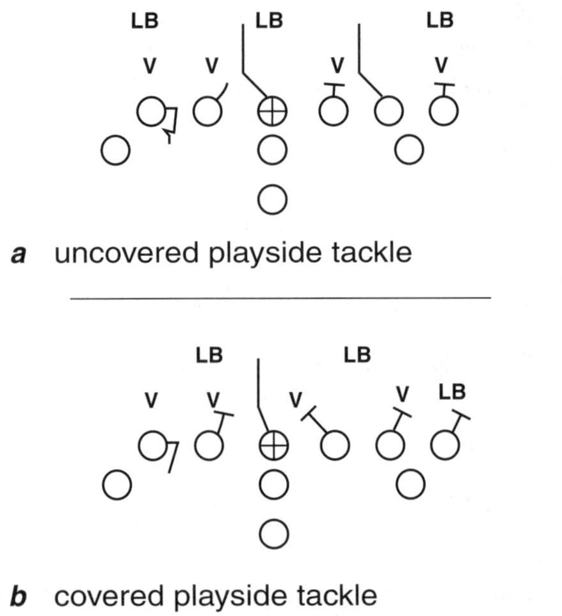

a uncovered playside tackle

b covered playside tackle

Play-Action Passes Off Triple Option

One of the most underappreciated parts of our offensive attack has been our passing game. Most defenses feel that if they stop our option game, they have a greater chance to win. In the same sense, we feel that if we can effectively use our passing game to take advantage of their aggressiveness in stopping the run, we can create big plays by throwing the ball and force them to play the option differently, giving us back our potent running attack. We may never be confused with Texas Tech in our ability to execute the passing game, but we take great pride in our schemes and execution and feel that in many games our ability to throw the ball has been the winning edge.

Pass Protection

As with any passing scheme, the first thing to be concerned about is protection. We try to abide by the KISS principle with regards to protection. Roughly 75 percent of our passing game comes from one protection. We try not to ask our guys up front to do too much or to do things they can't do. In 2003, we came close to setting a record that could never be broken—we allowed one sack in 12 ball games. That sack came in the last regular season game on a screen pass. The primary protection we use is a gap-hinge protection. Because the backs have such a great responsibility in this protection, I'll break the protection down into three phases: frontside line, frontside backs, and backside line.

The gap portion of the protection refers to the playside of the protection. The playside guard, playside tackle, and playside tight end (in unbalanced formation) are each responsible for the playside gap inside of them (figure 10.13). The center is always backside. They are not blocking a man until he declares as a rusher in their gap. They are also responsible to help the blocker to their outside if they're not immediately threatened in their gap. If their gap is immediately threatened, they step

with their playside feet and pin that rusher to the inside. In this protection, the quarterback usually sets up 5 yards deep over the playside tackle's inside leg, so that gives them a reference point. They never chase a rusher outside their inside gap unless they get their hands on him. If their inside gap is not immediately threatened, they step with their outside feet to the target outside of them and punch with their playside hands. Their eyes always stay in their inside gaps. They help the blocker to their outside and won't come off until their gap is threatened.

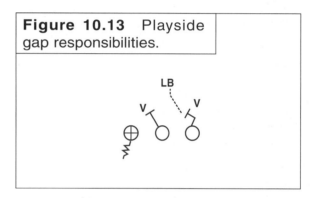

Figure 10.13 Playside gap responsibilities.

The backside of this protection is fairly simple. The center, backside guard, and backside tackle are responsible for their backside gaps (figure 10.14). They step with their playside feet and turn at a 45-degree away from the call. They want to widen the defender's rush lane in their gaps, and they are also aware of where the quarterback's release point is. Their rule is the same as for the frontside protectors. Once they get their hands on a defender, he is theirs. This is more passive than the front side, for obvious reasons. The front side must be aggressive to keep defenders on the line of scrimmage because of the quarterback's release point. The back side can be somewhat less aggressive to let the rush develop, but it must be aggressive once the rush has developed.

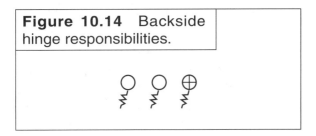

Figure 10.14 Backside hinge responsibilities.

The backs are just as important to the success of our protection as the offensive line is. They spend as much time in practice working on protection as anyone and take great pride in what they do. The three things we emphasize to them are to protect on the defensive side of the line of scrimmage with eyes up, to fit tight to the inside blocker, and not to chase outside their gap. The fullback always has the gap outside of the last frontside blocker (figure 10.15). His pathway is to the crack of the playside tackle or tight end (in unbalanced formation). He fits into the line of scrimmage off the tackle or tight end. His target is the hip of the defender in his gap. If he has no one in his gap, he places his eyes inside and expects pressure from the inside. One of the two halfbacks protect based on which one is in the route. If the frontside halfback is in the route, the backside halfback comes in pitch motion. As he passes the fullback, he works to the line of scrimmage and fits tight to the fullback at the line of scrimmage. He blocks just as the fullback does. If the backside halfback is in the route, the playside halfback steps with his playside foot to

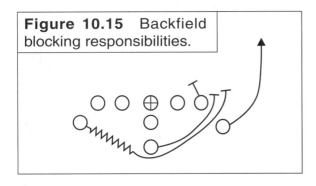

Figure 10.15 Backfield blocking responsibilities.

the line of scrimmage, and the fullback fits between the end man on the line of scrimmage and him. He should be tight to the fullback.

Routes

We have many routes off the same action designed to take advantage of how a defense is defending the option game. Because of space limitations, I'll discuss two frontside throws and one backside throw. In all three cases, the quarterback has one read—the corner-back. The quarterback takes his first step at 3 o'clock or 9 o'clock and ball flashes to the fullback. There will be no mesh because the fullback is working to the line of scrimmage outside the end man on the line of scrimmage in his protection scheme. The quarter-back gathers on his second step and then works back at a 45-degree angle from the line of scrimmage. He sets up over the playside tackle's inside leg at 5 yards deep. He must do a great job of selling the run by bending his knees and keeping his shoulders down. His eyes are on the corner back.

Frontside Post Wheel to X

The frontside X works to center the corner back up on his release (figure 10.16). At 12 to 14 yards, he gives a head-and-shoulders fake outside and works to the near goal post. The front-side halfback opens up on his arc

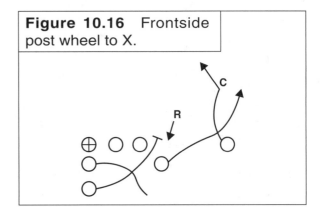

Figure 10.16 Frontside post wheel to X.

pathway and attacks the strong safety's outside leg. He will try to run his wheel outside the strong safety if he works at him. If he feathers or works upfield, the halfback will dip underneath him and then will immediately work back outside. He always looks for the ball over his inside shoulder.

Frontside Post Wheel to Y

This is identical to the previous play except it's thrown to the tight-end side (figure 10.17). The tight end gets the best release possible without getting jammed. He'll run a skinny post, never bringing the route across the original position of the ball.

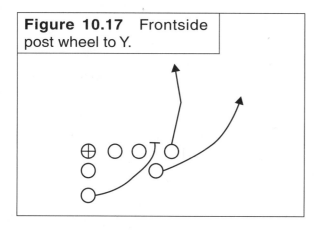

Figure 10.17 Frontside post wheel to Y.

Backside Post Wheel to Y With X Shallow Cross

This route has been a staple of our offense for 25 years. The quarterback's read and action are the same as in the frontside post wheel except it's a backside throw. Once he sets up, the quarter-

back must get his head and eyes around to see the corner back. The backside halfback comes in two-step pitch motion to the side of the quarterback's action. He plants, opens to the line of scrimmage, and runs a wheel backside (figure 10.18). The tight end runs a skinny post. The frontside X runs a shallow cross at 8 yards deep. His first priority is to get in the quarterback's view lane. He must avoid any linebackers underneath unless he has no choice, and then he'll go over the top.

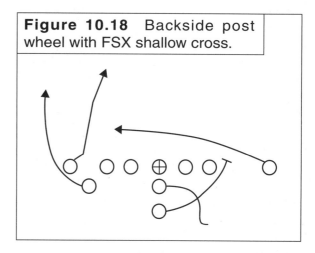

Figure 10.18 Backside post wheel with FSX shallow cross.

It has been our pleasure and a distinct honor to be a part of this book. I hope you learned some things to help you in your pursuit of excellence. This is such a great game, and we're all so privileged to be a part of it. If you ever need anything from us at the Air Force Academy, please don't hesitate to call or write.

PART V

Game Planning and Tactics

CHAPTER 11

Yellow Zone: Own Goal Line to Own 10-Yard Line

Dennis Franchione

Texas A&M University

Offensive football strategy and play calling in the yellow zone can be a precarious dilemma. The probability of the offense scoring points from this field position is low. The potential for a turnover and setting the opponent up for an easy score is disconcerting.

The momentum of the game at the time of yellow-zone possession must be considered, as well as the time remaining in the quarter, first half, or game. If you don't extend the drive more than a couple of first downs, the opponent will attain good field position on the change of possession. If you get to fourth down, do you punt or go for it? Are you ahead or behind, and by how much? What are the weather conditions? How about crowd noise? All of these factors and more are important considerations in developing a strategy for yellow-zone offense.

Play-Calling Philosophy

Our basic philosophy in the yellow zone is to be smart, not scared, with tactics. We take calculated risks, based on the circumstances at hand. All plays run in the yellow zone should be solid, sound plays that don't allow for structural mishaps. We run plays that account for all defensive tendencies and pressure possibilities, thereby reducing the chance of turning the ball over.

Two basic principles govern the mode of attack used in a yellow-zone possession series. Are we going to be in an offensive mindset based on the situation and try to move the ball into scoring position? Or are we going to be conservative in our approach in an attempt to protect our situation? Once we determine our approach, we select plays that will achieve our goal for that particular series.

Obviously, play calling varies a great deal depending on the situation. Maybe we need to score late in the game to win, or maybe we need to make one first down so the punter doesn't have to punt with his heels backed up close to the end line. Regardless of the situation, we make sure all of our plays in the yellow zone are structurally sound.

If the game situation dictates that we should try to move the ball into scoring position, the obvious problem is the amount of distance to be covered to get into scoring range. It's difficult for any offense to drive the ball 90-plus yards and score a touchdown. I've heard that if a team begins an offensive possession inside its own 10-yard line, the probability of scoring a touchdown is only about 1 chance in 30.

We believe that the offense must produce at least one big-yardage play to score from this field position. Over the years, we have had multiple 90-plus-yard drives that have culminated in touchdowns. In the majority of these drives we've achieved at least one big-yardage or explosive play. Our play calling includes plays that are sound and relatively safe, yet have the potential to create explosive yardage.

All of the plays we run from the yellow zone are part of our normal offensive system and part of our specific game plan. The plays chosen in the yellow zone are selected based on soundness and ability to produce a desired yardage. In the running game, these plays are typically perimeter oriented and option based. In the throwing game, these plays are play-action vertical concepts that allow the quarterback to throw the ball downfield. We feel secure in these two concepts; the option is part of our normal offensive system, and we're adept at handling the ball on pitches. We also don't mind launching one

deep with solid protection. In selecting option runs, we can generally have a good idea of which offensive player will end up with the ball based on defensive structure and can call plays in which a pitch is unlikely.

If we select a play-action deep shot, our thinking is that a downfield interception with minimal return puts us in about the same field position as a punt would. We like the calculated risk of this play selection based on the possible reward. Without an explosive play, it's unlikely that we would move the ball into scoring position, so we would have to punt the ball away, anyway.

In a game situation in which a more conservative approach is required, our thought processes change. We're thinking, "don't give them anything cheap" that could swing the game in their favor. We need to protect ourselves from a turnover, safety, or backed-up punt. With this in mind, we attempt to move the ball on a first-down basis. Let's make one first down and get the ball outside of the yellow zone before we think about opening up our play calling. Generally, our calls in this mode are less risky relative to ball security based on ball location. With the ball really close to our own goal line, nonexchange or quick-hitting plays are more advantageous and pose less risk of being tackled in the end zone for a safety. We want vertical runs that attack the line of scrimmage rather than horizontal runs. Vertical runs can be achieved from a variety of formations but are more secure from closed formations rather than from open sets.

Once we've determined our strategy for the game situation, other factors come into play. All of these factors must be considered, whether we're operating in a scoring mode or a conservative mode. Ball security in the yellow zone is of utmost importance. We select plays that, based on our execution, help us avoid turning the ball over to the opponent. We use plays from formations

that allow us to put a "hat on a hat" and not turn a forcing-unit defender loose to the football. The players who handle the ball must be well trained in the proper mechanics of ball security and must make proper decisions about maintaining possession of the ball. Whether we're attempting to score from the yellow zone or merely living to punt, we can't afford to sustain a turnover that would likely result in a game-changing score for the opponent.

Play selection is also determined to some degree by the weather. Are we playing with a wet or dry ball? Is rain sprinkling or pouring? How hard is the wind blowing? Is the wind in our face or at our back? Are conditions abnormally cold? Is it sleeting or snowing? Will the sun blind our receivers? A play caller needs to consider a lot of things. In a wet environment, plays in which the ball is exchanged directly from ball handler to ball handler make it easier

for the players to secure the ball. It's advisable to use plays that employ a direct center-to-quarterback exchange rather than a shotgun snap. Also, plays in which the quarterback exchanges directly with a ball carrier rather than pitching or tossing to a ball carrier are more desirable. These simple principles reduce the likelihood of mishandling the ball and causing a turnover. Obviously, wind becomes a big factor in the throwing game.

Crowd noise is a factor in play-calling decisions in the yellow zone. In some stadiums, the end zone noise can be brutal. Kyle Field at Texas A&M University is one of those stadiums. This works to our advantage offensively but can create real problems for our opponent's offense in yellow-zone situations. In this kind of environment, choose plays that require less verbal communication among players at the line of scrimmage. One-play huddle calls are advantageous. Don't let a lack of communication result in a self-inflicted mistake. Often plays are busted or time-outs burned because somebody couldn't hear an audible or missed a check call. It's also advisable in extreme noise to use what we call a silent snap count. We allow the snap when the quarterback is ready without using a normal verbal snap count. This allows for better communication among the offensive linemen, particularly in the shotgun formation.

The opponent's defensive tendencies play a significant role in yellow-zone play selection. When devising our game plan, we try to find defensive tendencies that we can exploit. These tendencies might involve field zone, down and distance, and formation. We might also be able to exploit a situational pressure defense with a timely play call. We choose yellow-zone plays by formation, plays that give us our best opportunity for success and are secure in gap integrity and number count.

You must have a grasp on what type of defensive approach your opponent will take in the yellow zone. Some teams lay back and defend in this circumstance, betting the odds that the offense can't successfully drive the ball into scoring position. Other teams take a more aggressive approach and pressure the offense, employing blitz and movement in an attempt to create a negative-yardage play and possibly a turnover. In either type of defensive strategy, focus on calling plays that can exploit what the defense is trying to do.

In addition to the opponent's general philosophy about defending this area of the field, defensive strategies in the yellow zone are governed by the down-and-distance situation. As always, third downs are crucial. The offensive play caller must be attuned to the possibility that the defense might do something out of character in this situation. A normal base rush-and-cover team might blitz on third down, which could affect the offense's play.

Unless the offense is extremely backed up (behind the 2-yard line), the call on first down is a very important call in the yellow zone. A successful first-down play can markedly improve the offense's ability to convert at least one movement of the chains by minimizing the risk of having an unmanageable third-down distance to make. If we're in a scoring mode mindset, first down is a great time to take a deep shot. A successful attempt gets the ball downfield in a hurry and has a tendency to put the defense on its heels. If the pass is incomplete, we still have two shots at achieving a first down before we have to punt away.

Game circumstances dictate whether a fourth-down play is attempted instead of a punt. Conventional wisdom usually wins out in this situation. However, some coaches employ the gambler mentality and make a fourth-down attempt in a game situation that doesn't mandate such a tactic. This is an uncalculated risk, which is usually not advisable.

The amount of time remaining in the quarter, half, and game are factors to be considered in yellow-zone play selection. Certainly, the score of the game in relation to time remaining is the most critical component relative to play selection. Are we ahead or behind? By how much? Do we need to be in scoring mode or conservative mode? Play calls in a situation with game time dwindling are inherent to that circumstance. If we need a score, and time is running out, we employ a "go for broke" mentality. Conversely, if we're trying to protect a lead, we might choose to take a knee with time expiring rather than run a normal play and risk a turnover. Time remaining at the end of a quarter affects play selection. At the end of the first half, we need to be able to gauge whether we realistically have enough time to drive the length of the field to score. If we conclude that we don't have the time remaining to make a realistic scoring drive and we can run the clock out to halftime, then we probably take a knee and get out of the half.

We must also be conscious of game situations that could lead us to choose to take a safety on fourth down instead of punting. This is obviously a conservative move and one that's rarely used, but it's a strategy that can minimize giving up points and extend the opponent's subsequent possession field position.

What we choose to do in the yellow zone is also determined by the emotional flow of the game—the momentum. How did we gain possession of the ball in the yellow zone? Was it through a great defensive play? A goal-line stand or a turnover certainly swings momentum in our favor and stimulates our squad. Equally, our opponent is dejected as a result of not scoring or of turning over the football and losing a scoring opportunity. This set of circumstances, coupled with the overall game situation, might put us in an aggressive mindset. We might want to go for the knockout punch. Play selection in this type of situation is more likely to be wide open with respect to looking for explosives on our call sheet. If we hit on a big play, we might break our opponent's spirit. If we attain ball possession in the yellow zone as a result of a kickoff, punt, or penalty, there's no appreciable momentum shift in our favor. Consequently, our play selection will be determined by whether we're in scoring mode or conservative mode as dictated by the overall game flow.

Yellow Zone Plays

Before discussing the plays we run in the yellow zone, let's address some specific systematic basics, beginning with personnel groupings. We use a number system to describe the personnel in a particular grouping. Two numbers are used. The first number represents how many backs are in the grouping. The second number tells how many tight ends are in the grouping. The 22 personnel grouping, for example, includes two backs, two tight ends, and one wide receiver. The 12 personnel grouping has one back, two tight ends, and two wide receivers.

Generally, we want the offensive line to use splits between 18 and 24 inches. We like to use an off-vertical alignment up front. Wide receivers take standard splits on most plays. If the ball is in the middle of the field, we split our receivers to the top of the numbers. With the ball on the hashmark, the wide-side receiver aligns between the hash and the top of the numbers, and the short-side receiver goes to the bottom of the numbers. The fullback aligns with heels 5 yards deep. The tailback aligns with toes 7 yards deep. If we're using the shotgun, the quarterback's heels are 5 yards deep. Backs are 6 yards deep.

The 22-personnel grouping is advantageous because it provides a closed formation and lets us successfully run or pass. We call this formation "flanker," and the split-flow inside zone play to the tailback (figure 11.1) is a solid running play. It's a downhill vertical run that attacks the line of scrimmage and is secure in blocking pattern and number count. We can get a hat on everybody in the forcing unit. Because it's a zone-principle play, we should be sound versus movement defenses. This play can be selected in a normal down-and-distance situation (first and 10, second and normal, third and short) and can be called anywhere in the yellow zone.

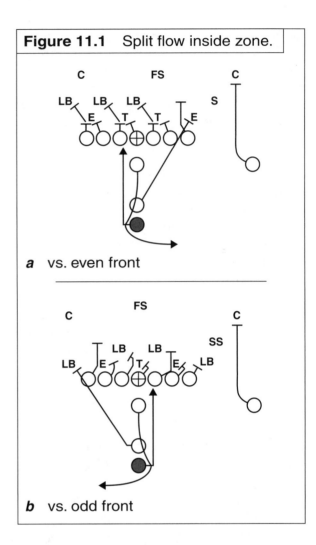

Figure 11.1 Split flow inside zone.

a vs. even front

b vs. odd front

However, we might not want to call it if we're extremely backed up because of the depth of the ball exchange.

A similar play that hits quicker and attacks defensive lateral pursuit is the fullback belly play (figure 11.2). The belly employs the same inside zone blocking pattern as the split flow, but it's a full-flow play that initially looks like the zone option. This play can really split a defense that pursues laterally if it's set up with some perimeter runs, such as the zone option or stretch.

The belly can be run in similar situations to the inside zone. It might be a better selection than the inside zone if the offense is extremely backed up because the belly hits quicker, and the exchange occurs closer to the line of scrimmage. The belly might also be a

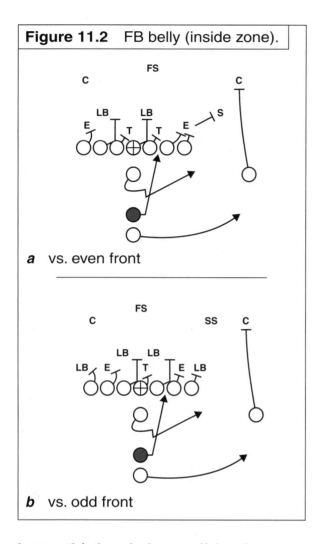

Figure 11.2 FB belly (inside zone).

a vs. even front

b vs. odd front

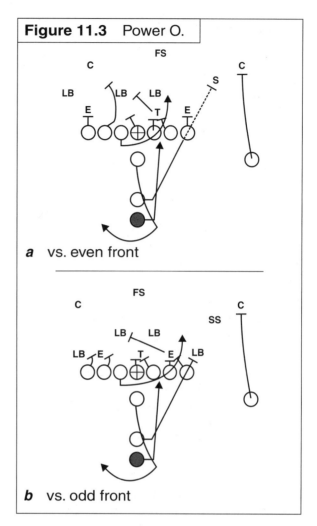

Figure 11.3 Power O.

a vs. even front

b vs. odd front

better third-and-short call for the same reason and because you can have a power runner (the fullback) carry the ball.

One of our most successful runs through the years has been the power "O" (figure 11.3). This play is a strong "in your face" type of run that's also vertically oriented. The tailback should hammer the playside A, B, or C gap, depending on defensive alignment and movement. In 22 personnel, the O is a sound gap principle frontside play that creates a double team at the point of attack. The pulling guard becomes an isolation blocker as he pulls through the hole onto the linebacker. The back side of the play is secure with the extra tight end using a gap-hinge technique along with the backside tackle. The

power O is a normal down-and-distance or short-yardage selection in the yellow zone.

We have also had good success running the iso draw (figure 11.4). This play is helpful because we aren't required to mash anybody in the defensive front. All defensive linemen and linebackers, except one, are influenced by pass action. The one defensive lineman to whom we do not pass influence is aggressively doubled to a linebacker. Again, with an extra tight end, we can account for an eight-man box if necessary and, ideally, get the ball to the second level of the defense. This play is solid on all downs except third and long. Because of the depth of the exchange, the play might be too risky when backed up inside the 1-yard line.

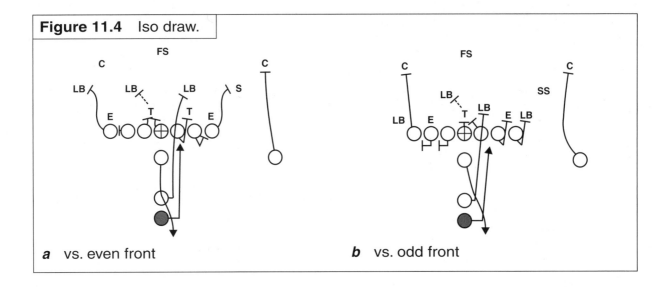

Figure 11.4   Iso draw.

a   vs. even front

b   vs. odd front

The stretch or outside zone from 22 personnel gives us a play to attack the perimeter of the defense (figure 11.5). This play employs a zone-blocking pattern by the line, which helps handle defensive movement and stunts. The fullback's block is key. We can affect his alignment or use short motion to put him in a better position to effectively block support. Because this is a horizontal run that doesn't immediately attack the line of scrimmage, we probably wouldn't use it when extremely close to our own goal line. It's a better call from the 5- to 10-yard-line area.

The zone-loaded option (figure 11.6) is another good perimeter run relative to field location. It can be used in the same fashion as the stretch. The quarterback options the secondary force defender and, in most instances, gets a keep read as the support player will predominately take the pitch back. As a result, we rarely pitch the ball on this play, and it becomes a quarterback sweep. Zone principles are used up front, and the fullback ensures that we get an edge before he secures a safety. The playside wide receiver blocks man-on versus a one-safety look, and he push-cracks against a two-safety defense.

Figure 11.5   Stretch.

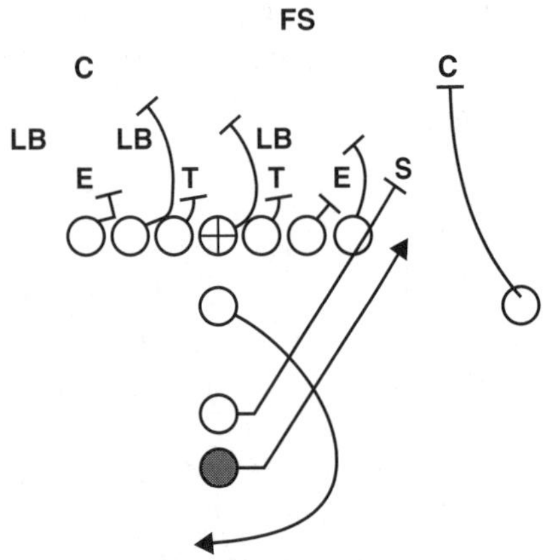

a   vs. even front

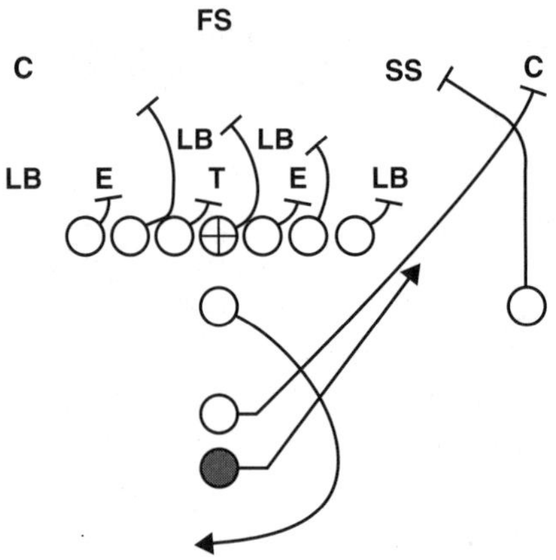

b   vs. odd front

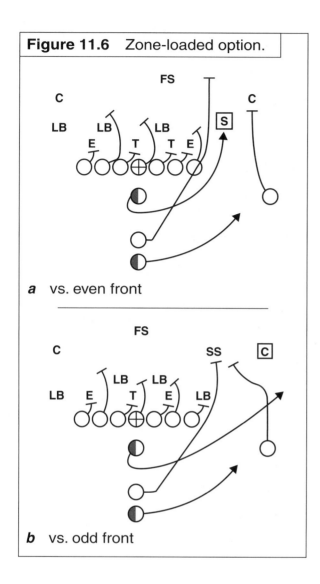

Figure 11.6   Zone-loaded option.

a   vs. even front

b   vs. odd front

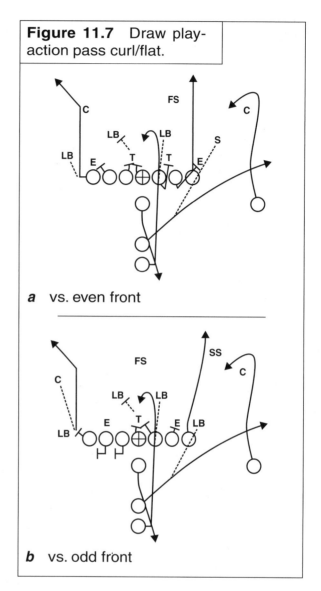

Figure 11.7   Draw play-action pass curl/flat.

a   vs. even front

b   vs. odd front

From 22-personnel, we have a couple of play-action passes we use in the yellow zone. We'll fake the draw and run a curl/flat concept (figure 11.7) on normal running downs. This play is also a good call on third-and-medium yardage. It's an eight-man protection, with both backs and the backside tight end using check-release techniques. The quarterback drops seven steps and makes a great ball fake. The playside tight end has a free-release vertical route, the flanker a 12-yard curl, and the fullback a check-release flat route at 3 yards deep. This play is a progression read by the quarterback: glance (vertical), high (curl), low (flat). This is

a securely protected play that rarely results in lost yardage.

A really good yellow-zone play-action play is the power pass (figure 11.8), in which we pull the off-guard just as in the power O run. The quarterback rolls to break contain after the ball fake, which makes this play a pass/run option. The playside tight end runs a 12-yard seam, and the flanker runs a 14-yard comeback, which will convert to a fade versus cover 2.

If we choose to down the ball by taking a knee, we call victory (figure 11.9) from 22 personnel. All line players explode

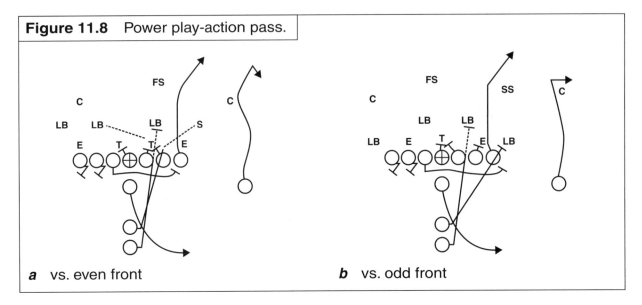

Figure 11.8 Power play-action pass.

a vs. even front   *b* vs. odd front

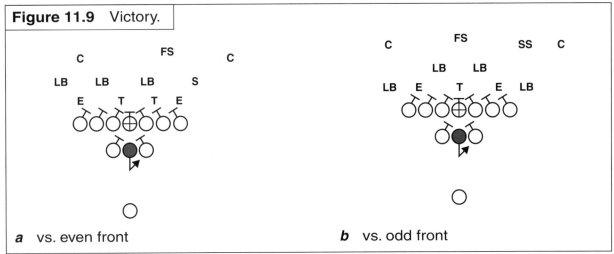

Figure 11.9 Victory.

a vs. even front   *b* vs. odd front

their inside gaps, and the quarterback takes the snap, steps back, and hits a knee. Both backs ensure the center-to-quarterback exchange and then step in front of the quarterback to protect him from contact. The flanker aligns 10 yards deep in the backfield as a safety, in case we mishandle the snap. Generally, we lose about 2 yards on this play, so we won't run it close to our own goal line.

Another good yellow-zone grouping is 12 personnel, which includes one back, two tight ends, and two wide-outs. We like three running plays from this grouping that match the same runs from 22 personnel. These runs include the

inside zone (figure 11.10), the stretch or outside zone (figure 11.11), and the zone option (figure 11.12). We can package these runs together or with passes to take advantage of defensive structure and get ourselves the best play at the line of scrimmage.

Figure 11.13 shows the inside zone play action we can use to launch one deep. This is a max protection (eight man) run-aggressive play action with a quick setup by the quarterback. He delivers the ball to one of the wide-outs based on the best look and matchup. We can get one-on-one coverage with a one-safety look or a two-safety look with low safeties. This play is a normal

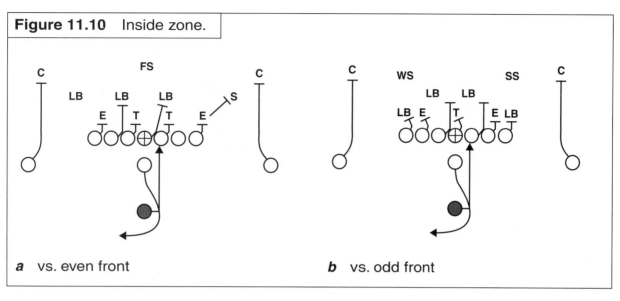

Figure 11.10 Inside zone.

a vs. even front *b* vs. odd front

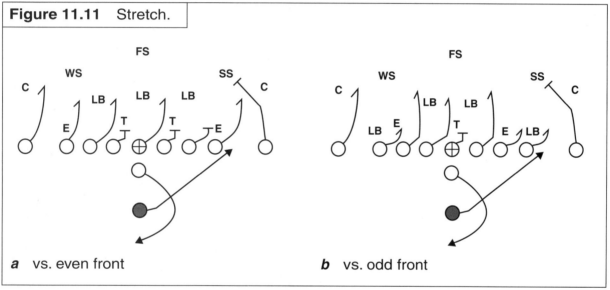

Figure 11.11 Stretch.

a vs. even front *b* vs. odd front

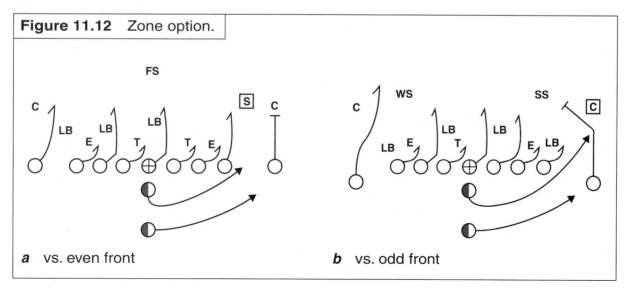

Figure 11.12 Zone option.

a vs. even front *b* vs. odd front

run down play action and can be a huge momentum changer if completed. It gets us out of a hole in a hurry. We can use the same play action and protection to throw the 10-yard hitch to either wide receiver if the corners are playing off-coverage.

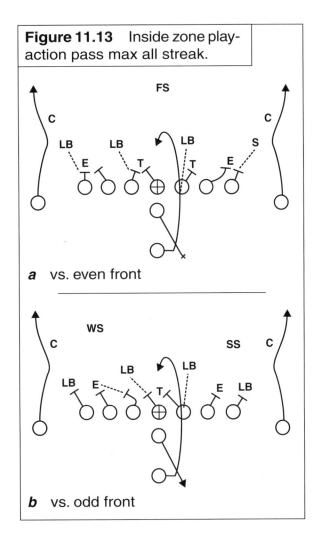

Figure 11.13 Inside zone play-action pass max all streak.

a vs. even front

b vs. odd front

If we get the defense in a run-stopping mode by previous play calls or down and distance, we like to run the boot (figure 11.14). This is a great play action that gives us a frontside route combination with a crossing route, and the option of a quarterback run if the defense loses containment. The playside wide-out runs a streak (we'll also use a comeback), the playside tight end runs a late flat at 3 yards, the backside

tight end drags at 12 to 14 yards, and the offside wide-out runs a take-two post. The quarterback progression read is glance (vertical), low (flat), high (drag). Boot protection allows the quarterback a great fake because he isn't worried about playside edge pressure in his face, as the pulling guard can secure it.

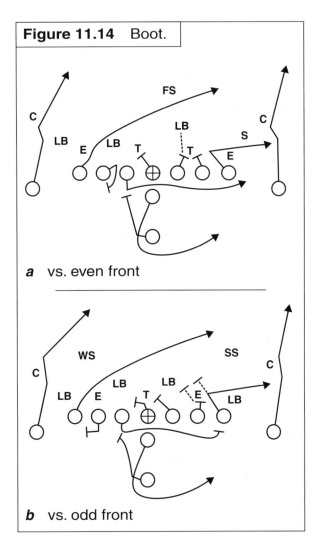

Figure 11.14 Boot.

a vs. even front

b vs. odd front

We open the formation and use our four wide-receiver grouping (10 personnel) in certain situations in the yellow zone. We like to run the quarterback sneak (figure 11.15) from this grouping because we can reduce the numbers in the box. We double an A-gap defensive tackle in an even front and wedge-block to that double team. Against a three-

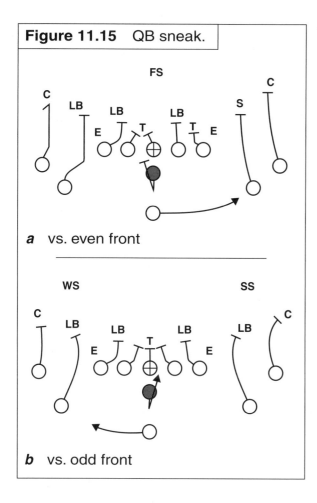

Figure 11.15 QB sneak.

a vs. even front

b vs. odd front

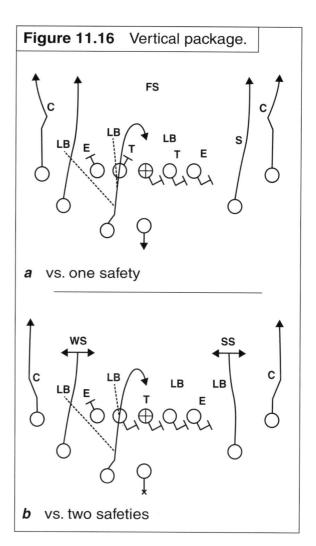

Figure 11.16 Vertical package.

a vs. one safety

b vs. two safeties

down look, we wedge to the nose tackle. We flare the tailback away from the quarterback's direction to influence the linebackers. The sneak is a good short-yardage call or can be used to get the ball out if the offense is extremely close to its own goal line (inside its own 1).

If we need to throw the ball on third and medium to third and long, we generally use 10 personnel and drop back. We employ six-man protection with the back using a check-release technique. We have a wide range of route combinations we can call in a variety of distance situations, but we like the vertical package because we can get the ball downfield versus a one-safety look (figure 11.16a) and have a chance to hit the inside receiver option routes for first-down yardage against a two-safety look

(figure 11.16b). The inside receivers will convert their vertical routes automatically when they see a two-safety look.

Possession in the yellow zone is an unwanted offensive situation. However, if our play selection is smart, not scared, we can successfully manage this critical field position area. Many factors determine our thinking in the yellow, but we'll either be in an aggressive or conservative mindset, and our play calls reflect this. It's important to include yellow-zone possessions as part of the normal practice regimen so that players know how the coach thinks in each situation and can base their play accordingly.

CHAPTER 12

Green Zone: Own 10-Yard Line to Opponent's 25-Yard Line

Ralph Friedgen
University of Maryland

Operating in the green zone, better known as the free-wheeling zone, is a major part of any game plan. More plays will be run in this zone than in any other. Every down-and-distance situation will occur, as well as formational tendencies and adjustments. The score, time remaining in the game, and the weather all influence play selection.

Our offensive philosophy is to balance the run with the pass. That doesn't mean we'll throw the ball 50 percent of the time and run it 50 percent of the time, but we want to be able to run and throw with equal efficiency. This allows us to attack a defense in its most vulnerable area.

We also want an offense that's flexible enough to be adapted to the strengths of our personnel, particularly our quarterback. It's important that the quarterback be able to pass the football, but if he can also run the ball, then we'll have some option elements in our offense. We want to have multiple formations and personnel groups while being able to execute the same runs and passes from these different looks. Mix in shifting and motion, and you get a lot of ways to attack the defense. The trick to this style of attack is to make the offense easy to execute but very difficult to defend.

Game Planning

Our approach to game planning is a little different from that of most teams. We try to anticipate how the opponent will defend our strengths and tendencies. Knowledge of our opponent's defensive philosophy and a great awareness of our own strengths and tendencies allow us to accurately predict what a defense will do in any situation. We don't base our game plan on how the opponent played its last game or the one before that but on how we anticipate the opponent will play us. The opponent had a game plan for the last team it played, but that team's offense might have been a lot different from our own. We try to break down tape of teams that have similar offenses to ours, but we always come back to answer the question: "What must our opponent do to stop our offense?" Once we understand the opponent's defensive philosophy, we can make an educated guess on how they'll try to stop us. We build our offensive plan around that assumption. Figure 12.1 outlines the factors we consider when self-scouting.

By being thorough in our self-scouting, we learn what the opposing defense knows. We want to be aware of our tendencies, to identify our successful and unsuccessful plays, to know what personnel groups and formations have been good or bad. If a play or formation hasn't been good, we find out why it hasn't been successful.

The use of videotape helps to identify what the opponent did to stop the play or defend the formation. We have found that coaches are great imitators and will repeat what an opponent has done in stopping a particular play or formation. This knowledge might be very valuable in anticipating how they'll attempt to defend us. It also might help us determine what we're doing wrong, which we wouldn't have known if we hadn't self-scouted.

Once we know our tendencies and determine how past opponents have defended us, we're ready to study the defensive scheme we'll face in the upcoming week. (Figure 12.2 is an outline of the factors we analyze when

Figure 12.1   Self-scouting outline.

I. Formations with motions
  A. Run-to-pass ratio
  B. Tight-end to split-end ratio
II. Best runs
  A. Consistency
  B. Yards per carry
  C. Tape
III. Passes
  A. Consistency
  B. Yards per throw
  C. Yards per catch
  D. Tape
IV. Down and distance
  A. Normal downs (first and 10, second and 4 to 6)
    1. Consistency
    2. Run-to-pass ratio
    3. Run consistency; tight-end to split-end ratio
    4. Pass consistency
      a. Drop-back pass percentage
      b. Play-action pass percentage
      c. Boot percentage
      d. Screen percentage
      e. Gadget percentage
  B. Second and long (second and 7 to 10, second and 11+)
    1. Consistency
    2. Run-to-pass ratio; tight-end to split-end ratio
    3. Pass consistency
      a. Drop-back pass percentage
      b. Play-action pass percentage
      c. Boot percentage
      d. Screen percentage
      e. Gadget percentage
  C. Short yardage (third and 1, fourth and 1) and goal line
    1. Formation and motion
    2. Run-to-pass ratio
    3. Strong-side to weak-side ratio
    4. Consistency
  D. Third down (third and 2 to 3, third and 4 to 6, third and 7 to 10, third and 11+)
    1. Consistency
    2. Pass routes
      a. Formation and motion
      b. Protection
      c. Consistency
      d. Completion percentage
      e. Yards per throw
      f. Yards per catch
      g. Sacks

scouting an opponent's defense.) The first thing we do is determine whether we're playing against a seven-man or an eight-man defensive front. Does the defense use three or four down linemen? This information is important in determining how we'll attack this defense. We want to be sure that we don't have any mismatches in personnel. We don't want one of our backs blocking one of their linemen.

We chart every one of the defense's pressures in the free-wheeling zone and note at which down and distance they occurred. These data are put up on a whiteboard in the staff room, known as our blitz board. Through studying the blitz board, we determine what protections to use each week

To get an indication of what plays have been effective in the past, we study all the runs over 5 yards and all the passes over 6 yards. This gives us an understanding of how other teams have attacked this defense, and maybe we can incorporate some of their thoughts into our game plan.

The next phase in game planning for the green zone is to study formations by down and distance. We sort the tape by one- and two-back formations, by normal downs (first and 10; second

---

Figure 12.2   Outline for scouting the opponent's defense.

I. Personnel
   A. 3-4 defense
   B. 4-3 defense
   C. 4-4 defense (eight-man front)
   D. 3-5 defense (eight-man front or nickel)
   E. 30 nickel or dime
   F. 40 nickel or dime

II. Runs over 5 yards (pinnacle)

III. Passes over 6 yards (pinnacle)

IV. Blitz board—select best protections

V. Two-back formations
   A. Sorted by normal downs (first and 10, second and 4 to 6)
      1. Formation by front
      2. Coverage frequency
   B. Sorted by second and long (second and 7 to 10, second and 11+)
      1. Formation by front
      2. Coverage frequency

VI. One-back formations
   A. Sorted by normal downs (first and 10, second and 4 to 6)
      1. Formation by front
      2. Coverage frequency
   B. Sorted by second and long (second and 7 to 10, second and 11+)
      1. Formation by front
      2. Coverage frequency

VII. Third down
   A. Third and 2 to 3
      1. Man percentage
      2. Zone percentage
      3. Pressure percentage
      4. Zone pressure percentage
      5. Man pressure percentage
   B. Third and 4 to 6
      1. Man percentage
      2. Zone percentage
      3. Pressure percentage
      4. Zone pressure percentage
      5. Man pressure percentage
   C. Third and 7 to 10
      1. Man percentage
      2. Zone percentage
      3. Pressure percentage
      4. Zone pressure percentage
      5. Man pressure percentage
   D. Third and 11+
      1. Man percentage
      2. Zone percentage
      3. Pressure percentage
      4. Zone pressure percentage
      5. Man pressure percentage

VIII. Short yardage
   A. Formations by front and coverage
   B. Coverage by man, zone, pressure, zone pressure, man pressure

and 4 to 6), and by second and long and extra long (second and 7 to 10; second and 11 plus). We examine each formation in these down-and-distance situations by sorting the most frequently used defensive front and coverage. This allows us to judge the fronts and coverages that the opposing defense likes to play against other teams.

When you sort the tape by most frequently used front and then coverage, you get to study the same defense versus the same formation over and over. Studying the defense in this manner helps you judge the personnel weaknesses and strengths, as well as adjustments to shifting, motions, and formations. For normal downs we search for weaknesses in the defense—anything that might give us an advantage to make

yards and first downs. The advantage might be a personnel matchup, a poor adjustment to motion or shifting, a formation into the boundary, or an unbalanced formation. Any advantage we gain in assessing formation is a starting point for our game plan.

Next, we to try to understand the opponent's defensive philosophy by breaking each down-and-distance situation into five categories: zone, man, pressure, zone pressure, and man pressure. We gain tremendous insight by breaking down a defense and categorizing the coverage into a percentage of zone or man. This helps us know how much pressure to expect and whether it will be zone pressure or man pressure. Analyzing the decisions made by the same defensive coordinator year in and year out regarding their use of zone or man coverage and the amount of pressure reveals how consistent they remain. The type of coverage might change with each game, but the philosophy of zone versus man and how much they pressure remains fairly constant.

Third-down situations in the green zone are critical; success here determines if the drive continues. We break third down into four categories: third and short (third and 2 to 3), third and medium (third and 4 to 6), third and long (third and 7 to 10), and third and extra long (third and 11 plus). Each category is broken down by zone, man, pressure, zone pressure, and man pressure. We're cognizant of the type of coverage the defense plays but will set our game plan on the percentage of zone, man, or pressure that we anticipate.

Short yardage is the next situation we must be prepared to attack. Short yardage is third and 1 or less or fourth and 2 or less. In college football, you must be ready for anything in these situations. As defenses gear up to stop the critical short-yardage play, beware of your own tendency because you can count on your opponent knowing it.

The advantages of this type of game planning are that we're not preparing for how our opponent game planned his last game but how we anticipate they will defend us. Knowing that coaches are great imitators and by thoroughly understanding our tendencies and how defenses have been successful against us, we can make adjustments and improvements on what we're doing. Understanding the defense's philosophy by situations and knowing that the defense will attempt to stop what the offense does best, we can anticipate how we think the defense will defend us and base our game plan on that assumption.

Going into each game, we prepare charts that reflect the previous game's percentages of down and distance, formation, and personnel groups. These charts are kept in the press box; at halftime we can tell if the defense is playing as we anticipated. If they're not playing as we expected, then we must adjust. If they are playing as anticipated, we note what plays have been effective and continue to emphasize them in the second half. We also try to anticipate what the defense might do to help stop our most effective plays. If the percentage of zone and man are the same, we check if the coverage is also what we expected.

Attacking the Defense With Personnel Groups

One thing we try to do is delay for as long as possible what personnel group is in the game. If we can force the defense to play the down and distance instead of matching up against our personnel, we gain another advantage.

We want to create mismatches with our personnel. On normal downs, if we have four wide receivers in the game, we like the defense to have their regular players in the game. On second and long, if the defense plays nickel or dime

because they expect us to pass with four wide receivers, and we come into the game with three tight ends and run the ball, we make it difficult for the defense to adjust to what we're doing by formation and personnel group.

In some years we've been blessed with players who can play multiple positions. This is when things really become fun, because defensive coaches think only certain formations can be run with the personnel on the field. If players can play more than one position, the defense can never anticipate what formation the offense will set up in. One year at Georgia Tech we had a tight end who could play fullback, a fullback who could play running back, and a slot back who could also play running back. Our formations included the wishbone, two backs and three wide receivers, and two backs and two wide receivers, all with the same personnel on the field.

Attacking the Defense With Formations, Motion, and Shifts

We attempt to gain the advantage through the use of formations, shifts, or motion. Formations are like weapons with which we can attack defenses. Knowing how a particular formation stresses a defense is invaluable when trying to gain an advantage. Some formations can outflank a defense or make it adjust and open up other areas. Other formations force a defense to expand and take defenders out of the box. Reducing a defensive front might create an advantage for a offense that runs the football. If the defense won't reduce, the advantage is in throwing the football.

Shifting and motion might force a defense to adjust if the offense can make the defense think. It might make the defense a little less aggressive. Some defensive adjustments might give the offense an advantage. If we determine standard adjustment in coverage or in defensive fronts, we try to incorporate them into our game plan. If the defense plays the field or the boundary and tries to keep their adjustments to a minimum, we have simplified the defense, and that can make it vulnerable.

Using Formational Strength Into the Boundary

How does a defense play with the strength of the formation into the boundary? Does it remain the same, overshift its defensive front, or rotate the secondary into the boundary?

If the defense remains the same as it would if the formation strength was to the field, the offense gains a numbers advantage into the boundary and should be able to run or throw with success.

If the defense overshifts its front and rotates the secondary into the boundary to have an equal number of people as the offense, the offense will have an advantage because it gains a larger field but the same number of people. If the defense has shown that they'll adjust in this manner, the use of an audible will get the offense back to the wide field. If the secondary is rotated into the boundary to balance up against the formation, the field favors the offense. Plays such as options, bootlegs, and screens to the field will be very effective.

Using a Wing to Outflank a Defense

When the offense uses a wing, the defense must adjust by widening its normal front (figure 12.3a) or rotating the secondary (figure 12.3b). If the defense fails to adjust, the offense can block down on the defense and run outside or pass the ball unimpeded.

Using the wing in a trips unbalanced formation or into the boundary puts more pressure on the defense. All of these formations are easily shifted or motioned out of or into.

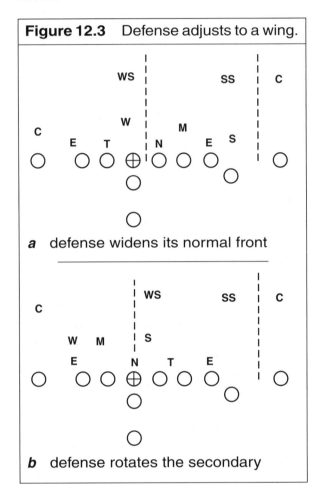

Figure 12.3   Defense adjusts to a wing.

a   defense widens its normal front

b   defense rotates the secondary

Using Formations to Reduce the Defense

Two tight ends and two wide receivers force the defense to defend another gap. A seven-man front must overshift or undershift their front and rotate the secondary the other way. Another way a seven-man front can play these formations is by balancing the secondary while the front stays the same.

Four wide receivers also force the defense to expand. Two receivers split out to either side (the wider, the better), forcing the defense to remove

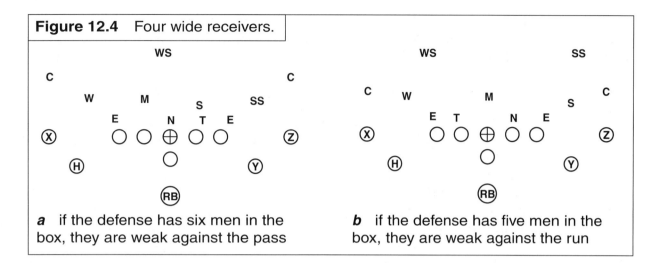

Figure 12.4 Four wide receivers.

a if the defense has six men in the box, they are weak against the pass

b if the defense has five men in the box, they are weak against the run

a linebacker from the box to play pass coverage. If the defense wants to play with a middle safety and six men in the box (figure 12.4a), they are very weak against the pass. If they double the outside wide receivers and play two-deep with five men in the box, they are weak against the run (figure 12.4b).

Running Game

We divided our running game into five groups—isolation, zone, power, option, and draw. Our goal is to be able to run most plays from all formations, strong and week. To be able to run most running plays from both two-back and one-back sets gives us tremendous flexibility in attacking defenses. Being balanced in the running game keeps

defenses honest and doesn't allow them to overplay the tight end or any tendency we might have. The use of audibles and checks by the quarterback allows us to run strong and weak and also helps reduce the defensive looks we have to block. If we can reduce the learning for linemen and use our formations, shifts, and motion to give us an advantage, we have succeeded in making our offense difficult to defend and simple to run.

Isolation

Our offense is at its best when we have a fullback or an H back who can lead block on linebackers. These plays give us a physical attitude and the ability to run right at defenses. We can run isolation plays strong from two- or one-back sets (figure 12.5). The use of audibles or

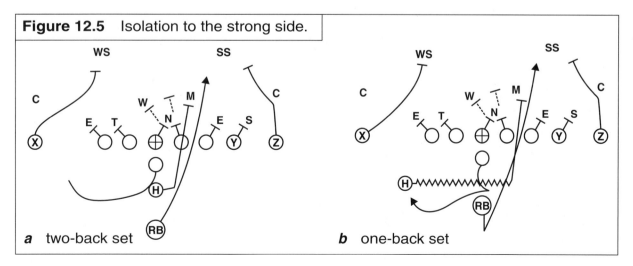

Figure 12.5 Isolation to the strong side.

a two-back set

b one-back set

checks allows us to run weak from one- or two-back formations as well. The use of motion may aid the isolation because the isolation blocks occur closer to the line of scrimmage.

Zone

The inside and outside zone plays have been a main part of our offense for years. We added a full-zone play that happens very quickly and that we can use in many formations.

The inside zone is designed to read the first down linemen from the tackle in. It can also be run from one- and two-back formations (figure 12.6). When the inside zone is run to the split-end side,

it must be run as part of an audible because if the defense outnumbers the offense, the play won't be successful. This also reduces the defensive looks that the inside zone can be run to, which cuts down the learning time for the offense.

The outside zone is designed to run off the read of the tight end's block. The play must be packaged if run out of a one-back set (figure 12.7) because the receiver to the tight-end side must block the most dangerous defender. If he's unable to block this defender, another play must be run. The interior line blocking remains the same when running the outside zone to a tight end, but we'll tag the one-back play to let the

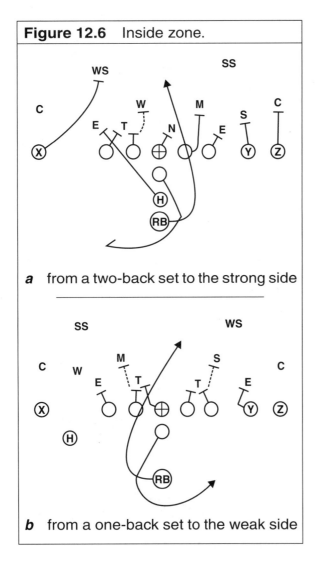

Figure 12.6 Inside zone.

a from a two-back set to the strong side

b from a one-back set to the weak side

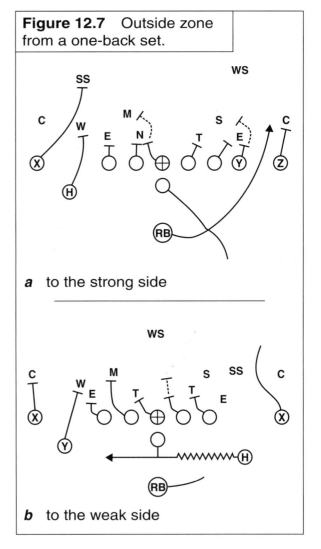

Figure 12.7 Outside zone from a one-back set.

a to the strong side

b to the weak side

playside receiver know that he must block run support, not the lead back.

The use of the full-zone play has allowed us to be able to run the outside zone to a split-end side. As in most split-end plays, we must be ready to check to a successful play if the look isn't right.

Power

We call these plays our power game because we double a defensive down lineman and pull a lineman from the back side to block on the front side. In other words, we double a defender at the point of attack and pull another blocker from the back side to help on the front side. We run these plays both to the tight-end and split-end sides (figure 12.8), and all of them can be run from either one- or two-back formations.

The first play in this series is to the tight-end side. A double team occurs on the first defensive down lineman. The fullback or H back kicks out the defender over the tight end, and the backside offensive guard pulls and blocks the frontside linebacker. This is a traditional power play that can also be run to the split-end side in certain situations.

We incorporate the power play and the counter trey concept. These two plays have the same blocking scheme; the difference is in which positions exchange assignments. We run the counter play with the backside offensive guard and tackle pulling and also with the backside guard and H back pulling. Hag counter trey indicates to the back that he's switching responsibilities with the backside offensive tackle (figure 12.9). This gives us maximum flexibility in how we can run the play and also solves certain defensive problems. When the defense overplays the tight-end side, we might be able to run the counter trey back to the split-end side. We call these plays *counter gap* or *hag counter gap* (figure 12.10).

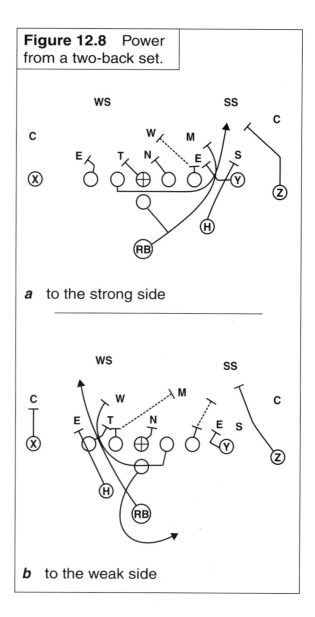

Figure 12.8 Power from a two-back set.

a to the strong side

b to the weak side

Figure 12.9 Hag counter trey to the strong side from a two-back set.

Figure 12.10 Hag counter gap to the weak side from a two-back set.

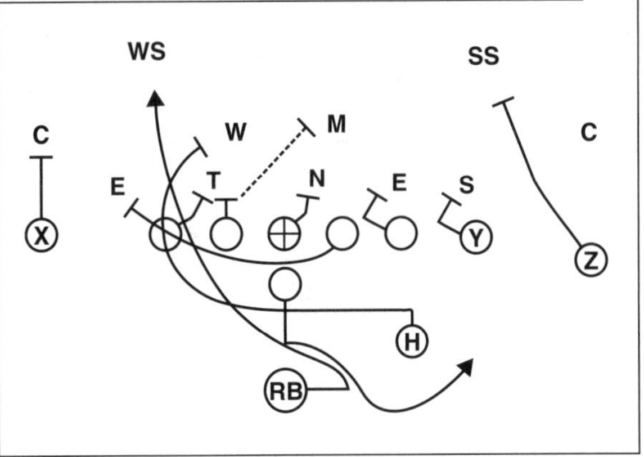

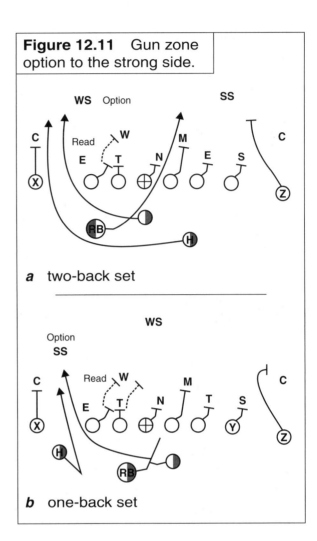

Figure 12.11 Gun zone option to the strong side.

a two-back set

b one-back set

Option

Over the years we have run quite a few types of options, including the inside veer, outside veer, midline option, and crack option. At this time we're running the gun zone option and the crack option. Both of these plays can be run either strong or weak.

We run the gun zone option from both one- and two-back formations (figure 12.11). The zone option allows linemen to block the inside zone. Instead of blocking the end man on the line of scrimmage, the quarterback reads the defender. If the defender closes with the running back, the quarterback pulls the ball and options the next defender to show. If the end man on the line plays the option, the quarterback hands the ball off, and the play becomes an inside zone with one less blocker. This gives us the ability to run the triple option with no new learning for the offensive line.

The gun zone option differs from the normal triple option in that the option takes place opposite the play action. In essence, this is a counter option, and we don't experience the pursuit that we would with a normal triple option. Another nice thing about this play is that you can run it to the split-end side and not have to audible.

The crack option is also run from both sets, but it's much more limited from one-back than from two-back formations. The load option is a play that we feature out of a one-back set. This play must be checked to or used as an audible.

Draw

The draw game is an important part of an offense. We run the lead draw from both one- and two-back formations. In two-back formations, one of the backs leads for the other (figure 12.12a). In the one-back formation, the remaining back blocks for the quarterback, and the play becomes a quarterback lead draw (figure 12.12b). We use the same blocking as in the weakside isola-

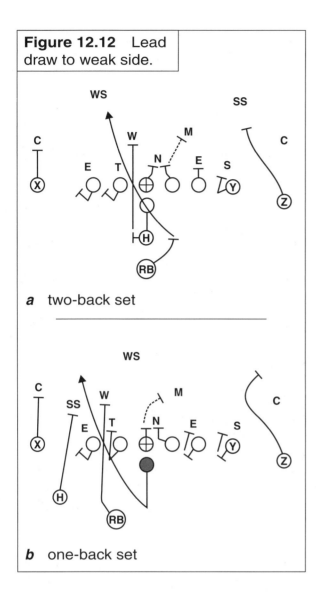

Figure 12.12 Lead draw to weak side.

a two-back set

b one-back set

Passing Game

In keeping with our philosophy, we want balance in the passing game. In the drop-back game, we use three-step, five-step, and seven-step drops. We feature play-action passes, including bootlegs and naked passes off the running game. We move the pocket with a sprint game both to the strong and weak sides. We employ a screen game to keep the defense off balance; we feature certain screens against zone and others versus man coverage.

To be able to throw the same passes from multiple formations, we divide passes into two groups. The first group is the three-by-one passes—three receivers released to the front side of these patterns (figure 12.13). The other group is the two-by-two patterns in which two receivers release on both sides of the pattern (figure 12.14).

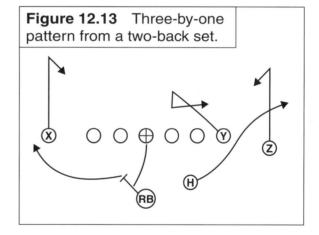

Figure 12.13 Three-by-one pattern from a two-back set.

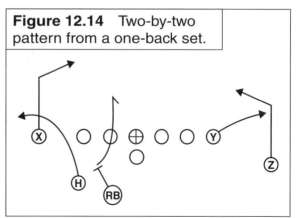

Figure 12.14 Two-by-two pattern from a one-back set.

tion play. Once again we have limited the learning required of the offensive line; only the blocking technique will change by showing pass and then run blocking.

The one-back draw will be run only with one back in the backfield. It's run with man blocking and used only as an audible.

By using these running plays to both the strong and weak sides and in all formations we create a lot of flexibility to attack the defense. Allowing the quarterback to make the decision at the line of scrimmage creates the best chance to be successful. It also cuts down on the overall learning for the entire team.

We also separate passing patterns by half-field routes and full-field routes. A half-field route is one that attacks one side of the formation. These patterns usually occur with three-by-one passes. In these patterns, the only time the quarterback goes to the other side is when he has a one-on-one situation. That situation occurs when there's a middle safety and the weakside outside linebacker is aligned over the weakside offensive tackle (figure 12.15). A full-field pass spans the entire field and occurs a lot with two-by-two patterns (figure 12.16). Full-field patterns are designed to go to one side. If the defense outnumbers the offense to that side, the quarterback takes the read to the other side of the field.

Protections

The most important part of a passing game is protection. We use quite a few protections; the defense will study our protections and find their weaknesses. There will always be problems that must be solved in picking up pressure. Instead of bastardizing a protection to solve a problem, we fit the protection to eradicate the problem. This way, players learn the protection, and it never changes. Changing protection also keeps the defense guessing about our protection. This is especially useful versus zone blitz teams who try to make us throw hot or sight adjust.

We have two six-man protections, three seven-man protections, and two eight-man protections. Some of these protections carry over to play-action pass; others, such as boot and sprint-out, must be learned. If we run a naked pass, then the line and backs execute the run, but the line does not go downfield.

Three-Step Drop Passes

These passes need to be very efficient; a pass-completion percentage of over 75 percent is acceptable. Three-step passes should be called when the wide receivers are in one-on-one coverage. They are an excellent complement to the running game when an extra man is in the box. When receivers are double covered, run the ball; when they're single covered, throw the ball (figure 12.17). Slants and fades accompanied with flat routes can be run versus double coverage. Hitches and outs are better to check out of. The quick-passing game should consistently yield 5- and 6-yard gains to be a productive part of an offense.

Figure 12.15 Half-field pass pattern to the strong side. Defense includes a middle safety and a weakside linebacker in the box. Wide receiver is one on one.

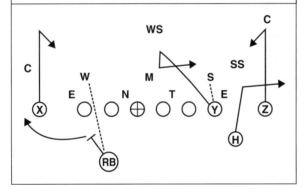

Figure 12.16 Full-field pass pattern to the strong side.

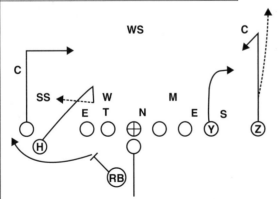

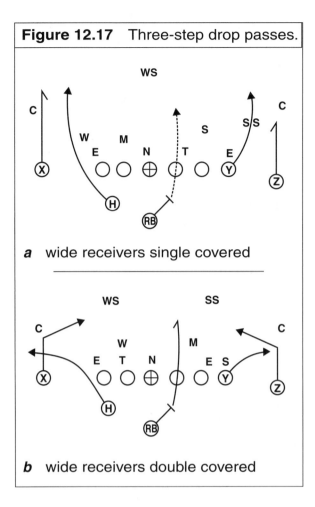

Figure 12.17 Three-step drop passes.

a wide receivers single covered

b wide receivers double covered

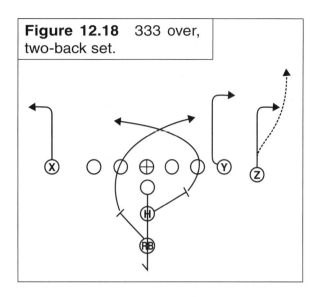

Figure 12.18 333 over, two-back set.

Five-Step Drop Passes

The five-step drop passes are an important part of the possession passing game. We like to complete over 60 percent of these passes, with a low risk of sacks. Many of these passes are timed routes and can be used in any down-and-distance situation. We use both six- and seven-man protections with these routes. We use the route in all formations and different personnel groups. We number routes starting from the boundary or the weak side of the formation. Odd-numbered routes break to the outside; even-numbered routes are inside routes. The back routes are named, for example, 333 over (figure 12.18). In one-back formations, the second and third receivers take on the back's routes.

Seven-Step Drop Passes

Many teams don't run seven-step patterns because of the high risk of sacks. These routes allow more sacks because of the time it takes to throw them and because of the long-yardage situations in which they're thrown. However, they are necessary because they can give you a chunk play that can sustain a drive.

Seven-step patterns also attack the defense in different ways; they can stretch the defense horizontally or vertically. When stretching the defense horizontally, the read is the flat defender, and the quarterback reads outside to inside (figure 12.19a). In the vertical stretch, the read is the deep playside safety. The quarterback reads deep to short, safety level, linebacker level, and check down (figure 12.19b).

Many of these routes are also used with play-action passes. The play-action fake slows down the rush and also controls the linebackers to get a greater stretch between them and the safeties.

Play-Action Passes

If you can establish the run and tie in the protection to fool the defense, big plays will be the result of a good play-action

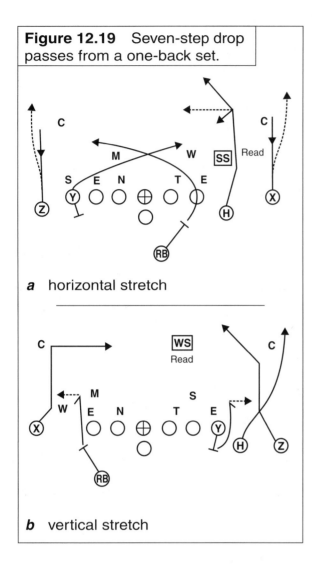

Figure 12.19 Seven-step drop passes from a one-back set.

a horizontal stretch

b vertical stretch

game. When game planning, we try to identify if there are any runs in which the defensive secondary supports the run too quickly. We also might employ a play-action pass to keep the secondary from stopping the run.

Any good play-action game features some key elements. The line blocking must be aggressive, especially on the front side, and the quarterback must take pride in his faking. We tell the quarterback that he can control more defenders with a good fake than with a good block. The faking back is also very important—he must make a good fake and, when possible, accelerate into the line. If the back has protection responsibility, this is not always possible. He must understand that he must make the best fake possible and execute his pass pick-up.

Bootlegs and Naked Passes

Counter plays are invaluable to an offense. Bootlegs and counter passes are great misdirection plays that really slow the defensive pursuit. The reason we call our counter trey running play a power play is because we don't get as much defensive pull as we do with bootlegs. Defenses read the pulling linemen so well that it's no longer a counter play but a power play. Many of our naked passes are run off counter trey plays, giving us great flow and acting as a tremendous complement to the counter. Any time you can force the defense to overreact and get them out of position, big plays will result. If nothing else, you make the defense play their responsibilities, which helps you in the running game.

Bootlegs and naked passes are best in running situations; however, we've had success running boots out of the shotgun with three and four wide receivers. We do run the ball out of these passing formations; I believe that's why we have been successful.

Sprint-Outs

Sprint-out plays have not been a big part of our offense, but they still create problems for the defense. First, a good sprint-out play moves the pocket, and the defense doesn't get to attack the quarterback in the same spot all the time. The protection is not difficult to learn, and there are no hots or break-offs. We sprint out to the split-end side with the running back blocking the edge or to a tight-end's side. The patterns are some type of flood or rub routes. We match the patterns to the man or zone tendencies.

Screens

When incorporating screens into our game plan, we try to consider that some screens are better versus man coverage and others are better versus zone coverage. By knowing what the defensive coverage tendency is in particular situations, we can match the appropriate screen pass.

The most successful screen for us in the last four years has been the double screen (figure 12.20). This screen is two screens in one and is good versus man or zone. It's a crack screen to one side and a jail-break screen to the other side. The quarterback takes a five-step drop, looking to the contain rusher on the crack-screen side. If by the third step the contain rusher doesn't peel with the swinging back, the quarterback throws the crack screen. If the contain rusher does peel with the screen, the quarterback turns immediately and throws the jail-break screen on the hash. Being able to run this screen out of multiple formations allows us to run it in almost any down-and-distance situation.

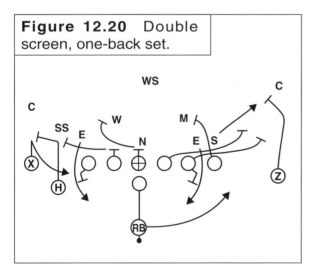

Figure 12.20 Double screen, one-back set.

We also run a flare screen, which is a traditional three-count screen (figure 12.21). The offensive tackle pass protects his responsibility and cuts the contain rusher at 5 yards deep. The two offensive guards and the center release in the screen. The lineman outblocks the outside man. The next lineman blocks the first inside linebacker. The third lineman looks to seal any defender pursuing the screen. The screening back must release into the screen when the backside offensive guard releases. This ensures the proper relationship with the back and the screening linemen. This relationship is critical to a good screen play. If the defenders must go through the blockers to get to the ball carrier, the blocks are more easily executed. If the defender can avoid the blockers and still make the play, the relationship of the screening back and the blockers is not correct.

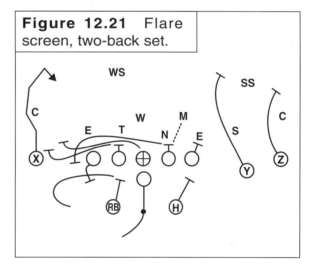

Figure 12.21 Flare screen, two-back set.

We run the flare screen from dropback, play action, and sprint-out. We prefer this screen versus zone coverage, but we will coach the screening linemen to block the linebacker if he's in man coverage. If the lineman blocks the backer, the play has a great chance of succeeding. If not, it's doomed.

The bubble screen (figure 12.22) is another screen we use to control defenders who try to play inside a slot receiver so that they can be a factor in both the running game and passing game. We use this play-action fake to freeze the perimeter defender and throw

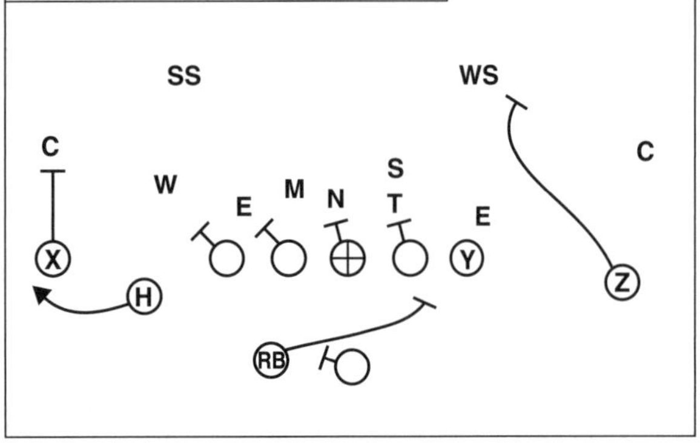

Figure 12.22 Bubble screen, one-back set.

the ball to the slot receiver. No linemen are involved in this screen.

Gadgets and Shots

Gadgets should be a regular part of an offense, something worked on weekly and not just put in for a given week. Reverses and fake reverses should be run once or twice a game. Passing gadgets should be installed in preseason and then brought out for the appropriate game plan. The halfback pass, flea flicker, reverse pass, fake-reverse pass, throwback to the quarterback, and tight-end hide play are examples. We won't carry all of these gadgets each week, but if we have installed them we include one in the game plan.

Shots are mostly passes that we think will make a big play. Some shots may be tied into a situation, such as waste a down or short yardage, and others to a tendency, such as anticipating pressure man or a particular coverage to a formation. We list these shots and when we want to apply them. We always like taking a shot after a turnover or big play, when the defense is down and maybe confused. Shots also stretch the field and keep the defense from overplaying the run or sitting on routes.

In this chapter, I have shown you the steps we would take to formulate a game plan for the green zone. We self-scout,

break down the defense, and not only study what they have done in the past but anticipate how they will play against us. I hope the explanation of our offensive philosophy and the description of the freedom and responsibility we give our quarterback have given you some insight into how we plan for each situation that arises in the green zone.

In the green zone, play calling depends on down and distance. On normal downs (first and 10, second and 4 to 6), we consider 4 yards running or passing to be a consistent play. This allows us to attack the defense with all elements of our offense. This is when we try to gain an advantage through the many ways we have discussed. Play calling is easy when you're on schedule. On second and long, we want to execute a play to get us at least half the distance. Obviously, on third down we must convert in order for the play to be successful.

Normal downs in the green zone avail the whole offense; that's why this zone is called the free-wheeling zone. We want plays to gain a minimum of 4 yards. We select plays after studying how to gain advantages by formation and personnel groups. We also study the defense's tendencies as they relate to man, zone, and pressure. For example, if a defense is a big zone coverage team in normal downs, what type of zone is it? Do they play a particular type of zone coverage to a particular formation? Can we expect them to play us the same way? If we like the way they play a particular formation, we might wish to incorporate that formation in our own game plan and have a plan for both the way they played the last opponent and how we expect them to play us. Our game plan consists of plays that would be good in either situation.

Let's take another example. Say we're facing a team with a pressure mentality. Understanding this allows us to be ready to attack this defense with plays that will be most effective. If a defense had a tendency for man pressure on normal downs, we want to know where that pressure would most likely come from. We would attack with the best runs, probably using audibles and the option game. The passing game would consist of getting the pass off quickly and using routes and play action to create man-coverage problems. Screens and sprints might also be effective.

In the green zone, we have no field restraints, so we can execute our entire offense. Knowing what our goal is for each down-and-distance situation, we can develop a game plan by anticipating what the defense is going to play and having an awareness of their defensive philosophy.

CHAPTER 13

Red Zone: Opponent's 25-Yard Line to Goal Line

Larry Kehres
Mount Union College

In 1990, our high-scoring offensive football team featured a great field-goal kicker, the closest thing to a sure bet in a field-goal situation our team ever had. Eight times in a 10-game season we took the opening kickoff, drove down the field, and kicked a field goal to take a 3-point lead. This All-American kicker was money in the bank. After winning 10 games, we went to the playoffs and learned the hard way that field goals are not enough to win playoff games. After two first-half trips inside the 10 resulted in successful field goals, we added a third-quarter touchdown. However, two fourth-quarter trips inside the 10 ended in two failed fourth-down plays. Although we were desperate for a touchdown, we could not score. Four first-and-goal series had produced only six points. Our offense was incomplete. We lacked aggressiveness and had virtually no confidence in the red-zone passing game. We spent too little time practicing red-zone plays. Planning for field goals resulted in field goals and a false sense of security. That playoff loss was a tough pill to swallow because it

resulted from an incomplete plan. Who's responsible for the plan—the equipment manager?

Developing a Red-Zone Plan

Determined to improve, and minus a surefire kicker, we reevaluated our thinking on red-zone offense. Losing does that to most coaches. It serves as a good kick in the butt, especially when a coach's shortsightedness cost the team. We wanted a fresh approach, one that was more aggressive and required throwing for scores.

As we investigated and planned strategies, we sought advice from other head coaches. We frequently heard, "Use your best player in the best matchup you can get." "Build around your best run and best pass" was a theme in several articles written by top offensive coaches. We decided to build a red-zone attack around what we did best and use the top players to accomplish this mission. A positive attitude was beginning

x points is better than three, ...ted six plus one. Maybe we ...playoff game if we ever got ...ance.

A new quarterback was our starter, and his strength was passing. Our number one wide receiver was a quality player. Maybe we could use the fade route more. The wide receiver was also excellent on the jailbreak screen in high school. Why not play to his strengths? The running game included a good counter play from split backs (figure 13.1), and we had a decent waggle off the counter fake (figure 13.2). Could we expand the waggle and develop some routes and patterns to use in the red zone? Staff discussions became more interesting and spirited.

As we developed the fade route, we learned what many other coaches already knew—for this pass to be effective, you need a matchup in your favor. Carefully assess your strengths before burning an irreplaceable red-zone down on a fade. Also carefully consider positioning on the field when working the fade. The three-step drop and longer throw works great for some quarterback–wide receiver tandems, while the one-step, shorter throw is better suited to others. Practice, practice, and practice some more. If a pass has only a 22 percent chance, maybe it should not be in the plan, unless the receiver is exceptional. Our game plan always takes into consideration the receiver's ability to separate, receive the pass, and get his feet down in bounds. We wanted a realistic chance for a completion, not a wing and a prayer.

The jailbreak screen (figure 13.3) in the red zone was an intriguing idea. Defenses frequently blitz in the red zone. The wide receiver had excellent running skills. If we could get an accurate throw to him, he could use that skill to score points. It proved difficult to get the offensive linemen in position to effectively block, but we soon realized the play often was successful even when not executed perfectly. A talented runner needs space and can frequently make a tackler miss in the open field. If the defense blitzed, open space resulted. We needed to make an effective block on the corner if he was playing man coverage, so we worked on ways to make that block. The jailbreak became a favorite red-zone play. If a defense just sat back, we were less likely to use it, but defensive coordinators are normally determined to make plays, and pressure is the norm in the red zone.

Adjusting the waggle pass to fit into the red zone proved to be our most demanding task. In the red zone, vertical passing distance is compressed, and the short field tightens the defense. We could not run the split end on a skinny

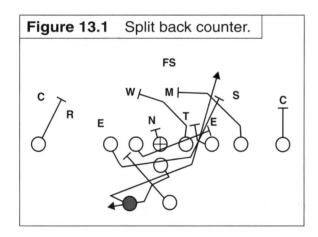

Figure 13.1 Split back counter.

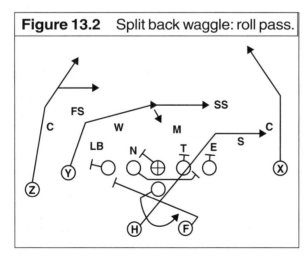

Figure 13.2 Split back waggle: roll pass.

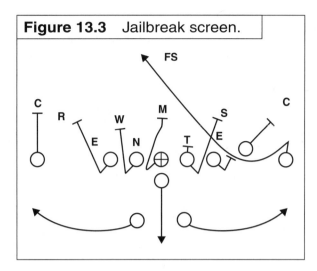

Figure 13.3   Jailbreak screen.

post with the ball inside the 25-yard line. The tight end might have to adjust the depth of his route if the ball was inside the 10. The flanker on the back side of the pattern would also have to adjust. We had a pattern designed to attack zone coverage, but we knew we would face pressure defenses in the red zone. Crossing routes (figure 13.4) seemed to be the simplest solution, so we experimented with those. We challenged receivers to improve their abilities to escape from tight man coverage. Techniques are fun to practice in drill work if players believe the opportunity to catch the ball for touchdowns may result. Our players poured tremendous effort into red-zone practice periods.

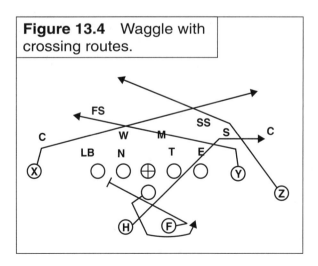

Figure 13.4   Waggle with crossing routes.

We challenged the quarterback with pressure from all angles and insisted that he practice patience in the midst of chaos as he waited for receivers to break free. Steadily, we gained confidence. As the seasons passed, we became an effective red-zone passing team. Table 13.1 shows the number of touchdown passes we completed as our players gained experience with a new approach to red-zone offense. First-year quarterbacks directed the offense in 1991, 1994, and 1998, which may explain the slight decline in touchdown passes in those seasons. Repetitions in practice, combined with game experience, are invaluable in the growth of a quarterback.

Table 13.1   Touchdown Passes 1990–2000

Year	Games played	Touchdown passes
1990	11	16
1991	10	27
1992	13	37
1993	14	55
1994	12	35
1995	13	49
1996	14	59
1997	14	64
1998	14	35
1999	13	41
2000	14	39

Adjusting the Plan

Defenses adjust. The 2000 season brought more change to our red-zone attack. Defenses began to attack and pressure less near the goal line. We adjusted to this change by featuring more rushing plays. The presence of a national player of the year at tailback made this adjustment a good fit. (Of course, maybe the additional rushing plays near the goal line helped make the tailback player of the year.) Here are some of the adjustments we made during the 1990s as our red-zone offense evolved.

Fade Route

Success with the fade in the red zone led to defensive adjustments to strengthen the defense on the top receiver. We found new opportunities when the defense overplayed the best receiver. If the corner played loose, we could match the inside receiver on a safety or linebacker. A three-step drop and a quick flat route gave the inside receiver a chance to make a catch and turn upfield quickly for additional yardage. The wide receiver was often in position to effectively block the soft corner (figure 13.5).

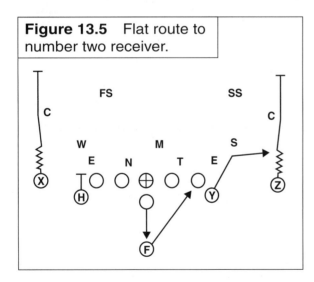

Figure 13.5 Flat route to number two receiver.

Jailbreak Screen

The jailbreak screen could not be planned, scripted, and then practiced to perfection. We tried. It's just too difficult to send offensive linemen downfield and expect them to outquick linebackers and deep backs. The jailbreak became a calculated gamble as a play call. If we had a scouting tip that the defense would pressure, and our receiver was elusive, we gambled and made the call.

Taking risks excited the team, and players bought into the plan. Players love the notion that they are part of an aggressive style of play, with big rewards waiting if risky calls are well executed. This concept removes some of the drudgery from the game. Like it or not, the way we repeat basic schemes can produce boredom and mental fatigue. Jump on the chance to persuade your team they are mavericks; just don't let the thought get out of control.

Practicing the jailbreak three or four times per week permitted guards and centers to run downfield. I made it a point to tell them they looked good running, and if the play were live they would have made a great block. Verbal positive reinforcement can be provided by each coach to any player at no cost.

Waggle Pass

The real work we enjoyed was in adjusting and adapting our version of the waggle, or roll pass. Figure 13.6 shows the roll pass with the back in the flat and the receivers crossing. The quarterback uses a reverse pivot and doesn't make a ball fake to the blocking back. Instead, he reverses out from center for two deep steps and pauses for a second with his back to the line of scrimmage. The intent is to freeze the inside linebackers. He keeps the ball against his chest, finding a comfortable grip. He then proceeds with steps three, four, and five to a passing position behind the B gap. Ideally, he should be 5 to 6 yards off the line of scrimmage. His presnap read should give him an indication of man or zone coverage, and from what position a blitz may be coming. It's imperative that he hold firm in the face of the pressure and go through his reads. Specifically he must stay under outside pressure, allowing the pulling guard to block the rusher out. If he must run, he moves forward to minimize the damage. The quarterback must not attempt to throw the ball away when a hit is imminent. "Live for another down" is our motto. A sack does not prevent a score, but an interception certainly does. The quarterback's progression is the running back in the flat, the receiver crossing to the playside (shallowest first if two are crossing), and the receiver crossing away (shallowest first if two are crossing).

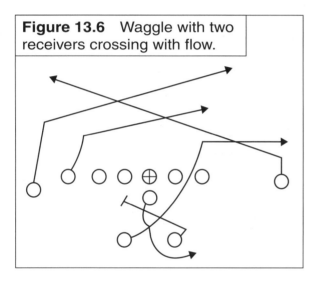

Figure 13.6   Waggle with two receivers crossing with flow.

The running back going to the flat has to scoot. His assignment is to find a seam through the B gap without getting knocked off course. It sounds hard, but we insisted. The backs are Division III men, usually no more than 190 pounds. When the payoff is a chance at a score, they become very resourceful.

The running back on the play fake did not worry about the fake. His assignment was to help protect the quarterback. He checked the backside A, B, and C gaps, in that order. If there was no pressure, he drifted back side and became the fifth receiver. I could show a highlight tape of the quarterback under pressure late in the play, moving toward the line of scrimmage, and then finding his fifth

choice in the red zone. Hitting the fifth choice was not just blind luck.

The receiver crossing against the grain ran an intermediate cross. His depth was determined by our distance from the goal line. If the ball was on the 25-yard line, he worked behind the inside linebackers to a depth of about 10 yards. He sprinted versus man coverage and was permitted to stop in a vacated zone versus a zone blitz. The inside receiver moving toward the playside ran a shallow cross under the inside linebackers. If the linebackers stepped into the line of scrimmage on the play action, he could run off their butts. He was not to make contact, because this would delay his route and could be called offensive interference. He was to stay alive, and we wanted him to be hungry for a touchdown catch. The wide receiver moving toward playside ran the deepest cross. If we were inside the 10, he worked within a yard of the end line. All receivers sprinted versus man and looked for seams in the zone.

We learned more intricacies as we grew. The constant thread was that we knew we had to be able to successfully pass in the red zone to win playoff games. Figure 13.7 illustrates various goal-line adjustments to our basic waggle pass.

The protection scheme for the roll pass is shown in figure 13.8. The pulling guard checks pressure in the A, B, C, and then D gap. We want him to pull under control so that he doesn't run past a blitz. We want the playside tackle to call loudly if he catches a presnap tip of outside pressure.

The blocking back has essentially the same assignment on the back side. We realized the defense could outnumber our blockers, so we added backside protection help by giving up a receiver. We tried to be deceptive when using this scheme by putting receivers in various motions. We gambled that our offensive practice repetitions would outnumber

Figure 13.7   Goal-line adjustments to waggle pass.

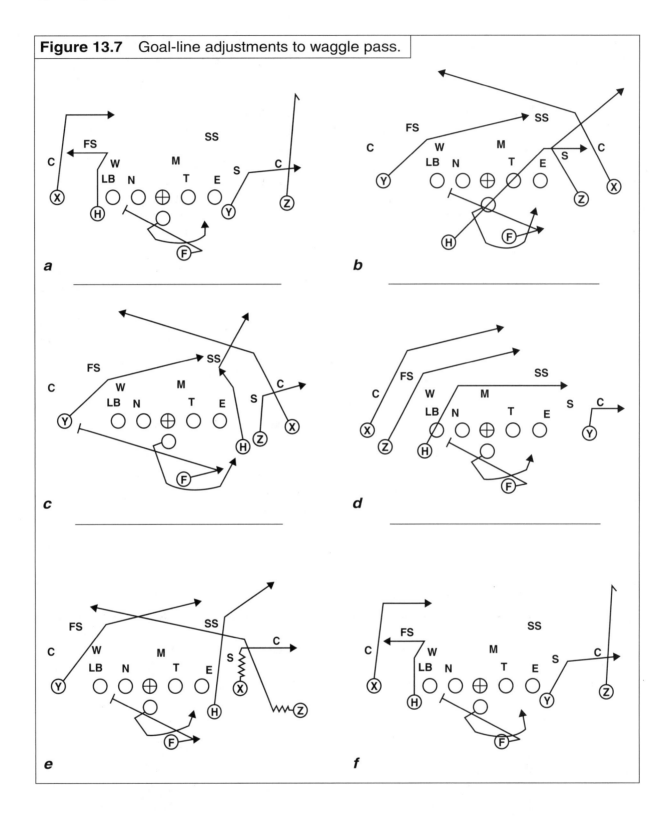

the defensive repetitions our opponents would get.

We had a thick skin about sacks in the red zone. Although we knew we would be sacked sometimes, we felt they would not defeat us. Sacks just make the defense hungrier for more sacks; ultimately, we would beat the heat.

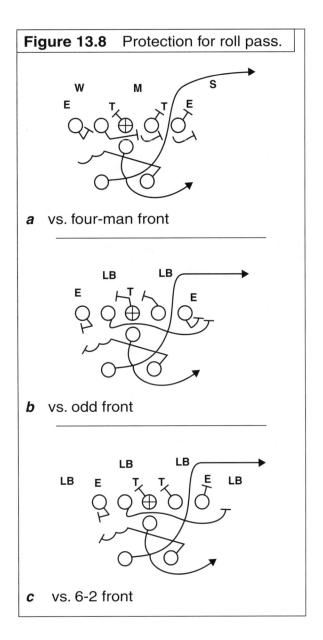

Figure 13.8   Protection for roll pass.

a   vs. four-man front

b   vs. odd front

c   vs. 6-2 front

Crossing Routes

An early adjustment to the crossing routes was to run a pivot. Usually the receiver who appeared to be running away from the flow ran the pivot. Imagine the defender fighting for inside leverage against the crossing route. The receiver tries to make the defender think he stymied the cross, then bursts in the opposite direction. This route also proved effective against some zone teams. Picture the playside corner seeing the wide receiver begin to cross. The corner looks for the back in the flat

and quickly closes on this route when it appears the quarterback is going to make that throw. Appearances can be deceiving. The wide-out plants on his inside foot and breaks to the deep corner of the end zone, giving the quarterback two receivers—one shallow and one deep—in the outside zone. This is a calculated gamble, usually best versus an inexperienced corner.

One-Back Sets

One-back sets are also used in the red-zone attack. Formations should be used for both runs and passes or not used at all. The balanced one-back sets that are so good for three-step drop passes and also for the jailbreak screen must also feature counter runs and roll passes. The basic roll pass from a one-back set is shown in figure 13.9.

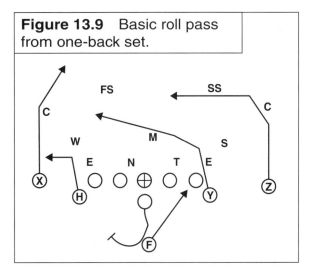

Figure 13.9   Basic roll pass from one-back set.

The personnel group doesn't change. A running back plays the slot position. Notice that the slots use a 1-yard position. The tight end also plays a slot. The slot running the playside flat route stings a D-gap rusher by using his outside shoulder. The intent of the sting is to slow the rusher, thus buying time for the pulling guard to make the block. If the pulling guard has a blitz inside the D gap, the sting serves to buy time for the quarterback to set his feet for the pass. All other receiver routes are the same as in the two-back set.

Defense can knowingly or unintentionally overplay the playside on the roll pass. If this tendency is detected, adjust the backside routes. If these routes use two backside receivers, a pivot route can be called to either receiver. Our preference is to pivot the inside receiver. Sell the crossing route. Let the defender get inside leverage and let him gain a position of advantage. Then exercise the pivot route by pressing against the defender and using his weight as a spring to redirect. This move should create separation. The pivot must be executed in a timely manner consistent with the quarterback being prepared to make the throw.

Motion

Motion can be used to make man defense more difficult to play. If two skilled receivers are positioned on one side of the ball, one can be motioned to a position behind the other. From this stacked alignment, both can release upfield together. The routes can become interchangeable in an attempt to confuse the defense. A pivot can be combined with a cross to create separation for one receiver or the other (figure 13.10).

Many other sight adjustments can be made to this play-action pass. If an offensive tendency is played by the defense, counter with an adjustment of your own. Try to stay one step ahead of the defense. Study your offense and anticipate defensive moves. This might prevent a play or two from being wasted. It might even prevent a loss.

Practicing Red-Zone Offense

Our approach to red-zone offense proved effective. We emphasized red-zone practice to the extent that the offense knew it was the pressure point of practice. We developed complete confidence in our ability to execute the fade, the quick flat, and the jailbreak screen versus certain defenses or specific opposing players. Players believed the roll pass would work in nearly all situations, and we refined and adjusted the play

Figure 13.10   Presnap motion makes it more difficult to play man defense.

over several years of consistent use. We believe in our red-zone offense.

To realize the rewards of using a select group of plays in the red zone, you must be dogged in your determination to effectively practice the plays. The creation of a practice environment that replicates a game environment is difficult. We tried several teaching methods. At times we used more than 11 players on defense. We wanted pressure on the quarterback, and we wanted five-under, man coverage. We used 55-gallon garbage cans in place of offensive linemen to permit the defensive line to penetrate to a point near the quarterback, thus producing the feel of pressure. (No contact with the quarterback, including his extended arm or hand, was ever permitted.) We created dead receivers by instructing receivers to fall a few steps into their routes, forcing the quarterback to progress deep into his possible choices. Use your imagination to create the opportunity to teach the lesson that needs to be learned.

Adding to the Red Zone Plan

Of course you need more than three plays in the red zone. My point here is that you need a few plays that you teach until they become great red-zone plays. When we needed more choices, our favorite was always some type of option.

The old counter option, which was a part of the split-back veer, served us well. There were several reasons for this. First, if a defense was great at man coverage, we wanted to run an option. Second, if the defense rolled coverage to our best receiver because of the fade and jailbreak, we felt an option to the other side would be strong. Third, a great football coach taught me the intricacies of the counter option, and I believed I could effectively teach the play to the team.

Calling Plays in the Red Zone

Obviously down, distance, score, and time remaining are going to influence play selection. Would it ever be wise to control the ball and run out the clock? Certainly. Picture this scenario. Team A takes a 10 to 9 lead with 2:32 left in the game. Team B fumbles the ensuing kickoff on its own 32-yard line. Team A has the ball, first and 10, with 2:20 remaining; team B has two time-outs. What does team A have to do to win the game? Does team A need either a touchdown or a field goal? In this case, which is from a real game, team A scored with 55 seconds left and kicked an extra point to go up by 8 points. Team B scored on the last play of regulation, made the two-point conversion, and won in overtime.

Clearly, there are times in the red zone when you need to use your four downs and keep the clock running. Determine what your best positive yardage running plays are versus a defense that expects the run and is desperate for a stop. We like the power play from an offset I formation with the tight end in a tight slot (figure 13.11). We complement this with the stretch to the strength side

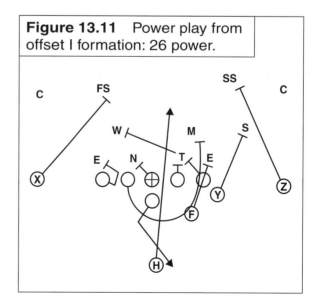

Figure 13.11   Power play from offset I formation: 26 power.

(figure 13.12) and a counter to the weak side (figure 13.13). If the quarterback has good speed and can get outside on a naked, we use a split end on the weak side. If not, we use a tight end and try to prevent being chased down by a fast backside defensive end.

Figure 13.12 Stretch play to strength side: 16 stretch.

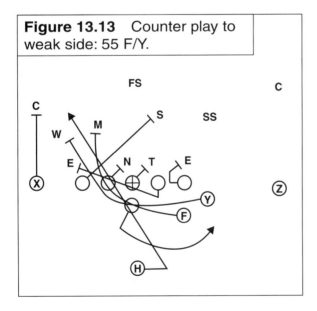

Figure 13.13 Counter play to weak side: 55 F/Y.

Some games seem destined to be decided by a field goal. Defensive teams often rise up and stifle even the best offense. This type of game will occur, so prepare for it. A part of a total goal-line offense is the play or series of plays designed to position the ball to give the kicker the best chance for an accurate kick. Understand that your kicker might be different from other kickers. Have the kicker chart kicks in practice so you understand where the ball should be for his best effort.

This is a sketch of our red-zone offense. We think first of players, then formations, and finally plays in all offensive planning. From this skeleton, this foundation, we build a more complete package for each season. The challenge for each of us who coach offense is to score the points the team needs to win.

CHAPTER 14

Gold Zone: Goal-Line and Short-Yardage Situations

Terry Malone

New Orleans Saints

We work very hard to build a balanced offensive attack. In all areas of the field, all downs and distances, we try to threaten with both the run and the pass.

However, that approach changes when we enter the gold zone. Inside the opponent's 3-yard line, we feature the ground game. Certainly the way in which we moved the ball to the goal-line area will affect our play calling, but not much. We are deeply committed to going with our big people and pounding the ball home. As has been covered in chapters 11 through 13, there are plenty of ways to move the ball down the field. In this chapter we'll discuss how to finish the job.

Goal-line football is about attitude. We must have a group of guys who believe they can gain 1 yard against anyone. We emphasize the following coaching points when we introduce our goal-line attack:

• **Allow no penetration.** Before we talk about knocking the defensive front off the ball, it's important that all our guys understand the defensive mindset. Their backs are against the wall and they'll do anything possible to get into our backfield. Our splits, steps, and leverage positions will determine our success.

• **Protect the edges.** We always assign blockers to secure the edges of the formation. It's crucial that we give maximum effort to our assignments. An unblocked defender pinching off the edge can spell disaster.

• **Put a dent in the defense.** Find a defender to combo or double-team and get movement. The chances of us scoring are slim unless we get some push off the line of scrimmage. The defensive front might determine where we need to combo, but study the defensive personnel to help determine the weakest defensive player.

• **Use the regular running game.** The gold zone is no place for cute little tricks. Make subtle adjustments to the normal running game to fit the demands of the goal line. We're an isolation and gap team in the open field. We call the same type of runs on the goal line. We will adjust some techniques, however, in anticipation of attacking defenses.

• **We can't block everybody.** Great goal-line running attacks must have a back who can find a way to get into the end zone, even when there's an unblocked defender. We coach backs to expect to beat at least one defender. Anyone can score when the entire defense is blocked, but the great ones score no matter what. We've had great success with big tailbacks in the gold zone. More important than size, however, is the desire the ball carrier has to get the ball in the end zone.

Don't beat yourself. Before you can win against a defense, you must first win against yourself. The challenge with offensive football is that you can beat yourself before the defense even has a chance to beat you. You can prevent beating yourself by adhering to five principles.

1. Secure the ball. Make the entire team responsible for protecting the ball. Missed assignments, poor technique, and penalties all contribute to turnovers.

2. Master the cadence. Mastering the cadence isn't simply a matter of not jumping offside. To master the cadence, a player must be disciplined enough to explode off the line of scrimmage on the snap count.

3. Play fast. Playing fast is not simply about physical speed. It's about being totally secure in all assignments, being able to adjust on the fly without hesitation, and playing with a controlled aggression. Playing fast keeps the team one step ahead of the bad guys.

4. Be the most physical team on the field. The foundation of our football program is the physical nature with which we play. Every time we play, our goal is to play as physically as possible. If we don't win the hitting battle, we'll have a hard time winning.

5. Play smart. Smart teams don't make foolish penalties. We have full control over presnap penalties, and there's no excuse for committing one. Habits are formed in practice. We hold players accountable. They must know their assignments and techniques and be willing to play with championship effort.

Running Game

We use our base running game to build the goal-line attack. Why come up with something new when we have a muscle run game already? In the open field, we feature gap schemes, man schemes, and full zone. All three have a lead-back design. I believe strongly in having a good, tough lead back on the goal line. Often, those guys are hard to find because they do all the dirty work and someone else gets the headlines.

Power Gap

The power gap is a great play to have in your goal-line package because it features a full-gap blocking scheme. We adjust the frontside blocking to prevent run-through defenders. In the open field, combo blocks are more upfield and designed to get movement off the line of scrimmage (figure 14.1a). We take a flatter angle on the goal line, which may hurt our movement, but we're in better position to pick up a downhill linebacker (figure 14.1b). We come off combo blocks flat and fast.

A critical ingredient to the power gap is the ability of the frontside tight end. If the tight end can win the battle for the C gap, this play has a great chance. Dan Henning at Boston College once told me, "If you have a tight end who can block the C gap, call the dogs home and put out the fire. The hunt is over." The challenge is finding that guy. Maybe you'll have to snag a guy from the defense who can get the job done.

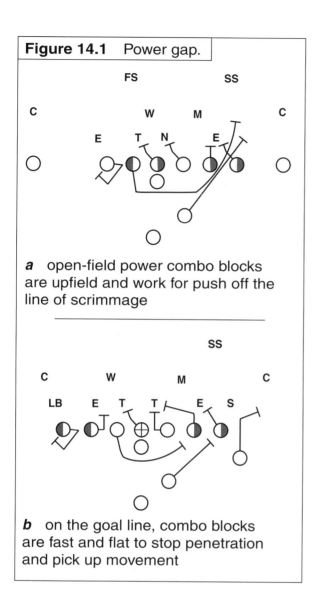

Figure 14.1   Power gap.

a open-field power combo blocks are upfield and work for push off the line of scrimmage

b on the goal line, combo blocks are fast and flat to stop penetration and pick up movement

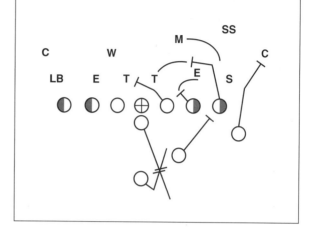

Figure 14.2 The tight end must block levels on the goal line—no sense in blocking a scrape LB when the loop tackle is making the tackle on the line of scrimmage. The frontside TE blocks from the defensive line to the looper, then works to the LB.

Figure 14.3 The tight end must have gap discipline.

We give our tight ends the best chance to be successful by making them responsible for an area and not a man. The tight end's job is to drive the C gap with power and leverage. If the C-gap defender pinches across the frontside tackle, the tight end is slow to go to the linebacker level. He stays flat and looks for any first-level twist before working to linebacker level (figure 14.2). If the C-gap defender loops outside, the tight end doesn't chase him. Instead, he stays on course to block the next defender who shows from the inside (figure 14.3).

Defenses won't allow you to gap block and get a kickout. Most teams will drive their end-of-line defender inside of the kickout block to force the ball to bounce outside. We must find a way to influence the end-of-line defender to lose his focus on the kickout. Against tight side eagle defenses, we adjust the tight end to become an influence blocker. Now we can kick out the C-gap defender, and the tight end blocks the edge (figure 14.4). This adjustment also gives us an answer against a really tough defensive end. It's not something you use as a steady diet, but it's a nice change-up scheme.

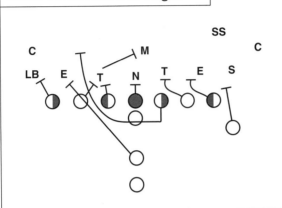

Figure 14.4 Combo front-side guard and tackle to LB level. TE blocks the edge.

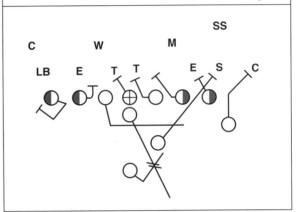

Figure 14.6 Wing influences outside LB. This play is great with motions and shifts. We're safe and sound off the edges.

At times, we tag the play to add a wing into the gap scheme (figure 14.5). By extending the gap scheme, we hope to kick out a defender who hasn't seen the block nearly as much as the outside linebacker has. It also gives the outside linebacker something to think about.

One of our base edge-blocking schemes is an influence with the wing position (figure 14.6). If we can get the outside linebacker to react to the influence block, we're in good shape because we have a kickout, we're protected off the edge, and we have enough blockers gapping inside.

We must keep the defense off balance and force defenders to play honest. Our first answer is to use motion and shifts to disguise our formation strength. We also change up our kickout blocker. At times, like most two-back teams, the fullback will block to the ball. We show our strength, motion away, and train the wing to kick out.

Our next answer is to go to the counter game (figure 14.7). It's great to have the counter in the package because it's easy to develop strong tendencies with the fullback. We teach the same gap techniques as the power. We can use the tight-end influence (figure 14.8), the wingback influence (figure 14.9), and the extended block scheme (figure 14.10). All these adjustments and most of our techniques are repeated from the power play.

Figure 14.5 Wing added to gap scheme. This is a great change-up scheme to offset aggressive Sam LBs.

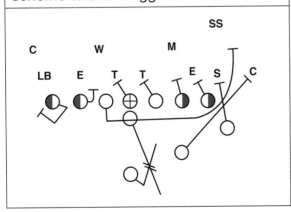

Figure 14.7 Counter. Handoff can be over the top or underneath.

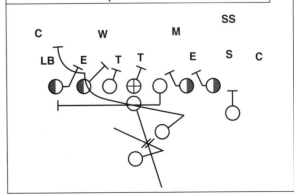

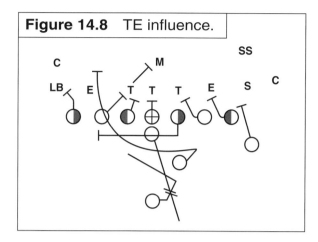

Figure 14.8   TE influence.

Figure 14.9   Wingback influence.

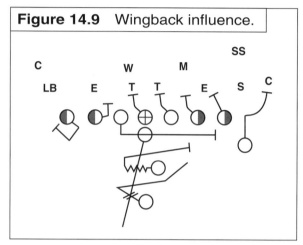

Figure 14.10   Extended block scheme.

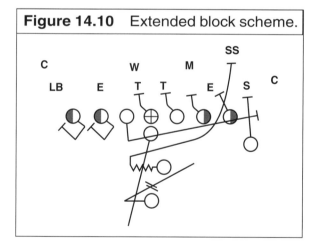

The back side of both the power and the counter must be secured. Tight splits will help cut off the backside gaps, but the offensive line must step off the ball on the snap count with proper steps and leverage. Some defenses will attack the backside A gap with a run-through linebacker. When you pull your backside guard, you do make yourself vulnerable to a run-through. The backside tackle must be aware of any threat inside and put his body in position to constrict the gap (figure 14.11).

Figure 14.11   If the backside guard pulls, the backside tackle needs to close the gap to cut off any inside threat.

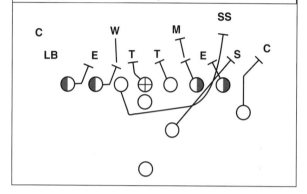

If we have a problem, our answer is to tag the play with a call that keeps the backside guard home to scoop the back side. The adjustment makes the wingback the kickout and the fullback the lead blocker (figure 14.12). This is a fairly drastic adjustment because we change base assignments, but it does give us an answer. The better answer, though, is to run the iso scheme against run-through defenders.

Figure 14.12   Backside guard scoops back side. Wingback becomes the kickout, and fullback becomes the lead blocker.

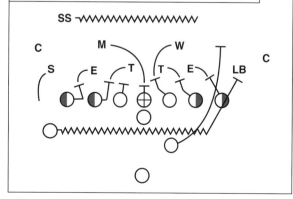

Isolation Run

The isolation is a great goal-line play because it's downhill, aggressive, and gives you an opportunity to cut the defense in two. You need a lead back who's willing to attack the linebacker. If you don't have a guy who will do the dirty work, move on to something else. We train all our tight ends to be able to replace the fullback so that an injury won't take us out of this part of our game.

It's vital to begin teaching the play by addressing the backside blocking. A large part of the success with iso running is cutting off the back side of the defense. This allows for the subtle cutback and protects the tailback from blindside hits.

We use man blocking on the front side, with a combination to the backside linebacker (figure 14.13). This not only helps secure the backside cutoff but also makes for an easier read for the tailback. When you take the combination front side, you risk a single-man cutoff in the A gap and no lateral displacement front side. Teams will tighten up their inside tackles to make it difficult to get any combination to the second level. Our first answer is to use a block back scheme (figure 14.14). We are slow to change from the combo scheme because teams will show tight alignments and then make out moves (figure 14.15).

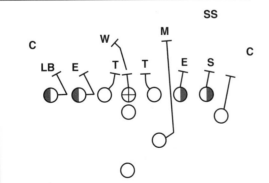

Figure 14.13 Man blocking front side, combo on backside LB.

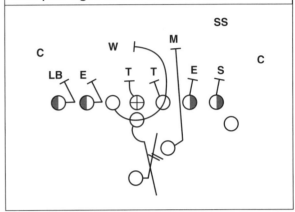

Figure 14.14 Keep the backside guard square to the line of scrimmage and pull tight to the back's block.

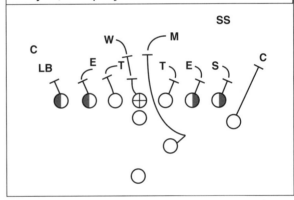

Figure 14.15 FB must see movement and adjust his course. If the center does his job, the play will be successful.

We preach hard that an isolation play blocked with combo blocking against out moves should be a walk-in score. I've seen some teams have their center leap-frog against tight shades and have success. I've just never felt good about asking the boys to do something out of the ordinary in such a crucial area of the field.

The frontside tight end and wing are looking to block the two most dangerous defenders to their side. Normally, we would make a fan call and man block. Then defenses started tucking the safety inside, and he became another linebacker (figure 14.16). By reading the support we can get a hat on the free man.

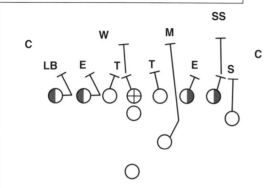

Figure 14.16 The frontside TE must keep eyes on the SS.

The isolation play against bear defense gets adjusted so that we'll not allow any run-through defenders (figure 14.17). The frontside guard takes a middle aiming point because his center will lead through the A gap. This gives us the best chance to get movement at the point of attack. The frontside tackle will drive through the near number to seal the first linebacker to the inside. It's tough sledding but should not be a negative play.

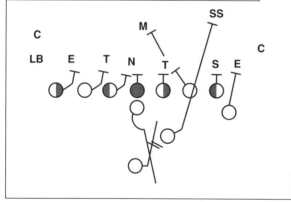

Figure 14.17 Movement at the point of attack is key. The frontside TE needs to keep his shoulders square and hold his ground.

Goal-Line Passing

We study our own tendencies in the running game to help us build a running action throw game. With only 10 to 12 yards of field to work with, we depend on a great run fake to fool the defense. Our protection is basically the same assignments as in the running play.

Snag

For the snag play (figure 14.18), the defense will see the same formation and motions that we run with the power. The quarterback will flash fake and look to the arrow. We would love to get a natural rub against any man coverage. The arrow route must get as much width as possible and not worry about getting downfield. If he has no throw to the arrow, the quarterback will read flag to the spot. This is only a six-man protection, so we must be on time. If the throws aren't there, shelve the ball and live for the next play (on first or second down).

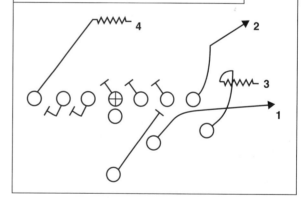

Figure 14.18 Snag. FB can sell the run with his course but should avoid contact.

Mexico

For Mexico (figure 14.19), the quarterback has the same action and reads as in the snag route. We take the easy throw to the arrow every time it's there. The quarterback checks the flag route, then comes back to the shallow route. This is an excellent route, with answers for everything. We must work hard to get solid releases off the line rimmage. The shallow route is a concept and provides blitz control. The backside tight end sits in a void against zone defense and stays on the run against man defense. Never give up on the over drag route; every now and then the wingback will get lost in the crowd only to find himself all alone in the back corner.

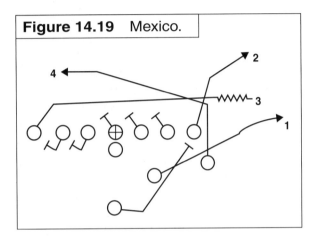

Figure 14.19   Mexico.

Iso Naked

The iso naked (figure 14.20) is a heavy run fake and hesitation by the quarterback. Everybody on the field is selling the isolation run. After the run fake, the quarterback sits and peeks at the tailback course to the line of scrimmage. He needs to be patient and overexaggerate the fake because we're not blocking defenders on the backside edge. The quarterback will get depth and bootleg

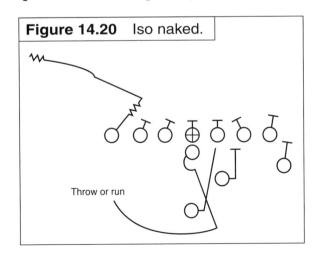

Figure 14.20   Iso naked.

Throw or run

to out-leverage the defense. The backside tight end will drive inside and drop flat to the ground. After a two count, the backside tight end will break to the back corner of the end zone. The quarterback must be a threat to pass or run. He needs to stay on the move and take what the defense gives him. The tight end needs to stay in the back corner of the end zone and stay available for the quarterback to dump him the ball late.

Zone Naked

The zone naked (figure 14.21) is a very good scheme against man coverage. The full zone action in the backfield should really test the discipline of the man defenders. The release and routes on the back side sell the outside zone play. The quarterback makes a solid ball fake and boots to outflank the defense. The fullback takes three steps, faking the zone play, then finds a way to slip out the back side. The wing slam releases to hook up on the linebacker level. Once the fullback clears to the backside flat, the wing can slide to an open void to the outside.

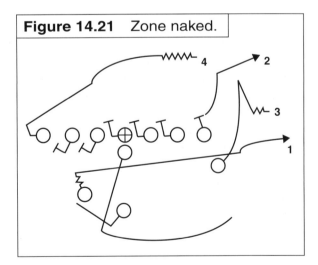

Figure 14.21   Zone naked.

Iso Pop Pass

For the iso pop pass (figure 14.22), everyone on the field must sell the isolation run. We are banking on the heavy run action to clear the middle of the field. The frontside tight end will slam release to get to the middle seam.

Figure 14.22   Iso pop pass. QB must sell the run but have the ball ready to deliver.

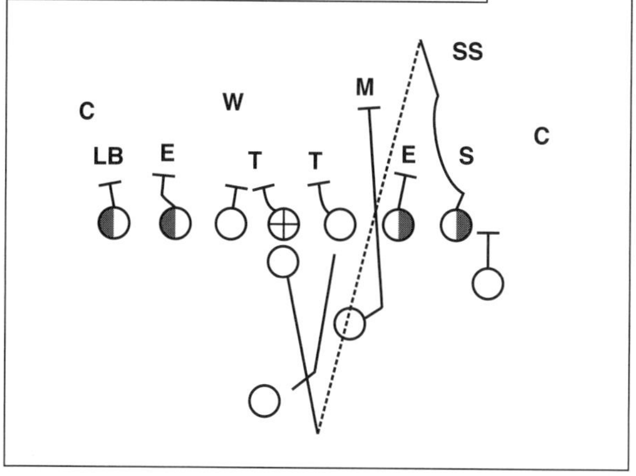

Short-Yardage Game Plan

We work hard to stay in advantage down and distances. Short-yardage situations in the open field certainly favor the offense, but the fact of the matter is that many factors weigh into our strategy. During game preparation, we study to find every strategic and personnel advantage we can. But as the game unfolds, some of those great Tuesday ideas get tossed into the garbage. Some days, the boys are winning the battles up front and the confidence is high. You can make all calls knowing that if you don't make it, plenty of other chances will follow. On other days, however, you're relieved simply to make a first down.

Often the team's comfort zone is affected by how its own defense is playing. In many games, our defense was playing such stifling football that my own confidence and play calling reflected it. It's a great feeling to know that no matter what you call, you'll get the ball back quickly. When the tide is running against your defense, you may think more about ball control and moving the chains. Either way, we give ourselves a much better chance to win when we consider what our defense is up against.

Like the goal-line strategy, the mark is 1 or 2 yards. The big difference, however, is the amount of field the defense must defend. Although we probably break down to 70 percent run in short-yardage situations, formations and personnel groupings still need to keep the defense honest. We must make the defense defend a long field.

When lining up in spread formations on short-yardage plays, we have the wide receivers protect the edges (figure 14.23). Defenses send an extra man to support the run, so we must have skilled players willing to go in the box and block. When using the power scheme from a spread set, we secure the backside gaps by using a wide receiver cut off the backside (figure 14.24). All our wide receivers are trained to protect the backside or frontside edges during group run periods. Our motion tags alert them to edge responsibilities, if necessary. We have had good success in short-yardage situations, and the wide receivers are a big part of it.

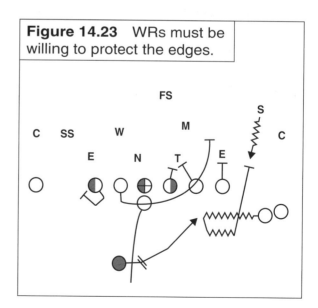

Figure 14.23   WRs must be willing to protect the edges.

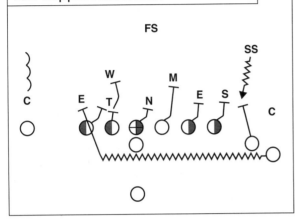

Figure 14.24 With the WR on the backside cutoff, the backside tackle is free to scoop to an extra run-support defender.

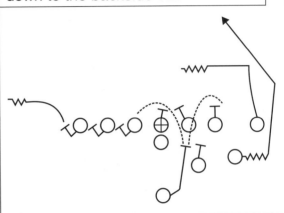

Figure 14.26 A heavy run fake gives us a possible big play over the top. The QB can always check down to the backside TE.

Our strategy for throwing the ball has much to with the type of defense we're facing. Typically, we choose from several areas. Our three-step quick passing game is a great weapon because it has solid protection and we have skilled players who can make extra yards after the catch. Nothing is magical about the routes except that we try to build in answers for all the defensive looks.

Our misdirection play-action pass (figure 14.25) is ready for teams that rely on safeties who react to our running

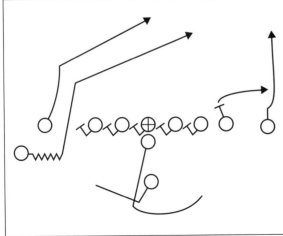

Figure 14.25 Misdirection play-action pass.

game. It's nice to have a possible big hitter, but also have easy dump-down passes to get the first down.

A heavy run action passing play (figure 14.26) gives us a chance to throw the ball down the field. We change the deep routes according to the defensive structure we anticipate, but the isolation fake and formations will match our running game.

To summarize these two areas of our offense, I must first emphasize that we'll always play to our strength. It's far more important to me that we give our guys a chance to execute. We'll run the things we believe in and feature our best players. Short yardage and gold zone are not the places to experiment with new schemes. Win or lose, you always want to know that you ran your best package with your best players.

It has been my pleasure to share these football thoughts with you. The great coaches at Michigan made coming to work every day a real treat. Andy Moeller, Fred Jackson, Erik Campbell, Scot Loeffler, and Terry Heffernan are all great coaches. I know that I learn more from them every day than they ever learn from me. It's their dedication and commitment that makes my job easy.

Mike Debord is a special friend, who no matter how big the storm has a tremendously calming effect on me. When you work at a place like Michigan, you have a tradition that's the foundation of everything you do. We're so fortunate to have Bo Schembechler still with us. He *is* Michigan football, and you could not ask a man to be any more supportive than he is to our staff. He's a daily reminder to me of how lucky I am to be able to coach this great game.

Best of luck to you and your teams. I'll leave you with a great quote from Coach Fielding Yost: "No man can be a football player who does not love the game. Halfheartedness or lack of earnestness will eliminate any man from a football team. The love of the game must be genuine. It is not devotion to a fad that makes men play football; it is because they enjoy their struggle."

CHAPTER 15

Two-Minute and No-Huddle Situations

Gary Tranquill
University of North Carolina

The two-minute drill is one of the most critical situations in football. Many games come down to success or failure depending on how well the drill is run. At the end of the first half, a successful two-minute drill creates momentum for the team in the second half. Scoring at the end to win a game is a great confidence builder for any team, sometimes resulting in a victory that makes a season.

Although most teams practice the two-minute drill two or three times a week, many situations come up that are difficult to practice. You could work on the two-minute drill for two hours a day for several weeks and still not cover every potential situation that might arise. That said, you must create and script different situations each time you practice it.

Everyone must be on the same page and understand what you're trying to accomplish. Communication, mechanics, execution, and clock management are the primary factors. The entire offensive unit must have total awareness of all possible scenarios involved in two-minute situations.

Our objective in a two-minute drill is, of course, to score. We use the same basic methods whether it's before the half or at the end of the game, when you must score to win. We prepare one personnel group for the two-minute drill. The premise is to keep the operation as mechanically simple as possible. By using just one group, we can effectively simplify the operation while retaining enough flexibility to accomplish the task.

We limit our mayday (our code word for our at-the-line, hurry-up system) offense to two formations: the rip and the rip wide (figure 15.1).

Everyone lines up in the same position except the slot (H). The tight end (Y) aligns off the ball for certain protection purposes. The slot (H) lines up either to the open side of the formation to create doubles or to the tight-end side to create trips. The tight end (Y) always aligns to the right along with the flanker (Z). The split end (X) always aligns to the left.

With a hand signal, the quarterback sets the slot (H) to the proper side of the formation call. Everyone else aligns in their spots with the flexibility to expand or to tighten the splits necessary to the play. The slot (H) is the only player who will change from one side of the formation to the other. This makes it easier to get aligned with minimal player movement.

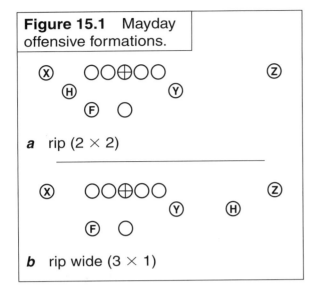

Figure 15.1 Mayday offensive formations.

a   rip (2 × 2)

b   rip wide (3 × 1)

We have a set number of plays from each formation (2 × 2 and 3 × 1) that we can call from the no-huddle mode. These plays are signaled to the quarterback from the sideline.

The quarterback will make a mayday call and signal to everyone that we won't huddle. The next call and signal sets the formation. The last call and signal sets the play.

It's the quarterback's duty to make sure the formation is set before he starts the play. The cadence is always the second sound, whether the quarterback is under the center or in the shotgun. We practice the drill without any verbal calls or commands. The whole process can be signaled by the quarterback.

The only other mayday command or signal that we use is "kill" to spike the ball and stop the clock. We do something a little different with our kill formation. All receivers line up on the line of scrimmage and on the same side as they did for the previous play. We should never get called for an illegal formation for not having enough men on the line of scrimmage. The back also aligns in the same spot as for the previous play. The quarterback goes under center to spike the ball. The line uses extra-point technique for the protection. We don't try any tricks when we kill the clock.

In our at-the-line mayday calls, we have three different protections: seven-man protection, gap three-step protection, and six-man protection, which is the protection we use the most. The quarterback uses a verbal command to call the protection.

These patterns are good versus most of the coverages we see. Some patterns give us a chance to run after the catch; others give us the opportunity to get the ball on the sideline to stop the clock; some give us the opportunity to take a shot.

In the mayday calls we have two screens, both of the fast flanker screen variety. We also have two runs, which might change from week to week. An inside zone and a draw of some kind round out our calls in an at-the-line mayday situation. This whole group of plays is also a part of our regular offense. We don't change the passes and screens the entire season. This group of plays forms the core of our two-minute offense. However, we also carry a short list of plays that we can go to when we huddle. The short list will vary from week to week based on our opponent's tendencies—blitzes, zone or man coverages, special looks, and so on—used in the two-minute defenses.

In a two-minute offense, you need to be at your best when the game is on the line. We prepare one personnel group for the two-minute offense, 11, which has one tight end, one back, and three wide receivers. In the 11 group, we align only in rip (figure 15.2) or rip wide (figure 15.3). The quarterback makes the call. The only receiver to change sides is the H. The two outside receivers won't change, nor will the Y. The quarterback calls rip or rip wide, the protection, and the play. We also have hand signals. F and Y must see the signals also. If the quarterback is under center, the snap count is always on the color (second sound). If the quarterback's taking the snap from the shotgun, the snap is on the color, or we use a silent count.

Figure 15.2 Rip (2 × 2) passes.

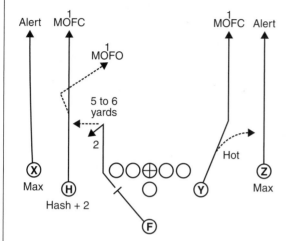

a 11 rip 92 Seattle

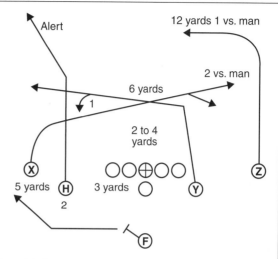

b 11 rip 92 mesh; Y is first at 6 yards, stop vs. zone in far TE area; X goes under Y at 2 to 4 yards, trying to rub vs. man

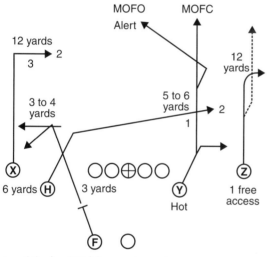

c 11 rip 92 H crash pole

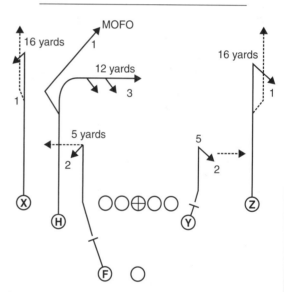

d 11 rip 5-50 (5s are locked vs. press)

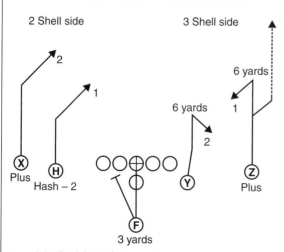

e 11 rip K-64/5 hurricane

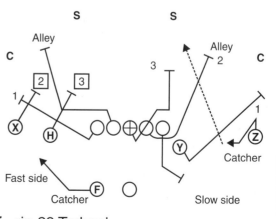

f rip 29 Tarheel

Figure 15.3 Rip-wide (3 × 1) passes.

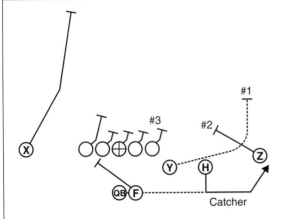

a 11 rip-wide 80 boom-boom

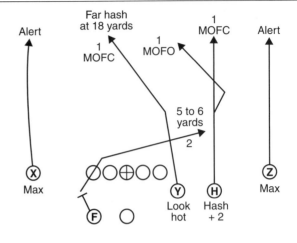

b 11 rip-wide 92 Seattle

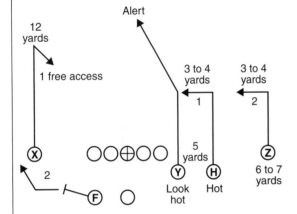

c 11 rip-wide 92 Chicago

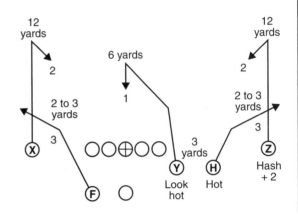

d 11 rip-wide 4-92

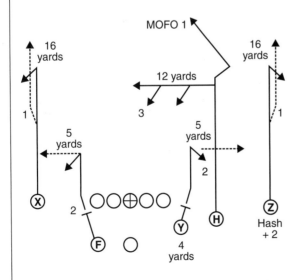

e 11 rip-wide 5-50 (5s are locked vs. press)

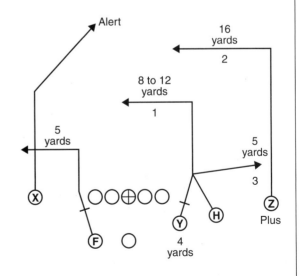

f 11 rip-wide 50 H Denver

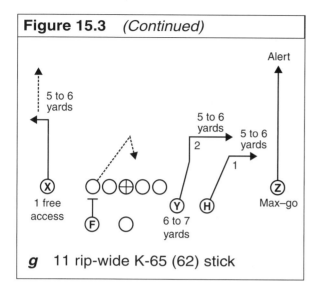

Figure 15.3 *(Continued)*

g 11 rip-wide K-65 (62) stick

The rip passes we use are 92 Seattle, 92 mesh, 92 H crash pole, 5-50, K-64 hurricane, and 29 Tarheel. The rip-wide passes we use are 92 Seattle, 92 Chicago, 4-92, 5-50, 50 H Denver, K-64 Y stick, and 80 boom-boom. We have two runs: roll 42 and 50 QB draw.

We also have chunk passes (figure 15.4) we use with limited time remaining—40 seconds or less and 70-plus yards to go. These patterns are designed to gain large amounts of yardage as we move the ball down the field quickly. We stay in the same formation for these passes regardless of lateral field position. The tight end (Y) flexes and moves onto the line of scrimmage, and the flanker (Z) moves off the line of scrimmage. We practice these every other week.

Last Plays

We also have a plan to throw the ball into the end zone when little time is remaining or it's fourth down and the clock is running. If the ball is outside the 20-yard line, we use the rocket play (figure 15.5).

We always go unbalanced with three receivers to the right side, aligned with the middle receiver on the numbers. That receiver is the jumper. The inside

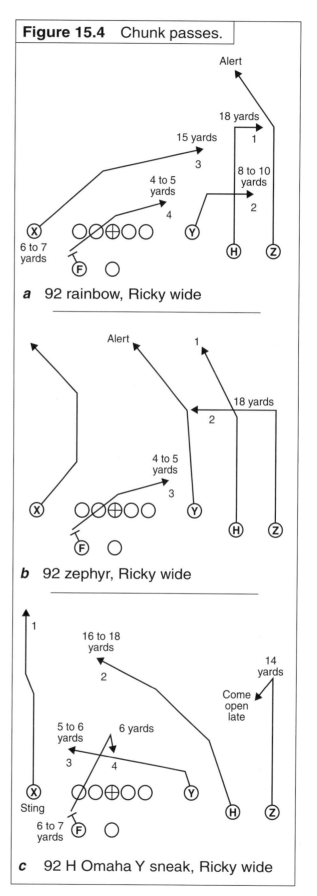

Figure 15.4 Chunk passes.

a 92 rainbow, Ricky wide

b 92 zephyr, Ricky wide

c 92 H Omaha Y sneak, Ricky wide

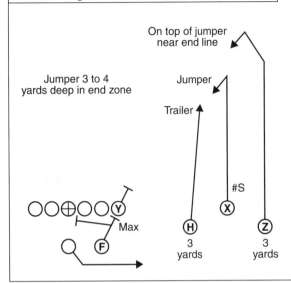

Figure 15.5   Trips right, 88 rocket. QB aims 3 to 4 yards deep in end zone. He must get air under the throw.

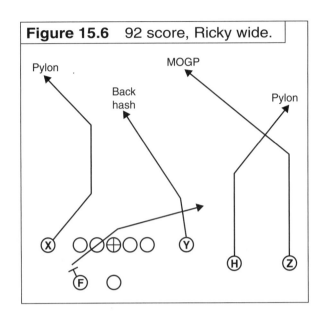

Figure 15.6   92 score, Ricky wide.

and outside receivers align 3 yards on each side of the jumper. The outside receiver sprints to a position behind the jumper in the back of the end zone. The inside receiver follows 3 to 4 yards behind the jumper. Both the outside and inside receivers get into position, looking for a tipped ball. We tell the jumper to try to catch the ball.

The quarterback rolls out to the right and sets up with depth behind the tight-end area. We use a reach-hinge protection. The back checks the frontside edge and then searches back to the inside. The aiming point on the throw is the numbers, 3 to 4 yards deep in the end zone. The quarterback must judge how long it will take the receivers to reach the end zone, and he must also have a feel for the trajectory of the throw.

When the ball is between the +20- and the +10-yard lines, we use a play called *score* (figure 15.6), which encompasses the entire play: formation, pattern, and protection. We practice score as the last play of the game on fourth down with the clock running. We have a primary read side based on coverage, but if the quarterback doesn't like what

he sees, he flushes or scrambles and throws the ball into the end zone, where one receiver is at each pylon and one receiver is under the goal post. He must throw it up in one of those directions as a last-ditch effort.

Inside the 10-yard line, our last play is an all-pivot pass we call Geronimo (figure 15.7). Geronimo, like score, encompasses the formation, pattern, and protection. We empty the formation; all receivers must be spaced properly and release 3 yards deep in the end zone before turning. These are muscle routes to gain position. The quarterback picks out his best choice and fires.

Figure 15.7   Geronimo, Ricky wide, low 68 turns. All receivers must get 3 yards into the end zone.

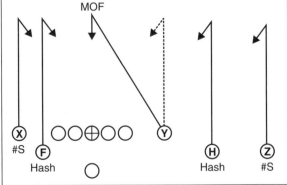

On both score and Geronimo, there's no blitz adjustment. The quarterback must, at all costs, throw the ball into the end zone.

Two-Minute Procedures

The team is notified by the coach or quarterback when the two-minute offense will start. The quarterback does all the talking in the huddle. We huddle when the clock is stopped or as time allows. In two-minute offense, be ready for a mayday call or signal. The mayday call indicates no huddle. Listen and look for the signal of the formation and the play. The snap count on mayday is always set—blue (second sound). The quarterback's call is mayday formation and then the play. There will be no dummy audible.

The quarterback may call two plays in the huddle. After the first play has been run, if the clock is still running, we line up quickly in the formation called in the previous huddle. If the second play stops the clock, we return to the huddle.

The word "kill" is called to stop the clock. When the quarterback calls kill, players line up quickly with receivers staying on the same side of the ball as they did for the previous play. All the receivers must line up on the line of scrimmage to eliminate any illegal formation penalties. The back lines up in the same position as for the previous play. The snap count is the second sound. The quarterback grounds the ball.

For the last play of the game (fourth down, clock running), we use the special plays rocket, Geronimo, or score, depending on field position.

All players must know the rules of the clock. We huddle if the previous play was an incomplete pass or went out of bounds or if a time-out is called. We no-huddle to the line of scrimmage if a penalty has been called on the previous play, if the officials have to measure, or if someone is injured.

Figure 15.8 is a checklist for the quarterback for the two-minute offense. These are the factors he needs to consider.

Figure 15.8 Quarterback checklist for two-minute offense.

I. General considerations
  A. Be absolutely positive about the number of time-outs remaining.
  B. Don't use a time-out until into the two-minute offense.
  C. Make certain the team knows we're in a two-minute situation.
  D. Know all the rules regarding stopping and starting the clock.
  E. Make the team aware of whether we're thinking touchdown or field goal.
  F. Be aware of down and distance.
  G. Follow the play closely so you'll immediately know down and distance.
  H. Think in terms of huddling when possible.
  I. Know situations in which you must have a play called at the line of scrimmage. Be ready to go when the official winds the clock.
  J. Know when a called time-out is necessary. Get to the nearest official quickly to call time-out.
  K. Recognize a situation in which you must intentionally throw an incomplete pass to stop the clock.
  L. Never take a sack, which results in an immediate time-out, if more than one time-out remains.
  M. Never go down with the ball on fourth down.
  N. Always be in the huddle. Let the alternate captain talk with the officials.
  O. Be aware of alignment by receivers and backs.
  P. Alert ball carriers to get out of bounds.
  Q. Know what to call in last-play situations.
II. What to consider at the end of the game when behind
  A. Know how many time-outs are left.
  B. Know if we need a field goal or a touchdown.
    1. If we need a field goal and no time-outs are left
      a. Get the ball in the kicker's range.
      b. If we have time and downs left, kill the ball.
      c. If 16 seconds left, run field-goal team on field (towel).
    2. If we need a field goal, we have one time-out left, and we're in the kicker's range, take the time-out with 5 seconds remaining.
III. Time-outs
  A. If three time-outs left, use first time-out to stop the clock.
  B. If two time-outs left, use one if you need the play more than the time-out.
    1. On first and 10 with 20 seconds, kill the clock.
    2. On third and 10 with 20 seconds, use the time-out. You need the play.
  C. If one time-out left, kill the clock. Save the time-out for the last 15 seconds.
  D. If no time-outs left, kill the clock with 7 seconds to get the last play.

No-Huddle Offense

If we wish to run a no-huddle offense at any time, we use the exact same mechanics as we use in the two-minute offense. We have the flexibility to incorporate different personnel groups and use more formations, motions, and plays than we do in the two-minute offense. We short-list plays for two or three different personnel groups based on our game plan. Usually, we try to establish two different tempos: one about 15 to 18 seconds, and the other as fast as we can go. The fast tempo is locked to a script of plays, though never more than five.

We can also use the two-minute tempo in different personnel groupings.

We don't go into a game with all of the ways to change the tempo. Some weeks we have only two-minute offense and maybe one other method of no-huddle offense. Practice time is the key factor in allowing you to do what you would like to do. Changing the tempo sometimes gives the defense problems and creates more interest and fun for the offense.

If you have a sound and simple system for your two-minute offense, you can easily adapt those methods to any change-of-tempo offense. Basically, when you're practicing one up-tempo drill, you're also working on the others, which gives you more return for your practice time.

The most important factors in our two-minute package are communication, mechanics, execution, and clock management. We try to streamline communications so that we don't have too many different signals and calls. By limiting formations, patterns, and protections, we can move from play to play at a quick tempo, which is our objective. The mechanics of the drill are simple because there's no confusion getting into the correct alignments. The small number of core plays in the package and the fact that they're part of the regular offense allow repetition, which results in better understanding and execution.

Clock management is probably the most difficult area because of all the different situations that can happen. Perfecting clock management comes only with practice and meeting time with the quarterbacks. Talking through different situations and getting quarterback feedback gives the coach an idea of how well quarterbacks are grasping the drill.

It's important for the coach to get a feel for the quarterback's comfort zone—what he likes and doesn't like. A good way to learn this is to allow the quarterback to call his own plays in a drill. This also builds his trust and confidence in the coach.

There are many ways to practice the two-minute drill, including walk-throughs, talk-throughs, execution on air for the rhythm, scripted situations on air, scripted situations against a scout defense, and scripted situations against the varsity defense. Practice the two-minute drill enough to be totally prepared so that you give yourself a chance to win.

CHAPTER 16

Automatics

Don Nehlen
West Virginia University

During my 43-year coaching career, I was exposed to several different ways to automatic at the line of scrimmage. This chapter presents the automatic system we used at West Virginia University.

When the quarterback gets to the line of scrimmage and sees that the defense has aligned perfectly to stop the play call, the quarterback must check out of that play and into a play that has a better chance for success. This is known as an audible.

With the tremendous technology available today and videotape exchanges by coaches, it's more important than ever to have a workable automatic system. Because of tape exchanges, the opponent knows everything about your offense and defense. Any tendencies that you have, your opponent will know and will be working to defend.

For an automatic system to be successful, certain principles must apply:

1. The system must be organized in such a way that you can practice against your own defense during the week without them knowing you're checking a play at the line of scrimmage.

2. All plays to be audibled must be in the game plan by Tuesday. Never add automatics after Tuesday's practice. To operate an audible system effectively, the quarterback needs the entire week for practice and recognition.

3. False audibles must be a regular part of the starting count.

4. The snap count must be written on the practice schedule during team time. We do this so that the snap count is constantly changing. Don't give the responsibility of the snap count to the quarterback. We did a study during spring practice. When the coaches did not control the snap count, 80 percent of the time the quarterbacks would go on 1. This has a tendency to become routine for the entire team with regards to the snap count.

5. Remember that it doesn't matter what you know regarding automatics—it only matters what the quarterback knows. Do no more than your quarterback can handle.

To fully understand our audible system, you must know the numbering system, cadence and snap count, color system, false audible starting counts, and our check-with-me system. For our numbering system, we number even (2, 4, 6, 8) to the right, odd (3, 5, 7, 9) to the left, and 0 or 1 in the middle. Any play in our offense that ends in an 8 (28, 38, 48, 58) is a sweep to the right. Any play that ends in a 6 (26, 36, 46, 56) is an off-tackle play to the right. Any play that ends in a 9 (29, 39, 49, 59) is a sweep to the left. We use this system to number all our plays.

For the snap count and cadence, we use a nonrhythmic base system:

- On quick—hit
- On one—hit, go
- On two—hit, go, go
- On three—hit, go, go, go

In the huddle, the quarterback calls the snap count, formation, and play, and then he repeats the snap count. The huddle might sound like this: "On one, red, 58 on one, ready, break." *Red* is the formation. For the formations, dark colors indicate right formations, and light colors indicate left formations. At the line of scrimmage, the quarterback might say "hit, go" and the ball would be snapped on the word *go*. The "ready, break" is our signal for everyone to break the huddle in unison.

In the color system we use, green indicates a run, and yellow and blue indicate passes. Yellow passes are quick routes off three-step drops by the quarterback (60s series). Blue passes use the normal five-step drop (70s and 80s series). We use red and white for directional calls. In our check-with-me package, red means right, and white means left.

The false audible system is used to confuse the defense. This is the false audible system we use:

- On 10—hit, color number, color number, go
- On 20—hit, color number, color number, go, go
- On 30—hit, color number, color number, go, go, go
- On ready hit—color number, hit, go, color, ready hit

Our team knows whenever the snap count is 10, 20, or 30 colors, it means nothing, and we'll run the play called in the huddle. If the snap count is "ready hit," the team knows the quarterback is free to call anything at the line of scrimmage he wants before the second ready hit. This system of snap counts makes it virtually impossible for the defense to know when the quarterback is using automatics at the line of scrimmage.

For our check-with-me package, the quarterback calls two plays in the huddle at the same time. The coaches decide which plays will be called while preparing the game plan. We like to call companion plays, for example, two sweeps (58/59 check with me) or two zone plays (14/15 check with me). If the first play called in the huddle is the desired play, the ball is snapped at two (hit, go, go). If the second play called is the desired play, the ball is snapped on 20 (hit, white play, white play, go, go).

Green Calls

Defenses are so sophisticated and quick that you need to be able to have the right play called against a particular defense. We give quarterbacks some general rules regarding the running and passing games. The green call gets us out of a bad play in the running game. For example, let's say we called a sweep to the right in the huddle (figure 16.1). When he gets to the line of scrimmage, the quarterback sees that we're running the play into a defensive alignment that's stacked against the play. He makes a green call and changes the play to a 43, an isolation play to the left.

It's obvious when looking at figure 16.1 that the sweep right is a bad play. The defense has five men to our four. The quarterback greens to 43. Although 43 is not a great play, it's not a bad play.

Let's look at another example. Say we called 43 in the huddle (figure 16.2). Again, a bad play—the defense has four

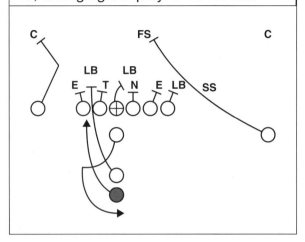

Figure 16.1 58 sweep right called in huddle. Defense is overloaded to the playside. The QB calls green 43, green 43, changing the play to 43 iso left.

men to our three. The green call gets us into a better play, maybe not a great play, but not a bad play. The quarterback recognizes the defensive alignments and greens to the 58 play. The green call would sound like this at the line of scrimmage: "Hit, green 58, green 58, go, go." The play is changed from 43, the huddle call, to 58, a sweep right.

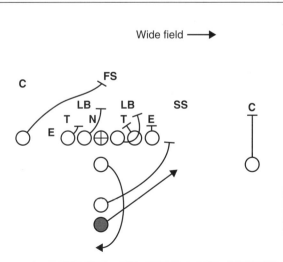

Figure 16.2 Play 43 was called in the huddle. Defense is overloaded to the playside. QB calls green 58, green 58, and we sweep right.

Yellow and Blue Calls

To use the yellow and blue calls effectively, you must be willing to have a 15- to 20-minute blitz period every day. The quarterback must feel comfortable with the plan. He also is going to have to spend at least seven to nine hours a week looking at the opponent's blitz package. If he can't recognize what's coming, you'll be running and throwing into some overloaded defensive alignments. Our reads are always the safeties. The free safety tells the quarterback what's coming.

Yellow is our 60 passing game, a three-step quick-passing game. We run an out, a hitch, a fade, and a slant. The quarterback and receivers must all be on the same page in the quick game. With the yellow call, we incorporate hand signals by the quarterback

- Closed fist—5-yard out
- Open hand—5-yard hitch
- Crossed arms, closed fist—fade
- Crossed arms, open hand—slant

We practice hand signals every day, and communication between our quarterbacks and receivers has always been excellent. Keep in mind—if you're going to use hand signals with the yellow call, the quarterback has to use them once in a while in the running game so that the defense has no idea when the signals are live.

Figures 16.3, 16.4, and 16.5 show examples of our yellow calls. All of these examples of yellow calls can be practiced daily in drill periods.

In figure 16.3, the quarterback recognizes the defensive corner is playing 9 yards off the receiver. He makes a yellow call, signaling a 5-yard out route with a closed fist. The quarterback releases the ball on his third step.

In figure 16.4, the quarterback recognizes the defensive back is playing

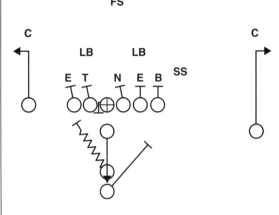

Figure 16.3 Yellow call, closed fist. Receivers run 5-yard out routes.

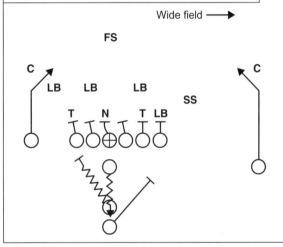

Figure 16.4 Yellow call, crossed arms, open hand. Receivers run 5-yard slant routes.

Figure 16.5 Yellow call, crossed arms, closed fist. Receivers run fade routes.

wide on the receiver. He makes a yellow call and signals a slant—crossed arms, open hand.

In figure 16.5, the quarterback recognizes the defensive back is playing press coverage and is up tight on the line of scrimmage. He makes a yellow call and signals a fade—crossed arms, closed fist. With the corners up tight, the receivers run fade routes, staying 4 yards inside the sidelines.

Protection for the 60 quick-passing game or the yellow call is quite simple. Linemen set hard to the inside, and

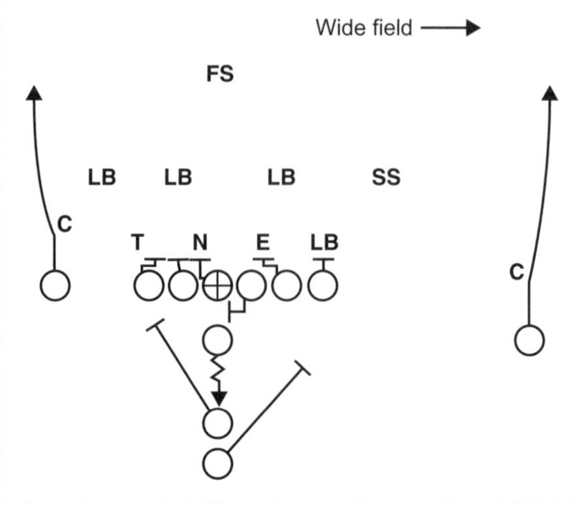

backs block the end of the line. The fullback always goes to the split side, the tailback to the tight-end side. The protection is very similar to extra-point protection.

The blue call is used in the 70 and 80 passing games. The 70 passing game is a five-step drop with zone protection. The 80 passing game is a five-step half-roll with maximum protection. We use the 80 passing game with the blue call to defeat the blitz.

In figure 16.6, the quarterback goes to the line of scrimmage and reads the secondary. He sees that the secondary is blitzing with the strong safety and playing man to man on the receivers. The recognition comes from the alignment of the free safety. The quarterback calls, "Hit, blue 82, blue 82, go, go." The offensive line blocks, using 80 protection. The receivers run the 82 route. The ball is snapped on 2. The quarterback throws on his fifth step, looking for a spot on the boundary at 21 yards.

In the blue call shown in figure 16.7, the quarterback goes to the 86 route. His read is the same as shown in figure 16.6. The quarterback throws the ball on his fifth step.

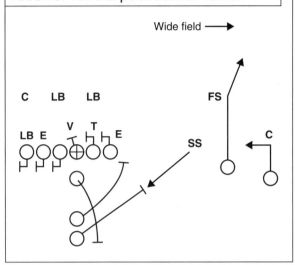

Figure 16.6 Blue 82. Outside receiver runs a 4-yard hitch route. Inside receiver runs a post corner route.

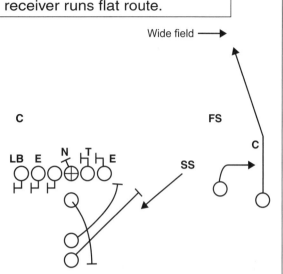

Figure 16.8 Blue 84. Outside receiver runs skinny post. Inside receiver runs flat route.

In figure 16.8, the quarterback goes to the 84 route. His read is the same. The outside receiver runs a skinny post route, looking over his shoulder at 10 yards. The inside receiver runs a flat route to 4 yards. The quarterback throws on his fifth step.

In figure 16.9, the quarterback reads a three-deep defense against our double formation. The quarterback has been

taught to automatic to four verticals against a three-deep alignment. This would be our 79 route in the 70 passing game. The quarterback looks off the free safety to make him move. The outside receivers run streak routes, staying 4 yards from the boundary.

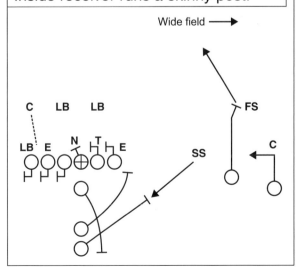

Figure 16.7 Blue 86. Outside receiver runs an under route at 3 to 4 yards. Inside receiver runs a skinny post.

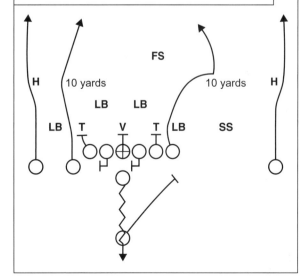

Figure 16.9 Blue 79. Outside receivers run streak routes. Inside receivers run streak routes and then bubble out two to three steps and look over their inside shoulder.

The inside receivers run streaks at 10 yards, bubble out two to three steps, then look over their inside shoulders. The quarterback throws opposite the free safety.

Check-With-Me Package

Our check-with-me package was my favorite way for us to automatic. It reduced mistakes made by the team and the quarterback. We seldom, if ever, went into a game with more than two or three run packages and no more than one or two run/pass packages.

After scouting our opponents, we always had a good idea when the blitz would come. We tried to help the quarterback by anticipating what the defense would do, and we would put our offense in a favorable formation. The formation would always make the quarterback's read easier.

In the check-with-me system, the quarterback calls two plays in the huddle at the same time. We like to call two zone plays (such as 14/15 check with me) or two sweeps (such as 58/59 check with me). If the first play called in the huddle is the desired play, the ball is snapped on 2 (hit, go, go). If the second play called is the desired play, the ball is snapped on 20 (hit, white 15, white 15, go, go).

Figure 16.10 shows the zone play 14/15 check with me. (The 14/15 plays are cutback plays for the tailback.) The quarterback knows that on all inside zone plays, he's to take the play to the offset nose tackle. In figure 16.10a, the nose tackle is to the right. The quarterback runs the desired play (14) and takes the play to the nose tackle. In figure 16.10b, the nose tackle is to the left. In this case, the desired play is 15. The quarterback calls, "Hit, white 15, white 15, go, go" at the line, the ball is snapped at 20, and the team runs 15.

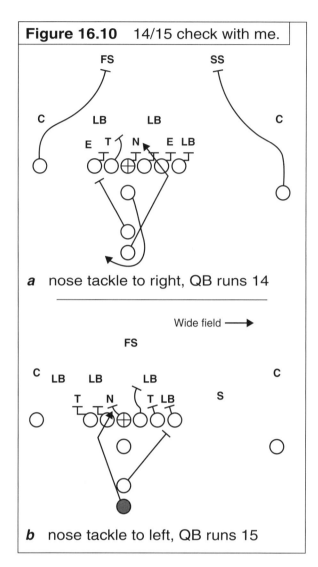

Figure 16.10   14/15 check with me.

a   nose tackle to right, QB runs 14

Wide field ⟶

b   nose tackle to left, QB runs 15

For the 58/59 check with me play (figure 16.11), the quarterback knows to run the play away from the shaded nose tackle. When the nose tackle is on the right (figure 16.11a), the desired play is 59. The quarterback calls, "Hit, white 59, white 59, go, go," and the ball is snapped on 20. The sweeps run to the 3 technique or opposite the nose tackle. When the nose tackle is on the left (figure 16.11b), 58 is the desired play. The quarterback knows to take the sweep opposite the nose tackle. He calls, "Hit, go, go," and the ball is snapped on 2.

In our check-with-me package, we package the run and pass together. The pass is play action off the running play,

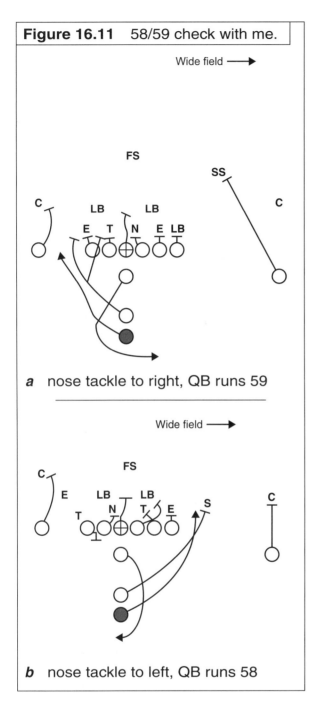

Figure 16.11   58/59 check with me.

Wide field ⟶

a   nose tackle to right, QB runs 59

Wide field ⟶

b   nose tackle to left, QB runs 58

quarterback throws the 42 pass (figure 16.12a). The quarterback calls, "Hit, blue 42, blue 42, go, go" on the line of scrimmage, and the ball is snapped on 2. The wide receiver runs a 7-yard out route. If the strong safety aligns wide, the quarterback runs 42 (figure 16.12b). The quarterback calls, "Hit, go, go" on the line of scrimmage, and the ball is snapped on 2.

The check-with-me package can give the offense an edge against the opponent's defense. When studying an

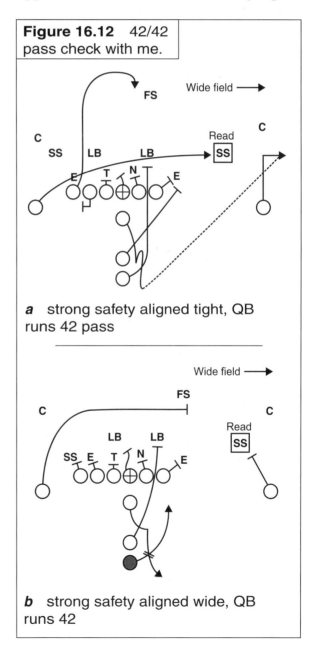

Figure 16.12   42/42 pass check with me.

Wide field ⟶

Read

a   strong safety aligned tight, QB runs 42 pass

Wide field ⟶

Read

b   strong safety aligned wide, QB runs 42

such as the 42/42 pass check with me (figure 16.12). In setting this package in the game, we like to run it against some form of a 4-4 defense. With this package, the formation is put into the boundary. By doing so, the quarterback's decision becomes more clear. At the line of scrimmage, the quarterback reads the alignment of the strong safety. If the strong safety aligns tight, the

opponent's defense, you'll find alignments that your top three plays will work well against. We make a staff decision on what alignments to run against and teach the quarterback to recognize those alignments. This ensures we'll always run plays against a desirable defense.

The blue and yellow passing game against the blitz must be practiced every day for the team to execute it properly. Hand signals can also be practiced during skeleton drills.

With the use of the color system, the check-with-me system, and all the different snap counts, it's impossible for the defense to know what the offense is doing at the line of scrimmage. Remember —you get what you emphasize in football. If you want to run the best play against a particular alignment, you must work on it every day. Never overburden your quarterback.

INDEX

Note: The italicized *f* and *t* following page numbers refer to figures and tables, respectively.

ABOUT THE AFCA

Since its establishment in 1922, the American Football Coaches Association (AFCA) has provided a forum for the discussion and study of all matters pertaining to football and coaching. It also works to maintain the highest possible standards in football and the coaching profession. These objectives—first declared by founders Major Charles Daly, Alonzo Stagg, John Heisman, and others—have been instrumental to the AFCA's becoming the effective and highly respected organization it is today.

The AFCA is the professional organization for coaches at all levels, from high school to the National Football League (NFL). Its international membership includes coaches from Canada, Europe, Australia, and Japan. Through annual publications and several newsletters, the association keeps members informed of the most current rule changes and proposals, proper coaching methods, innovations in techniques, insights on coaching philosophy, and business conducted by the board of trustees and AFCA committees.

The AFCA works closely with the National Collegiate Athletic Association, the National Association of Collegiate Directors of Athletics, the National Association of Intercollegiate Athletics, the National Football League, the National Football Foundation and Hall of Fame, Pop Warner, and other organizations involved in the game of football. Indeed, one of the goals of the association is to build a strong coalition of football coaches—Team AFCA—who speak out with a unified voice on issues that affect the sport and profession.

For more information about becoming a member of the AFCA, please visit the AFCA Web site (www.afca.com) or write to the following address:

American Football Coaches
    Association
100 Legends Lane
Waco, TX 76706
254-754-990

ABOUT THE EDITORS

Bill Mallory ranks first on Indiana University's all-time victories list, having amassed a 69-77-3 record in his 13-year tenure as head coach. While compiling a 165-121-4 record at Miami (Ohio), Colorado, Northern Illinois, and Indiana, Mallory became one of only a handful of coaches in history to guide three different programs to top 20 finishes in national polls. He was twice named both Mid-American Coach of the Year and AFCA District Coach of the Year, and in 1987 he became the first coach to be awarded back-to-back Big Ten Coach of the Year honors. While at Indiana, Mallory led the Hoosiers to six bowl games, including victories in the 1998 Liberty Bowl and the 1991 Copper Bowl. He also led IU to a top 20 ranking in 1988. Mallory is a Hall of Fame member at Miami University, Northern Illinois University, and Indiana University. He holds a bachelor's degree from Miami University and a master's degree from Bowling Green State University. Mallory and his wife, Ellie, have four children—three of whom coach college football—and 10 grandchildren.

Don Nehlen, who achieved the most wins in West Virginia University's history, served as the Mountaineers' head coach from 1980 to 2000 and posted a 149-93-4 record. Nehlen's career record of 202-138-8 (including nine seasons as head coach at Bowling Green from 1968 to 1976) made him one of only 17 coaches in NCAA history to record 200 wins. Taking WVU to 13 bowl games and 17 winning seasons, Nehlen coached 15 first team All-Americans, 82 all-conference players, six first team Academic All-Americans, and 80 players who went on to professional football. He received Coach of the Year honors from numerous groups and was the unanimous choice as the 1993 Big East Coach of the Year. A member of the Mid-American Conference, Bowling Green, and Gator Bowl halls of fame, Nehlen has a bachelor's degree from Bowling Green and a master's degree from Kent State. A native of Canton, Ohio, Nehlen and his wife, Merry Ann, have two children and five grandchildren.

ABOUT THE CONTRIBUTORS

John Bond has been the Northern Illinois University offensive coordinator since 2003, when he steered the Huskies to single-season school records in points (421), touchdowns (53), first downs (261), and total offense yards (5,265). Bond boasts 22 seasons of experience, including three years as the offensive coordinator and quarterbacks coach at Army (2000-2003), where he installed a one-back system that set 35 records, and at Illinois State University (1996-99), where he helped lead teams to the NCAA 1-AA playoffs twice (1998-99) and the Gateway Athletic Conference title (1999).

Al Borges, regarded as one of football's top offensive minds, has more than 31 years of coaching experience. The offensive coordinator for Auburn University since 2004, Borges helped his team finish first in the SEC in scoring offense in his first year. During his previous two years at Indiana, he helped the Hoosier offense set a school record for passing yards and take a third-place ranking in Big Ten passing offense. In five seasons as UCLA's offensive coordinator and quarterbacks coach from 1996 to 2000, Borges helped guide the Bruins to three consecutive NCAA bowl games and two Pac-10 championships (1997, 1998). Borges is a two-time finalist for the Frank Broyles Assistant Coach of the Year Award (1997, 1998), and he received Football Coach Quarterly's Offensive Coordinator of the Year in 1997.

Gregg Brandon became the 16th head coach in the history of Bowling Green State University's football program in 2002 and guided the Falcons to back-to-back bowl wins for just the second time in school history after winning in the GMAC Bowl in 2004. The Falcons also boasted the most potent offense in MAC history, finishing second in the country at 506.3 yards per game and fourth nationally in scoring offense at 44.3 points per game. Both established new league records. Brandon was hired after more than 22 years of coaching experience at the Division I level, including two years as assistant head coach at BGSU.

Mitch Browning has worked as the assistant coach to Glen Mason for 20 seasons at three different institutions: Kent State, Kansas, and Minnesota. During Browning's reign at Minnesota, the Gophers have finished among the top 35 in total offense in the nation in five consecutive seasons. In 2003 he helped the Gophers set a Big Ten record for total offense (6,430) and finish with the fourth-highest rushing total (3,759) and sixth-highest point total (503) in Big Ten history. Browning was selected as a finalist for the Frank Broyles Award, given annually to the top assistant football coach at the NCAA Division I level.

Jim Chaney reached the NFL level in February 2006, when he was hired as the assistant offensive line coach for the St. Louis Rams. Chaney spent the previous nine seasons as the offensive coordinator for Purdue, during which time he helped the Boilermakers lead the Big Ten in passing offense for five of his last eight seasons (1997, 1998, 1999, 2000, 2004) and in total offense on three occasions (1997, 1999, 2002). He also worked as the Boilermakers' tight ends coach. Chaney is a native of Holden, Missouri, and played college football as a nose guard at Central Missouri State.

Fisher DeBerry has been the Air Force head coach since 1984 and served as the Academy's assistant coach from 1980 to 1983. He has led 17 of his 22 teams to winning records, and 12 have captured a bowl bid. His career record of 165-100-1 is the best in school history in terms of games won and winning percentage. DeBerry has coached the Falcons to three conference championships, and his team won a share of the Western Athletic Conference championship in both 1985 and 1995. In 1998 DeBerry guided the team to its first outright title with the WAC Mountain Division championship, and in 2003 he reached the 150-win mark.

Mike Dunbar joined the University of California at Berkley football staff in February 2006 as the offensive coordinator. He previously served as the offensive coordinator for Northwestern University since 2002, where he helped to bolster the Wildcat offense to elite status. Dunbar came to Evanston from Northern Iowa, where he compiled a 29-15 record as head coach from 1997-2000. He has a 83-24-1 career head coaching record, including a 54-9-1 mark in six seasons at NAIA Central Washington. While at CWU, his teams earned two number one national rankings, made the playoffs six times, and extended a regular-season win streak to 40 games.

Dennis Franchione was named Texas A&M's 26th head coach in 2002. A 32-year coaching veteran, Franchione has a career record of 166-86-2 (a .657 winning percentage), which ranks him 13th among active head coaches. His 166 career victories rank him seventh among active head coaches. Franchione has won nine conference or division championships and 11 conference or regional Coach of the Year awards. He has also received two National Coach of the Year awards and is a two-time finalist for the Paul "Bear" Bryant National Coach of the Year Award (2000, 2002). Starting his head coaching career at Southwestern (Kansas) College in 1981, Franchione finished with a 14-4-2 record before moving to his alma mater, Pittsburg (Kansas) State, in 1984, where he was twice named NAIA Coach of the Year and led teams to five straight conference titles, five consecutive playoff appearances, and a regular-season winning streak of 45 consecutive games.

Ralph Friedgen became the winningest fourth-year coach in Atlantic Coast Conference history as he entered his fifth season at the University of Maryland in 2005. Friedgen continues to build his alma mater's football program, guiding the Terps to a 36-14 record and a trio of major bowl appearances—including two decisive wins—in his four seasons as a collegiate head coach. In his first three seasons at the helm of the Terrapin program, Friedgen also became the first coach in conference history to lead a team to three straight seasons of 10 wins or more. His 36 wins in four years rank him in the top 10 in NCAA history.

John Hayden Fry compiled a record of 232-178-10 during his 37-year career as a head coach. Best known for sparking a resurgence at the University of Iowa, Fry led the Hawkeyes to a record of 143-89-6 over 20 seasons. In 1981 he led the team to its first winning season in 19 years with a Big Ten co-championship and a trip to the Rose Bowl. The 1981 season was the first of eight straight winning seasons for the Hawkeyes and 14 bowl game appearances. When he retired as coach of the Hawkeyes following the 1998 season, Fry was ranked 10th on the all-time list. Fry graduated from Baylor University with a degree in psychology in 1951 and received his first head coaching job at Southern Methodist University from 1962 to 1972, where he led the Mustangs to their first Southwest Conference title since 1948. He then went on to coach at North Texas State University (now the University of North Texas) from 1973 to 1978. Fry was inducted into the College Football Hall of Fame in 2003.

Larry Kehres is the head football coach and director of athletics at Mount Union College in Ohio. During Kehres' 20-year tenure, his teams have captured eight national championships and broke Mount Union's own NCAA all-division record for consecutive wins when the squad won its 55th game in a row (2000-2003) in the semifinals of the Division III playoffs in 2003. The Purple Raiders also set the NCAA all-division record with 54 consecutive wins from 1996 to 1999. Kehres was named 2005 Ohio Football Coach of the Year, finishing the season with a career record of 231-20-3 (.915). In 2002, Kehres became the first coach in AFCA history to win seven AFCA National Coach of the Year Awards, and he was elected to the AFCA Board of Trustees in 2001.

Terry Malone was hired as the New Orleans Saints tight ends coach in 2006 after serving as the University of Michigan's offensive coordinator and tight ends coach from 2002 to 2005. During his nine-year tenure with the Wolverines, Malone helped lead teams to five Big Ten championships, one national championship, 16 All-Big Ten first team citations, and eight second team honors. During Malone's four years as offensive coordinator, the Wolverines won two Big Ten championships and produced two Big Ten MVP winners. Michigan's 2003-2004 offensive unit ranked second in the Big Ten in scoring and 24th nationally with an average of 30.83 points per game. Malone was offensive line coach at Boston College in 1996 and served as offensive line coach, tight ends coach, and offensive coordinator at Bowling Green from 1986 to 1995.

Glen Mason has led the University of Minnesota football program to six bowl games in the past seven years, becoming the first coach in school history to do so. With a victory in the 2004 Music City Bowl, Mason helped Minnesota earn three consecutive bowl victories for the first time in school history. He is one of only six active coaches with at least 40 victories at two different Division I schools and one of four active coaches with at least two bowl wins at two different Division I institutions. Mason has directed three of the most monumental turnarounds in college football at Kent State, Kansas, and Minnesota. He is one of only three coaches in NCAA history to be named the conference Coach of the Year in three different conferences: Big Ten (1999), Big Eight (1995, 1991), and Mid-American (1986).

Joe Novak has served as the head football coach at Northern Illinois University since 1995. In 2004, he led the Huskies to a 9-3 record, a share of the Mid-American Conference Western Division title, and a victory in the Silicon Valley Bowl, marking the program's first bowl appearance in 21 years. Novak earned AFCA Regional Coach of the Year honors in 2003 when the Huskies finished 10-2, setting a school record for regular-season wins. In 2005, he was elected to the AFCA Board of Trustees, and he received the prestigious Ray Meyer Coach Award. Novak previously served as defensive coordinator and linebackers coach at Indiana University (1984-1995), where he led teams to six bowl games.

Chuck Petersen has been a varsity assistant for the Air Force Academy football program since 1991, serving as offensive coordinator since 2000 and quarterbacks and fullbacks coach since 1997. With Petersen at the helm, the Falcons led the conference in total offense, scoring, rushing, passing efficiency, and third- and fourth-down conversions in 2000. In 2002, Air Force won its first national rushing title and led the conference in scoring. In 2003, Petersen was named Assistant Coach of the Year for Division I by the AFCA.

Harold R. "Tubby" Raymond's retirement in 2002 ended an era that spanned 36 seasons as head coach at the University of Delaware and seven decades in the coaching profession. Under Raymond's direction, the Blue Hens compiled a 300-119-3 (.714) record, making him one of only nine coaches in the history of college football to reach 300 victories and just the fourth to do so at one school. He led teams to three national championships, 14 Lambert Cup trophies, 16 NCAA playoff appearances, and six Yankee Conference/Atlantic 10 Titles. Raymond received awards for NCAA College Division Coach of the Year four times, EFAC I-AA Coach of the Year twice, and AFCA District II and Region I Coach of the Year seven times. He received the Vince Lombardi Football Foundation Lifetime Achievement Award in 1999, was recognized by *Sports Illustrated* magazine as No. 3 on the top 100 sports figures of the 20th century in the state of Delaware in 2000, and was inducted into the College Football Hall of Fame in 2003.

Rich Rodriguez has been the head football coach at West Virginia University since 2001, during which time he has led teams to three Big East championships (2003, 2004, 2005), two Gator Bowls (2003 and 2004), and a Sugar Bowl victory and top 5 national ranking following the 2005 season. Previously Clemson University's associate head coach and offensive coordinator (1999 to 2000), Rodriguez guided a Tiger attack that set 26 school records—more than any Clemson team since the NCAA modern era of record keeping began in 1936. He also served as Tulane University's offensive coordinator and quarterbacks coach from 1997 to 1998 and as Glenville State University's head coach from 1990 to 1996, leading teams to four West Virginia Intercollegiate Athletic Conference titles, two NAIA playoff appearances, and one berth in the NAIA championship game.

Greg Studrawa is the assistant head coach and offensive coordinator at Bowling Green State University. In 2005, he oversaw an offense that finished second in the league in passing (283.9) and scoring (33.8) and was third in the league in pass efficiency (142.4). In 2004, BGSU finished second nationally in total offense with a MAC record 506.3 yards per game, securing him as a nominee for the Broyles Award, given annually to the nation's top assistant coach. A former starter at left tackle for the Falcons, Studrawa returned to Bowling Green after spending three seasons as offensive line coach at Arkansas State. He also was an assistant offensive line coach at Cincinnati for two years (1989 and 1990) and was the offensive coordinator at Wilmington from 1991 to 1996.

Joe Tiller became Purdue's 33rd head football coach in 1996. Taking the reins of a program that had just one winning season and no bowl game appearances since 1984, Tiller engineered eight consecutive bowl berths, an average of nearly eight wins per season, and a Big Ten championship in 2000. His teams have qualified for eight of the 13 bowl games in school history, making Purdue one of only eight schools in the nation to play in a bowl game each of those consecutive eight years. After his first season at Purdue, Tiller was named National Coach of the Year by both *Football News* and *Kickoff* magazines, the GTE Region 3 Coach of the Year (Big Ten, Mid-American Conference, and Conference USA) by the AFCA, and the Big Ten Dave McClain Coach of the Year.

Gary Tranquill has 44 years of collegiate and professional coaching experience, becoming North Carolina's offensive coordinator and quarterbacks coach in 2001. Tranquill has a diverse coaching background that includes 14 years of experience as an offensive coordinator at five different schools, three years as a defensive coordinator, and five years as a Division I head coach. In his four years at Carolina, the Tar Heels have set numerous passing records. In 2004, Carolina finished second in the league with 390.7 yards per game. Tranquill was inducted into Wittenberg's Athletic Hall of Fame in 1986.

Randy Walker was hired as Northwestern University's football coach in 1999, after becoming Miami of Ohio's all-time victory leader, and now stands as the second-winningest coach in Northwestern history. In just his second season at the Wildcat helm, Walker took Northwestern from last to first in the Big Ten. For his 2000 achievements, he was named the Dave McClain Big Ten Coach of the Year and the Region 3 Coach of the Year by the AFCA. In 2003, Northwestern earned a trip to the Motor City Bowl by winning four of its last six Big Ten games. With a 2005 bowl appearance, Walker has become the first NU mentor to guide three different teams to the postseason and the first coach ever to guide three straight teams to four or more Big Ten wins.

Bill Yeoman served as head football coach at the University of Houston from 1962 to 1986, and his greatest legacy may be the invention of triple option that resulted in the veer offense. Yeoman's 160 victories are the most in Houston's history and rank 51st on the NCAA all-time wins list. The Cougars won four Southwest Conference titles and 11 bowl games, posting a 6-4-1 bowl record under Yeoman's guidance and leading the nation in every facet of offense from 1966 to 1970. Named Texas Coach of the Year in 1976, Yeoman helped the Cougars finish the season ranked in the top 10 four times and in the top 20 ten times. In 1985, Yeoman was inducted into the Southwest Conference Hall of Honor and was the first representative from the University of Houston to be inducted into the College Football Hall of Fame.

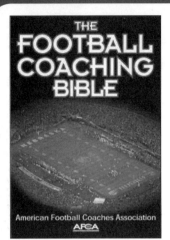
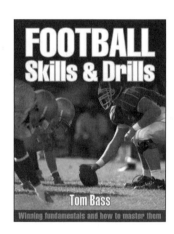
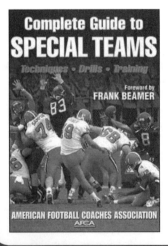